Essays On Hinduism

Third Edition

The Spiritual Heritage Series Volume I

Essays On Hinduism

Third Edition

KARAN SINGH

Bahá'í Chair for World Peace
Center for International Development
and Conflict Management
University of Maryland at College Park
USA

First published 1987
Second revised edition 1990
Reprinted 1993
Third Edition 1998

ISBN 81-7070-100-7

Published by
the Bahá'í Chair for World Peace, University of Maryland,
in collaboration with Insights Press,
5010 Austin Road, Chattanooga, Tennessee 37343
Printed at Chattanooga, Tennessee.

Editor's Foreword

The Spiritual Heritage of the Human Race

In this time of global transition the spiritual traditions of the world live in much closer proximity to each other than ever before. Space does not separate cultures and beliefs to the extent it once did. Modern technology and communications have reduced distances, and related changes in patterns of immigration have intermingled believers from different traditions as never before. These conditions make mutual understanding and respect between the world's spiritual traditions imperative, but reducing the divisions created by distance does not necessarily produce that result. Understanding still remains incomplete and imperfect, and respect sometimes non-existent.

The English poet John Dryden once wrote of a new age that he saw emerging:

> All, all of a piece throughout:
> Thy chase had a beast in view: --
> Thy wars brought nothing about:--
> Thy lovers were all untrue:--
> 'Tis well an old age is out,
> And time to begin anew.

Whether the global transition will be all of a piece is ultimately unknowable. One hopes it will avoid wars. Most probably it will have its chases and lovers. But if its chases are not to bring the beast into view and its lovers to be untrue, then spiritual understanding and respect must become as basic to the human condition as mastery of technology.

This series has been established to make available studies of the major spiritual traditions that combine knowledge, respect, and understanding. Each book in the series will be devoted to one of the world's major spiritual traditions and written by a scholar and believer from that tradition.

The Spiritual Heritage Series is an attempt to construct from the diverse spiritual traditions and the different religions — both divine and non-divine — a continuum that creates a holistic view of those powerful forces that have inspired humanity in its long history.

SUHEIL BUSHRUI

College Park, Maryland
July, 1998

Preface

Over the last few years I have had occasion to write and speak fairly extensively on various aspects of Hinduism, both in India and abroad, and these pieces have from time to time been published in various books and journals. Several friends have suggested that in view of the growing interest in Hinduism, not only in India but worldwide, these should be made available in a collected form to a wider reading public. In many of the universities I visited in the United States there was a substantial interest in such a book.

I have slightly edited and added some new articles for this revised edition, although the reader will inevitably come across a certain amount of repetition. In particular, I have constantly stressed what I consider to be the broad, universal aspects of Hinduism which are specially relevant in this nuclear age. Indeed, Hinduism is so vast and multi-faceted that all one can hope to do is to explore some of its more significant elements, so that the reader can gain a glimpse into its beauty and power. If I have helped in doing this even to a small degree, it will give me tremendous satisfaction.

It is my firm conviction that mankind today is transiting into an entirely new phase of civilization, which may be called the global society, a transition as important, if not more so, as the earlier ones from nomadic to agricultural, from agricultural to industrial and from industrial to post-industrial society. Besides, with the rate of change having immensely accelerated due to the technological explosion, major transformations, which in an earlier age would have taken several centuries, are now compressed into a few decades. This gives human consciousness insufficient time to adjust to the new situation; hence the dangerous lag we witness today between the emergence of a global society and its acceptance by the vast mass of humanity.

While science and technology are central to this entire process, the great religious traditions of mankind also have an important role to play because of their impact on the minds and hearts of billions of human beings. My interest in Hinduism, therefore, flows not only from the fact that I am a Hindu but also because, as a global citizen, I am convinced that the universal aspects of Hinduism— particularly the Vedānta — can provide an invaluable input into the emerging global consciousness.

It is my hope that the essays that follow, which include a translation and commentary on the *Mundaka Upaniṣad,* one of the seminal texts of the Vedānta, will be of some value not only to scholars but to lay people throughout the world who are interested in this great religious tradition.

New Delhi
15 April 1990

KARAN SINGH

Contents

EDITOR'S FOREWORD V
PREFACE VII
1. Hinduism — An Overview 1
2. Vedānta in the Nuclear Age 44
3. The Message of the Upaniṣads 49
4. The Message of the Bhagavad-Gītā 59
5 The Insights of the Mystics 69
6. Hinduism and Humanity 78
7. Yoga: An Integrated Philosophy of Life 87
8. Moral and Spiritual Values in New India 93
9. Religion Today 98
10. American Gurus 103
11. Secularism: A New Approach 108
12. Restructuring Education 112
13. Declaration on Nature: The Hindu Viewpoint 117
14. The Ethics of Conservation 120
15. Transition to Global Consciousness 125
16. The Need for Human Unity 130
17. The Way to Peace 133
APPENDIX: MUṆḌAKA UPANIṢAD 137
INDEX 187

TO LORD SIVA

I am your plaything.
You can breathe into me
the fire of eternal life,
and make me immortal;
or You can scatter my atoms
to the far corners of the universe
so that I disappear for ever.

You can fill me with light and power
so that I shine like a meteor
against the darkness of the midnight sky;
or You can extinguish my spirit
so that I sink for ever
into the deep and fathomless ocean of time.

You can set me among the eternal stars
resplendent with your divine fire;
or You can hurl me
into the abyss of darkness,
so that I can never again be visible
to mortal eyes.

You can come to me
with the glory of a thousand cupids;
or You can turn from me
and leave me stranded
in a grey and ghastly desert of despair.

You can smile at me
with the radiance that kindles the universe;
or You can open your eye of fury
and reduce me to a heap of ashes.

I am your plaything;
the choice is yours.

KARAN SINGH

1

Hinduism—An Overview

The religion that has come to be known as Hinduism is certainly the oldest and most varied of all the great religions of the world. The word 'Hinduism' itself is a geographical term based upon the Sanskrit name for the great river that runs across the northern boundaries of India, known as the Sindhu. For those living on the other side of this river, the entire region to the south-east of the Sindhu, which the Greeks called the Indus, came to be known as the land of the Hindus, and the vast spectrum of faiths that flourished here acquired the generic name Hinduism. In fact, Hinduism calls itself the *Sanātana Dharma*, the eternal faith, because it is based not upon the teachings of a single preceptor but on the collective wisdom and inspiration of great seers and sages from the very dawn of Indian civilization.

The Scriptures

The Sanskrit word for philosophy is *darśana* or 'seeing', which implies that Hinduism is not based merely on intellectual speculation but is grounded upon direct and immediate perception. This, in fact, distinguishes Indian philosophy from much of Western philosophical thought. The oldest and most important scriptures of Hinduism are the Vedas, which contain inspired utterances of seers and sages who had achieved a direct perception of the divine being. The Vedas are considered to be eternal, because they are not merely superb poetic compositions but represent the divine truth itself as perceived through the elevated consciousness of great seers.

The four Vedas—the *Rg* the *Sāma*, the *Yajur* and the *Atharva*—contain between them over a hundred thousand verses, which include some of the greatest mystical poetry ever written. For example, the famous Hymn of Creation in the *Ṛg-Veda* (X. 129/1–7) is an extraordinary utterance. It has been translated by Griffith as follows:

> Then was not non-existent nor existent:
> there was no realm of air, no sky beyond it:
> What covered it, and where? and what gave shelter?
> Was water there, unfathomed depth of water?
>
> Death was not then, nor was there aught immortal:
> No sign was there, the day's and night's divider.
> That One thing, breathless, breathed by its own nature:
> apart from it was nothing whatsoever.
>
> Darkness there was: at first concealed in darkness
> this All was indiscriminate chaos.
> All that existed then was void and formless:
> by the great power of Warmth was born that Unit.
>
> Thereafter rose Desire in the beginning,
> Desire the primal seed and germ of Spirit.
> Sages who searched with their hearts' thought discovered
> the existent's kinship with the non-existent.
>
> Transversely was their severing line extended:
> what was above it then, and what below it?
> There were begetters, there were mighty forces,
> free action here and energy up yonder.
>
> Who verily knows and who can here declare it,
> whence it was born and whence comes this creation?
> The gods are later than the world's production,
> who knows then whence it first came into being?
>
> He, the first origin of this creation,
> whether he formed it all or did not form it,
> Whose eye controls this world in highest heaven,
> He verily knows it, or perhaps he knows not.

The Vedas contain beautiful hymns addressed to various powers of nature such as the Sun, the Moon, the Ocean, the Rain, the Dawn, all pervaded by a deep intuitive awareness of the essential unity and interconnectedness behind these phenomena. Portions deal with the ritual worship of the early Aryans, the *yajña* sacrifice revolving around the sacred fire which was looked upon as the intermediary between the human and the divine powers. There is also a fascinating array of medical prescriptions, specially in the *Atharva-Veda*, and a great deal of other social material including hymns to matrimony and friendship, prayers for progeny, longevity, cattle and prosperity. Taken together, they constitute a unique document of the religious consciousness of all humanity. It is virtually a miracle that they came down intact through thousands of years entirely by memory, a fantastic feat of mnemonics for which countless generations of Brāhmaṇas deserve unqualified gratitude. It was only in the middle of the nineteenth century that the great orientalist Friedrich Max Müller brought out the first printed edition of the *Ṛg-Veda*.

The Upaniṣads are known as the Vedānta, or the end of the Vedas both, because they come at the end of the Vedic collections and also because they represent the culmination of Vedic teachings. One hundred and eight Upaniṣads have been preserved, of which at least fourteen are of major importance. These remarkable dialogues between the teacher and one or more pupils deal with the deepest problems of human existence, of death and other realms of being, of the goal of life and the stages of spiritual realization. The *Īśā Upaniṣad*, though containing only eighteen verses, is considered to be probably the most important such text. Its famous first line, 'This entire cosmos, whatever is still or moving, is pervaded by the divine', contains the very essence of Hinduism.

The *Muṇḍaka Upaniṣad* (2.2.3) has a beautiful verse which brings out the essential role of the Upaniṣads as vehicles for spiritual realization:

> Having taken as a bow the great weapon of the Upaniṣads, one should fix on it the arrow sharpened by constant meditation; drawing it with a mind filled with That (Brahman), penetrate, O handsome youth, the Imperishable as the target.

The *Kaṭha Upaniṣad* contains the memorable dialogue between the boy Naciketas and Yama, the God of Death, and represents a remarkable formulation of the Vedāntic gospel. It is significant that in Hinduism death is not something to be looked upon with horror and hatred, but is rather considered to be as essential an aspect of existence as life, part of the inescapable dualities of day and night, heat and cold, good and evil, joy and sorrow that are woven into the very texture of manifested existence. It is only by transcending these dualities and attaining the *brahmasthiti*, the state of Brahman, that the human being can finally fulfil his cosmic destiny.

Contrary to a popular misconception often encountered in the West, Hinduism is not a passive, world-negating religion. It is verily a vibrant, life-affirming faith, using 'life' in the deeper sense of that supreme poise that transcends the dualities of life and death. According to the Hindu view, there is a supreme state into which it is possible for the human consciousness to enter and which, once achieved, places one above the endless cycle of rebirth in which the entire cosmos is imprisoned. The sage Śvetāśvatara says in the great Upaniṣad that bears his name (3.8): 'I know that Great Being, effulgent like the Sun shining on the other shore beyond the darkness.' And Lord Kṛṣṇa also describes the supreme goal as 'the light of lights beyond the darkness' in the *Bhagavad-Gītā* (13.17).

The attainment of this exalted state of consciousness is not incompatible with action in this world. While it is true that there has always been a significant stand of renunciation in Hinduism, which found fuller expression in the Jain and Buddhist traditions that flowed from the mother faith, it is useful to remember that the goal of Hinduism is a luminous, glowing state of supreme bliss, not a negative self-annihilation.

There are five basic tenets that underlie Hinduism which, if properly understood, provide the key to an understanding of a faith that is bewildering in its apparent diversity and complexity. The first is the concept of Brahman, the unchanging, undying reality that pervades the entire cosmos. The Vedic seers saw that everything in the universe changes, and they called the creation *saṁsāra*, that which always moves. But they also perceived that behind this change there was an unchanging substratum from which the changing worlds emanated like sparks from a great fire. This supreme, all-pervasive entity known as Brahman has been beautifully described in various Upaniṣads. Thus the *Muṇḍaka Upaniṣad* (2.2.12) has the following verse:

> Brahman verily is this immortal being.
> In front is Brahman, behind is Brahman.
> to the right and to the left.
> It spreads forth above and below.
> Verily, Brahman is this effulgent universe.

Similarly, the following important passage in the *Śvetāśvatara Upaniṣad* (4.2–4) shows clrealy that, although the Hindus worshipped many manifestations of the divine, they realized that behind them all there was the same all-pervasive Brahman:

> Thou art the fire,
> Thou art the sun,
> Thou art the air,
> Thou art the moon,
> Thou art the starry firmament,
> Thou art Brahman Supreme:
> Thou art the waters—Thou
> The creator of all!
>
> Thou art woman, thou art man,
> Thou art the youth, thou art the maiden,
> Thou art the old man tottering with his staff;
> Thou facest everywhere.
>
> Thou art the dark butterfly,
> Thou art the green parrot with red eyes,
> Thou art the thunder cloud, the seasons, the seas.
> Without beginning art thou,
> Beyond time, beyond space,
> Thou art he from whom sprang
> The three worlds.
>
> Filled with Brahman are the things we see;
> Filled with Brahman floweth all that is;
> From Brahman all—yet is he still the same.

The second great insight of the Vedic seers was that, as the changing universe outside was pervaded by the Brahman, the changing world within man himself was based upon the undying Ātman. They realized that 'like corn, a mortal ripens and like corn is born again' (*Kaṭha Upaniṣad*, 1.1.6). The human entity is born again and again across the aeons, gathering a multitude of experiences and gradually moving towards the possibility of perfection. This immortal spark they called the 'Ātman'.

Having perceived the existence of the undying Brahman without and the undying Ātman within, the great seers were able to make the critical leap of realizing through their spiritual insight that the Ātman and Brahman were essentially one. In the *Chāndogya*

Upaniṣad, there is the famous story of Śvetaketu, who is taught by his father in a series of statements which end with the famous words *Tat tvam asi*—'that thou art'—meaning that the Ātman was essentially the Brahman. What the exact relationship between the two is has been the basis of various great schools of Vedānta, some holding with Śaṅkarācārya that in fact the two are identical (the Advaita Vedānta), some with Rāmānujācārya that they are both unitary and dual (the Viśiṣṭādvaita) and some with Madhvācārya that they are similar but always separate (the Dvaita).

Having established the existence of the Brahman, the Ātman and their relationship, the fourth major tenet of Hinduism is that the supreme goal of life lies in spiritual realization whereby the individual becomes aware of the deathless Ātman within him. The realization of the Ātman at once brings an entirely new dimension into the picture, and the realized soul transcends the cycle of suffering, illness, old age and death which are inevitable concomitants of ordinary life, the wheel of change and decay of the manifested universe. He may still choose to stay within the limits of manifestations and by his presence sweeten the bitter sea of suffering, but he is no longer bound to do so.

The fifth concept which lies at the very heart of the Hindu way of life is that of *karma*, a concept that includes action, causality and destiny. Action being inevitable, the human individual is bound by the results of his actions, pleasant fruits flowing from good deeds and unpleasant consequences from evil ones. *Karma* can thus be considered the moral equivalent of the law of conservation of energy or the equivalence of action and reaction in the field of natural sciences. While it is true that what we are today is the result of our past deeds, it also follows that we are the makers of our future by the way we act at present. Thus, far from implying fatalism as is often wrongly believed, *karma* gives tremendous responsibility to the individual and places in his own hands the key to his future destiny. Naturally, the unerring law of *karma* can work itself out only over a sufficiently long period of time; therefore the Hindu belief in reincarnation with the Ātman being reborn in a long series until the attainment of liberation. Indeed, if man were to have only one life, there would seem to be no moral or spiritual justification at all for the tremendous disparities and evidently undeserved suffering, even of children, which is so evident all around us. As the *Bhagavad-Gītā* (2.23) has it: 'As a man casts off his worn-out garments and takes others that are new, so the Ātman casts off worn-out bodies and enters others that are new.'

The Key Concepts

In addition to the Vedas and the Upaniṣads, Hinduism has a vast corpus of auxiliary scriptures including the two great epics, the *Rāmāyaṇa* and the *Mahābhārata*. Between them they express the collective wisdom and history of the entire race, and have had a profound influence on all aspects of Hindu life and culture in India and throughout South-east Asia for thousands of years. Then there are eighteen Purāṇas, rich in myth and symbol, of which the best known is the *Śrīmad-Bhāgavatam*; the *Brahma-Sūtras* which contain Vedāntic philosophy in the form of aphorisms, and the Tantras dealing with the esoteric aspects of the spiritual quest. There are also the codes of conduct, including the elaborate *Manu-Smṛti*, which seek to relate religion to the social and individual lives of Hindus.

Embedded within the huge compass of the *Mahābhārata* is that crestjewel of Hindu thought and one of the great religious classics of mankind, the *Bhagavad-Gītā*. Before going into the teaching of the *Gītā*, however, it will be useful to mention five sets of concepts which are an integral part of the Hindu ethos, as some understanding of these is essential if one is to grasp the main thrust of the teaching of the *Gītā*. Briefly, the concepts are as follows.

The Four *Yugas* or Cycles of Time

The Hindu concept of time is cyclical, not linear. The universe is *anādi-ananta*, without beginning and without end, going through recurrent phases of manifestation and dissolution. It is quite extraordinary how the Hindu concept of time is becoming more comprehensible with recent developments in extragalactic cosmology. Each day of Brahmā, the creator principle in the Hindu trinity, consists of four billion, three hundred and twenty million years, and the night of Brahmā is of a similar duration. Thus, the entire universe is a process of the outbreathing and inbreathing of Brahmā, corresponding to alternating periods of manifestation and dissolution. Each manifested cycle is divided into four *yugas* or aeons—*Satya, Tretā, Dvāpara* and *Kali*. In the *Satya-yuga*, virtue is in the ascendant, but this diminishes progressively until in the *Kali-yuga* it virtually disappears. At the end of each *Kali-yuga*, there is tremendous destruction, *pralaya*, after which the golden age appears again. The four *yugas* taken together form a *Maha-yuga* or a great cycle. We are now believed to be living in the *Kali-yuga* of the present cycle.

The Four *Āśramas* or Stages of Life

In the Hindu view human life is divided into four *āśramas* or stages—Brahmacarya, Gārhasthya, Vāṇaprastha and Sannyāsa. As the ideal life-span of the Hindus was a hundred years, each of these stages consists of twenty-five year period. The first twenty-five years would be student life, when the young man is expected to spend his time and energy upon the attainment of education at the feet of a qualified teacher, and to observe sexual abstinence. Once this is completed, he moves on to the Gārhasthya *āśrama*, or householder stage, wherein he marries, raises a family and participates in economically productive activity for the welfare of society. By fifty, he is ready to move on to the Vāṇaprastha stage of semi-retirement, in which he gradually brings himself to detach himself from worldly activities and to concentrate upon the study of scriptures and meditational practices. Finally, at seventy-five, he is ready to withdraw entirely from social life and become a *sannyāsīn* or ascetic by renouncing the world, freeing himself from all social responsibilities and concentrating exclusively upon the spiritual quest. Sannyāsa *āśrama*, however, can be entered into even at a younger age by a person who renounces worldly life and joins one of the many monastic orders that exist in Hinduism.

The Four *Puruṣārthas* or Goals of Life

According to Hindu thought, these four goals are *dharma, artha, kāma* and *mokṣa*. *Dharma* is a word that has often been translated as 'religion', but, in fact, it is more comprehensive. It implies not only a religious and philosophical framework but a total world-view, including a scheme of right conduct under various circumstances. It comes from the root *dhṛ* which means to uphold, and in the broadest sense is used for the universal laws of nature that uphold the cosmos. It also implies such concepts as justice, virtue, morality, righteousness, law and duty. It is the first of the four goals, because it is the most comprehensive and is valid throughout the life of a human being. *Artha*, or wealth, is the second goal. It is interesting that Hinduism not only tolerates the importance of wealth but accepts it positively as one of the four main goals of life, provided its acquisition and utilization are in accord with the broad principles of *dharma*. The third goal is *kāma* or sensual enjoyment. Here again, Hinduism gives an important place to sensual enjoyment, realizing that, while renunciation may be suitable for the ascetic, it is certainly not suited to the common man. Therefore, the concept of *kāma* is incorporated in the Hindu ethos, and indeed it has its own Śāstra in the form of the famous *Kāma-Sūtra* by Vātsyāyana. The final goal in Hindu thought is *mokṣa*, or release from suffering, old age and ultimately from death itself. As mentioned earlier, *mokṣa* is not simply a question of survival after death, which in any case is taken for granted in Hinduism; it implies transcending both life and death by the attainment of that spiritual poise whereby man is liberated from the wheel of *saṁsāra*.

The Four *Varṇas* or Castes

According to the traditional Hindu view, human beings are divided into four categories on the basis of their intrinsic qualities. The highest caste consists of Brāhmaṇas, the thinkers, philosophers, priests, whose role it is to provide spiritual guidance and intellectual sustenance to society. Next come the Kṣatriyas, or warriors, whose *dharma* revolves around ruling the nation and defending it against aggression. Third are the Vaiśyas, or traders, who are involved in agricultural and commercial operations, while all that falls within the sphere of service is the responsibility of the fourth category of Śūdras, or labourers. It is interesting that the word *varṇa* also means colour, and, if one looks back over the history of early India, it is clear that the problem of colour as between the Aryans, the great existing Dravidian civilization, and the numerous aboriginal tribes was a major factor in the development of this caste concept. There were certain categories beyond the pale of the caste system which were known as the outcastes, and whose ill-treatment over the centuries is a standing disgrace to the otherwise remarkable achievements of Hindu civilization.

The Four *Yogas* or Paths to the Divine

The word *yoga* is derived from the root *yuj* meaning to join or yoke, and it involves the joining of the Ātman with the Brahman, of the individual soul with the universal divine being. In the Hindu view, there are several methods of this union, and each spiritual aspirant chooses the one that is best suited to his inner and outer conditions. While the path is essentially one, it varies to the extent that emphasis is placed upon different human faculties. Over the ages, four main *yogas* or paths have developed—*jñāna, bhakti, karma* and *rāja*. *Jñāna* is the path of intellectual discrimination, suitable for those whose intellects are highly developed and who are taught constantly to discriminate between the real and the unreal, the ephemeral and the eternal, until they reach spiritual realization. *Bhakti*, or the path of devotion to a personal form of God, is based on the emotional urge and involves harnessing of the sovereign power of love to spiritual quest. In this path, there is a deep emotional relationship between the human and the divine, beautifully expressed by Arjuna in the *Gītā* as the combined relationship of a father to a son, a friend to a dear friend and a lover to his beloved. *Karma*, or the way of action, is best suited for people who are particularly drawn by social service, alleviation of human suffering and organizational activity, and whose constant compulsion for work is directed towards the divine. Finally, *Rāja-yoga* involves various spiritual practices, including physical and psychic exercises set out in Patañjali's classic, the *Yogā-Sūtra*. These paths are by no means mutually exclusive, and can, indeed, enjoy a benign symbiosis.

Another important aspect of Hindu thought is the concept of the *avatāra*, or descent of God in human form. In keeping with its concept of cyclic time, Hinduism holds that there have been numerous such descents in the past and will be more in the future. As Kṛṣṇa himself says in the *Gītā* (4.7–8):

> Whensoever righteousness declines, O Bharata, and unrighteousness arises, then do I manifest myself upon earth. For the deliverance of the good, for the destruction of evil-doers and for the re-establishment of righteousness, I am born from age to age.

With these concepts in mind, we can now turn to the *Bhagavad-Gītā*. The teaching of the Upaniṣads is in a peaceful setting, usually in the forest *āśramas* or retreats of the teacher. The setting of the *Bhagavad-Gītā*, however, is entirely different. Here the teacher and the disciple—Śrī Kṛṣṇa and Arjuna—are placed in the very centre of the battlefield. The conches have been sounded, the flight of missiles has begun and, poised between the two armies, Arjuna suddenly suffers a failure of nerve when he sees arrayed against him his kinsmen and teachers. He is overcome by a great wave of revulsion, and at that critical juncture implores his friend and teacher to show him the correct path. The setting of the *Gītā* is thus similar to the present human predicament. Man today finds himself in the midst of serious conflicts, both outer and inner; and it is on the battlefield of life that he needs correct guidance. This explains the special appeal of the *Gītā* to modern man.

Another unique feature of the *Gītā* is that it fuses the four paths into a single integral movement towards the divine. It deals with all the four *yogas*, but constantly seeks to integrate them around the overriding relationship between Arjuna and Śrī Kṛṣṇa, the human and the divine. While the Brahman of the *Upaniṣads* is impersonal and is, therefore, referred to as 'That', in the *Gītā*, Śrī Kṛṣṇa himself appears as the Divine Being that transcends both the manifest and the unmanifest in his all-encompassing consciousness. The divine in the *Gītā* is not a non-personalized concept, but involves the personality, raised as it were to the nth degree. Thus at the end of the teaching, Śrī Kṛṣṇa instructs Arjuna in these words (18.61–2):

> The Lord, O Arjuna, is seated in the heart of all beings,
> causing by His divine power the entire cosmos
> to revolve as if mounted on a machine.
> Take refuge in Him with your entire being, O Bharata;
> by His Grace you will gain supreme peace and the
> eternal abode.

Having thus spoken of the divine in the third person, Kṛṣṇa completes the teaching with the following memorable verse (18.65–6):

> Fix your mind on Me, be devoted to Me,
> Sacrifice to Me, bow to Me and to Me shall you come.
> This is My pledge to you, for you are dear to Me.
> Abandon all dharmas and take refuge in Me alone.
> Fear not, I will deliver you from all sin.

The *Bhagavad-Gītā* is a remarkable fount of inspiration and power. Among its many memorable passages is the famous scene in the Eleventh Chapter where Kṛṣṇa reveals to Arjuna his Divine Form which encompasses the entire cosmos and yet includes the great calm that lies behind all manifestation. It is this vision that is described as having the splendour of a thousand suns risen simultaneously in the sky. The *Gītā* also contains the celebrated and oft-quoted statement with regard to action and its fruit. While man should work constantly for the welfare of the world, he should not be attached to the fruits of his action and should repose them in the divine. The *Gītā* thus teaches unceasing involvement in action while retaining an inner core of detachment, and dedicating the totality of human life to the divine will. Involvement without obsession is the key concept.

While there are many *avatāras* in the Hindu scriptures, including manifestations of Śiva in the South Indian tradition, the best known list is a set of ten incarnations of Viṣṇu known as the *Daśāvatāra*. These have had a profound influence on popular Hinduism, and include two of the most popular and widely worshipped figures in the Hindu pantheon, Rāma and Kṛṣṇa. Interestingly, these ten incarnations represent the evolutionary ladder in a most remarkable manner. They start with Matsya the fish; then Kūrma, the amphibious tortoise; then Varāha, the boar; then Narasiṁha, the man-lion; then Vāmana, the dwarf; then Paraśurāma, the wielder of the great axe; then Śrī Rāma, the noble hero of the *Rāmāyaṇa*; then Śrī Kṛṣṇa, the divine flutist and charioteer of the *Mahābhārata*; then the Buddha, and in the final incarnation of this cycle yet to manifest, the Kalki *avatāra*, depicted as a magnificent youth riding a great white horse with a meteor-like sword raining death and destruction on all sides, perhaps symbolizing some cataclysmic nuclear conflict.

The inclusion of the Buddha as the ninth incarnation needs special comment, because it reveals the great capacity in Hinduism to absorb even heretical movements. Evidently the fame and influence of the Buddha were so great that he could not be ignored, and yet his teachings were in some respects antithetical to classical Hinduism. He was, therefore, absorbed into the Hindu pantheon, so that he is revered today by Hindus with no difficulty at all. Indeed, although technically the number of Buddhists in India is very small, this is partly due to the fact that many of his teachings, such as his stern condemnation of animal sacrifice, have become part of the Hindu mainstream itself. To some extent, the same can be said about Christ, and most Hindus have no difficulty in accepting him as one of the incarnations of God. What Hinduism is not able to accept is the exclusive claim of any one teacher to the monopoly of divinity and wisdom for all time to come.

Classical Hinduism

With the Vedas, the Upaniṣads and the auxiliary scriptures culminating in the *Bhagavad-Gītā*, the major contours of Hinduism became clearly defined. But in Hinduism there has been through the last two thousand years a continuous process of reinterpretation and restatement by a series of remarkable men and women. Some were kings and erudite scholars, others were common folk, often unlettered and unsophisticated. Some belonged to the 'higher' Brāhmaṇa and Kṣatriya castes, others to the 'lower', including the 'outcastes'. Some spoke chaste Sanskrit, that most magnificent of human languages; others sang in the local dialects. Some lived in great palaces and temples; others in simple cottages, or roamed the countryside with neither home nor shelter. Some were devoted to Śiva, the great Lord seated in majestic solitude on the mountain peak; some to Kṛṣṇa, the eternal lover playing his divine flute in the forests of Vṛndāvana. Some worshipped the great Mother in one of her innumerable forms, beauty enthroned upon the seat of power; others offered their homage to one or the other numerous deities in the Hindu pantheon rich with an inexhaustible store of symbol and image.

And yet, running through all these remarkable persons like a golden thread, is the overriding common factor—their realization of the divine. Hinduism has always reserved its deepest veneration for those who have in some way realized the divine. Scholars are respected, rulers are feared, but real veneration is reserved only for the realized ones who constitute a race apart, the race that never dies. And it is a remarkable fact, largely responsible for the continued vitality of Hinduism through the ages, that it has in every century produced a number of such realized souls. Spread from Kashmir in the North to Kerala in the South, from Gujarat in the West to Assam in the East, these great souls have by the sheer force of their spiritual realization kept the inner power of Hinduism intact and reillumined Hindu society in times of incredible adversity and ordeal. Had it not been for these great ones, truly the salt of the earth, Hinduism which had to undergo such savage persecution for centuries would have vanished from the face of this earth.

The Great Ācaryas

Space permits only a rapid survey of the more important developments in Hinduism over the last twenty centuries. The first outstanding figure that comes to mind is Tiruvalluvar (*c.* A.D. 300), the great Tamil saint, whose classic work, the *Tirukural*, is generally known as the Veda of the Tamils. Then came Ādi Śaṅkarācārya (*b.* A.D. 686) the extraordinary philosopher from Kerala, who wrote illuminating commentaries on the great Hindu texts, innumerable hymns to various deities in beautiful Sanskrit, and a number of treatises on the philosophy of non-dualism or Advaita Vedānta. He also founded four *pīṭhas* or monastic centres in the four corners of India—at Śṛṅgerī in the South, Dvārikā in the West, Badrīnātha in the North and Puri in the East—which have played a profound role in sustaining classical Hinduism down the ages. Śaṅkara stressed the supreme importance of liberation achieved through knowledge which, in turn, is born of asceticism and meditation. In his system, devotion and action could only play a preparatory and subsidiary role.

In sharp contradistinction to Śaṅkara's monistic philosophy was the theistic approach of the great Tamil scholar Rāmānuja (*b.* A.D. 1017) who advocated qualified monism and proclaimed that the way of devotion was the supreme path. The seeker must develop a devotion to God so intense that he realizes that he is only a fragment of Him and wholly dependent on His grace. Thus Rāmānuja held that, however high the individual soul may rise, it will always remain in some degree separate from the divine, so that the intense interpersonal relationship can subsist for ever.

Another great South Indian Ācārya was Madhva (*b.* A.D. 1199), whose system can be described as dualistic in that he held that God and individual souls are eternally distinct, and the salvation consists not in the merger of the two but in the soul dwelling eternally close to God and enjoying the contemplation of His glory. Madhva also held a doctrine, not generally found in Hinduism, that souls who consistently indulge in evil can ultimately get so weighed down that they can be permanently expelled from the universe to a state of eternal damnation.

These great teachers and their followers wrote original commentaries upon the *prasthānatrayī*, the three foundations of Hindu philosophy—the Upaniṣads, the *Brahma-Sūtras* and the *Bhagavad-Gītā*. In addition, for intellectual and academic classification, Hindu philosophy has been divided into six systems of thought, each associated with a great teacher, which are generally reduced to three categories. The Vaiśeṣika of Kaṇāda and the Nyāya of Gautama form one group; the Sāṅkhya of Kapila and the Yoga of Patañjali the second; and the Pūrva-Mīmāṁsā of Jaimini and the Vedānta (also called Uttara-Mīmaṁsā) of Vyāsa the third. These schools are regarded as *āstika* or orthodox, because they accept the overriding authority of the Vedas, while the two other great schools of Indian philosophy, Jainism (whose twenty-fourth great teacher, Mahāvīra, lived in the sixth century B.C) and Buddhism (founded by Gautama Buddha in the same century) are regarded as *anāstika* or heterodox because they repudiate the authority of the Vedas.

Almost contemporaneous with these great sons of Indian spiritual movements there developed in the northernmost state of Kashmir a unique and extremely rich tradition, known to the world as Kashmir Śaivism. Based on the Tantras—esoteric spiritual texts—rather than the Vedas, it produced a series of great teachers, the most outstanding of whom was Ācārya Abhinavagupta (*b. c.* A.D. 950–975) who must rank as one of the greatest spiritual masters in the entire Hindu tradition.

The Forms of the Formless

It is necessary to point out, however, that while learned scholars proclaimed and disputed these various schools of philosophy, for the common man, the mainstay of Hinduism has always been devotion to a deity representing some aspect or incarnation of the divine. Hinduism has a wealth of imagery, symbolism and iconography, and has produced a dazzling array of images and concepts which often baffles non-Hindus. This has led to the erroneous view, still extant in some quarters, that Hinduism is polytheistic. It certainly encourages the worship of many forms and symbols, but it must be understood that behind these myriad forms is the same all-pervasive divinity mirrored in a thousand different ways.

Very briefly, popular Hindu worship today revolves around three major deities—Śiva, Viṣṇu as himself and his major incarnations, and the goddess. Śiva Mahādeva is the great primeval lord, and there is reason to believe that he is of a pre-Aryan origin because on the still undeciphered seals of the Indus Valley civilization (*c*. 5000–3000 B.C.), there is a figure seated cross-legged with several of the features associated with Śiva. Śiva is invariably worshipped along with a *lingam*, a powerful symbol representing the creative force behind all manifestation. He is generally portrayed as a resplendent ascetic sitting in meditation on a mountain peak, his body smeared with ashes, deadly snakes entwined around his neck and the sacred Ganges flowing from his matted locks. He is also worshipped in his role as the cosmic dancer, Naṭarāja, whose dance symbolizes the eternal wheel of the cosmos where millions of worlds are destroyed every moment and millions other spring into existence to the best of the eternal rhythm. Indeed, the magnificent image of the dancing Śiva represents one of the high watermarks of human art.

Despite his fearsome appearance, Śiva (the very word means 'auspicious') is easy to please, Āśutoṣa, and is generous with his boons even to the titans who often misuse them. He is neither born nor does he die, being the master of birth and death. In South India, there is a tradition in which Śiva is believed to have appeared in human form on several different occasions, either to help his devotees or to impart esoteric teachings. He is the *mahā-yogī*, the great ascetic, and the patron-saint of those practising *yoga*.

Śiva is the third god of the Hindu trinity—Brahmā the creator, Viṣṇu the preserver and Śiva the destroyer—but again it must be remembered that these are not three different gods but three aspects of the same divine being. This is beautifully portrayed in the magnificent monolithic sculpture of *Trimūrti* on the Elephant island off the coast of Bombay. One of the world's great artistic creations, this massive sculpture shows clearly the three aspects integrated in a single, divine entity. In fact, the great art of India provides as useful a way of approaching an understanding of the theistic concepts as the texts themselves. Apart from sculpture and painting, the great classical dance forms of India, particularly the Bharata Nāṭyam, can bring to life concepts which may appear abstruse and unidimensional when approached purely through the written word.

Viṣṇu is depicted as lying on a great serpent that floats on the vast, endless ocean of milk, the *kṣīrasāgara*. In this form he is worshipped in many temples, specially in the South, but elsewhere in India he is more widely worshipped in two of his most popular incarnations associated with the two great epics—Śrī Rāma and

Śrī Kṛṣṇa. Indeed, these two names have carried the undying message of Hinduism to billions of men and women for thousands of years now, not only in India but wherever the Hindu cultural impact has been felt in the world. Śrī Rāma is depicted with a bow in hand, accompanied by his noble wife Sītā, his faithful brother Laksmana, and his devoted follower the monkey god Hanumān. Śrī Kṛṣṇa is depicted in numerous forms, commencing with his early childhood as a baby, Bāla Kṛṣṇa, and terminating as the charioteer of Arjuna, Pārthasārathī. But his most popular and appealing form is as a beautiful cowherd youth, Gopāla Kṛṣṇa, dark and resplendent, standing with one foot crossed over the other and playing his magic flute. He is generally worshipped along with Rādhā, the shepherdess who has come to symbolize the essence of the Kṛṣṇa cult of devotion. Viṣṇu is also worshipped in some of his lesser known incarnations such as Narasiṁha, the man-lion, who appeared to rid the world of the demon-king Hiraṇyakaśipu and save his son, the great boy-devotee Prahlāda.

The third major focus of devotion in India is the goddess in her numerous forms. She is worshipped as Pārvatī, the consort of Śiva; Lakṣmī, the consort of Viṣṇu; Sīta and Rādhā along with Śrī Rāma and Śrī Kṛṣṇa. But, and this is a point of considerable significance, she is not only worshipped as a consort, but in her own right as the essence of power and beauty; as Durgā with eighteen arms riding a lion and scattering the demon hordes like chaff; as Kālī, the fierce, naked goddess standing upon a corpse and drinking the blood of her freshly slain enemies; as Sarasvatī, the goddess of art, poetry and music, the patron of all learning and wisdom. The worship of the great mother is, of course, known throughout the world in one form or another, but it is in Hinduism that she appears in all her splendour.

There is a Paurāṇic myth about the birth of Durgā which is full of symbolic significance. Once a great demon, the buffalo-headed Mahiṣāsura representing the evil forces of brute materialism, succeeded in defeating all the gods (*devas*: the shining ones) and established his supremacy over creation. The gods despaired, because despite all their efforts, they could not vanquish this terrible monster. At last they gathered together on a mountain peak and decided to pool their divine powers. Each god contributed his own power symbolized by a weapon, led by the lord of the gods, Indra. At the end of the great ritual, when all the divine powers had been pooled, there arose a dazzling light which spread its glory throughout the three worlds, and in the midst of the light appeared Durgā, the great goddess, with a weapon in each of her eighteen arms and riding a ferocious tiger. She then gave battle to Mahiṣāsura, and after a terrible conflict lasting nine days and nine nights, she finally slew him and rid the world of this great terror. These nine nights, the Navarātri, are still celebrated every year by Hindus as symbolizing the victory of divine power over the forces of evil.

In addition to Śiva, Viṣṇu and the goddess, there are numerous other deities who are the object of devotion and worship by Hindus down to the present day. These include the elephant-headed Gaṇeśa, remover of obstacles, whose worship is essential before any auspicious undertaking can begin; Kārtikeya or Subrahmaṇya, the younger son of Śiva and Pārvatī who is widely worshipped in South India as a young boy with a spear, riding a peacock; Hanumān, the devoted follower of Śrī Rāma who despite his simian appearance is wise and powerful; Dattātreya, the three-headed deity who is the patron-saint of *yogis* engaged in esoteric practices; and Ayappan, a South Indian deity, believed to be the result of a union between Śīva and Viṣṇu in his female form as Mohinī. Sūrya, the sun-god, is known as the *pratyakṣa-deva*, the visible god, and is generally worshipped through the famous *gāyatrī mantra*. Curiously, Brahmā, the first god of the Hindu trinity, has only one temple in Pushkar dedicated to him in the whole of India, his worship having evidently fallen into disuse along with that of the other Vedic gods such as Indra and Varuṇa.

An important point to remember is that the worship of these various deities is by no means mutually exclusive. While each Hindu usually has a special family deity—the *īṣṭa-devatā*—he often worships three or four different deities during his daily prayers, and pays homage to any deity in a temple he may visit. Also, apart from anthropomorphic deities, some Hindus in addition use certain symbols for purposes of meditation. The most important of these is the *Aum* which is described in the scriptures as being the audio-visual symbol of Brahman itself and is endowed with a wealth of symbolism. An entire Upaniṣad—the *Māṇḍūkya*—has been devoted to the word *Aum*.

Meditation on the symbol and sound of *Aum* is an important aspect of *yoga*, a word that has gained much currency of late throughout the world but is generally imperfectly understood. As has been mentioned earlier, *yoga* implies the joining or yoking of human consciousness to the Divine Being, and in this sense it can be applied to the four major paths of spiritual attainment. In a more specialized sense, *yoga* involves physical and mental disciplines directed at control over mental and physical functions, specially breathing. The classic text of this *yoga* is the celebrated *Yoga-Sūtra* of Patañjali, one of the world's great religious classics.

The *sūtras*, or aphorisms of Patañjali lay down an eight-fold path *aṣṭāṅga-yoga* of physical, psychological and moral discipline that, if properly adhered to under the guidance of a qualified teacher, results in the consciousness of the seeker being gradually raised until the Ātman shines forth in its pristine glory as pure consciousness. This path also involves arousal of the *kuṇḍalinī śakti* or serpent power, believed to be located at the base of the human spine. As this power rises through a series of occult centres or *cakras* located in various parts of the body, the consciousness is correspondingly elevated, until finally it bursts into the highest *cakra* at the top of the brain—the *sahasrāra* or thousand-petalled lotus—where the merger between the Ātman and the Brahman takes place and the seeker is plunged into the highest bliss. This elevated state, known as *samādhi*, is the goal of all yogic practices.

Numerous other texts on various aspects of *yoga* are to be found in Hindu literature, all basing themselves upon the foundations laid by Patañjali. These include the Tantras or esoteric texts which deal with the various practices and techniques of *kuṇḍalinī* arousal and acquisition of psychic powers. These miraculous powers, or *siddhis*, are accepted as an important aspect of yogic practices, but their misuse or even excessive demonstration is frowned upon as a hindrance to the achievement of the supreme goal. Through the ages, as today, there have been in India a fair number of persons who possess these powers, and miracle-mongering has always been an occupational hazard for *yogis* which it is not always easy to avoid.

An important aspect of Hinduism, whether it is *yoga* or any other system of philosophy, discipline or teaching, is the critical importance that is assigned to the *guru* or teacher. The *guru* in the Hindu tradition is to be venerated even more than one's parents, because while our parents give us physical life, it is the *guru* who brings about our spiritual rebirth whereby alone can man fulfil his cosmic destiny. This notion, which appears to many to be somewhat exaggerated, will become clearer when it is understood that the human *guru* is but a symbol of the divine power that already resides within us. The word *guru* itself means dispeller of darkness, and by bringing the light of spiritual wisdom into the material darkness of normal human consciousness, the *guru* indeed performs a unique and priceless function.

Needless to say, in Hinduism, as in so many other religions, there is the usual quota of charlatans and even criminals masquerading under the guise and habit of spiritual teachers. Generally, a person gets the sort of *guru* he deserves, and there is a well-established tradition that when the disciple is ready, the *guru* will appear. In the *Mundaka Upanisad* two essential qualifications of a true *guru* are laid down, both of which must be fulfilled if a person is really to occupy that elevated status. The *guru* must be *śrotriya*, learned in the scriptures, and *brahmaniṣṭha* established in the Brahman or divine consciousness. Hinduism believes that spiritual attainment is not possible without a *guru*, although sometimes in place of a human *guru*, a book or scripture may suffice. There have also been instances in which people have been initiated by some high being through a dream rather than in the flesh.

The Bhakti Movement

Despite great turmoil for many centuries in the North, due to foreign invasions and conquests, Hinduism continued to develop. Indeed, an important aspect of its development during Muslim rule was a two-fold movement: a turning inwards to preserve itself in the face of widespread, often severe, persecution by Muslims whose religion forbade many of the practices central to Hinduism, specially image-worship; and a syncretic movement in which at the mystical level there could be a synthesis between the two faiths. Both these factors led to a tremendous devotional revival which has collectively come to be known as the Bhakti movement, one of the most interesting movements in the long and eventful history of Hinduism.

Throughout the Middle Ages there arose a series of extraordinary saint-singers who preached the gospel of divine love and ecstasy. While previous Hindu teachings had been almost exclusively in Sanskrit, this new movement broke away from the rigid and conservative Brāhman-dominated tradition, and used the regional languages and dialects to propagate their message. This also involved a revolt against the rigid caste restrictions and taboos that had become a negative feature in classical Hinduism. The saint-singers not only came from all castes and communities, including Muslims and some remarkable women, but their message was addressed to the common people irrespective of caste or creed.

In Islam also, as against the *ulama* or clergy, there has always been a mystical tradition of seekers intoxicated with the love of God. These were known as Sufi, and it was with the Sufi tradition that the Bhakti movement developed close affinity. The first major Sufi teacher to come to India was the great Khwaja Moinuddin Chishti (*b.* 1142). He arrived in Delhi towards the end of the twelfth century, and finally settled in Ajmer where he had many disciples, both Hindu and Muslim. His great shrine there, the Dargah Shareef, is today one of the most important centres of Muslim pilgrimage and draws numerous Hindu pilgrims also year after year. In Hinduism the first great figure of medieval mysticism was Rāmānanda (*c.* 1370–1440). Although a disciple of Rāmānuja, Rāmānanda moved away from traditional orthodoxy, challenged caste divisions and began preaching in Hindi rather than in Sanskrit. One of his most illustrious disciples was Guru Ravidās who was a cobbler by profession. By sheer dint of spiritual merit, he rose to become one of the most respected religious teachers of his time, and still has millions of followers.

Rāmānanda's disciples came mainly from the lower castes, the most famous being Kabīr, who is claimed both by the Hindus and the Muslims. The son of a Muslim weaver, Kabīr (1440–1518) was drawn into the Bhakti movement at an early age. His songs struck at the root of religious orthodoxy, ritualism and intolerance. Kabīr combined in himself the best of the Sufi and Bhakti traditions. One of his songs (translated by Rabindranath Tagore) contains the following stanzas:

> O servant, where dost thou seek me?
> O! I am beside thee.
> I am neither in the temple nor in mosque;
> I am neither in Kaaba nor in Kailasa,
> Neither am I in rites and ceremonies,
> Nor in yoga and renunciation.
> If thou art a true seeker

Thou shalt at once see me,
Thou shalt meet me in a moment of time.
Kabir says, O Sadhu, God is the breath of all breath,
There is nothing but water at the holy bathing places,
I know that they are useless, for I have bathed in them,
The images are all lifeless, they cannot speak.
I know, for I have cried aloud to them.
The Purana and the Koran are mere words;
Lifting up the curtain, I have seen.
Kabir gives utterance to the words of experience;
He knows well that all other things are untrue.

Kabīr had a tremendous influence upon the India of his day. Despite the fact that he was a lowly weaver, the sheer force of his spiritual realization made him a focus of great veneration. There is an interesting, perhaps apocryphal, story about his death. Both the Hindus and the Muslims claimed his body, the former insisting that he be cremated and the latter that he be buried. When the shroud was removed, however, the body had disappeared and in its place was a heap of flowers. These were then divided between the contending parties; the Hindus carried off their share and cremated them with great devotion, while the Muslims buried their share with equal veneration. Thus, in death as in life Kabīr taught the gospel of spiritual communion and brotherhood to India's two largest religious communities.

Kabīr had many disciples, but two teachers who were greatly influenced by him deserve special mention. The first was Nānak (1469–1538) who went on to found the Sikh faith. He constantly emphasized that in the sight of God 'there was no Hindu and no Mussalman', and many of the hymns contained in the *Granth Sāhib*, the sacred book of the Sikhs, echo this concept. Another of Kabīr's followers was Dādu (1544–1603) who also founded a powerful movement based on his teachings known as Dādu-panth. He wrote many beautiful hymns, and in one of them he says:

God is my ancestor, the creator is my kinsman,
The world-guru is my caste, I am a child of the Almighty.

The Bhakti movement produced a profusion of great literature. Two figures of particular importance in the vast Hindi-speaking

Indo-Gangetic plain are Tulsīdāsa (1527–1623) and Suradāsa (1478–1581). Tulsīdāsa produced the first and greatest classic in Hindi, the *Rāmacaritamānasa* (Holy Lake of Rāma's Deeds), which is the story of the *Rāmāyaṇa* retold in Hindi verse with a wealth of poetry and deep devotion. There are many versions of the *Rāmāyaṇa*, the most important being the original Sanskrit version of Vālmīki and the Tamil version of Kamban. But the *Rāmacaritamānasa* has had a unique impact. For millions of Hindus in North India, it has provided for centuries the main cultural and religious foundations, and down to this day verses from it are sung in every village and town. It was this great religious classic that the indentured labourers who went from India to Fiji, Surinam, Mauritius and other plantations during colonial rule took with them, and which remains their religious umbilical cord linking them to the land of their origin. Tulsīdāsa looks upon Śrī Rāma as the supreme incarnation of the divine being, born for the salvation of mankind and worthy of total devotion and dedication.

Suradāsa, considered by some critics to be an even greater poet became blind in early childhood. Nonetheless, he composed beautiful devotional poetry directed towards Śrī Kṛṣṇa. The descriptions of Kṛṣṇa's childhood, his youthful pranks, his dalliance with the *gopīs* (milkmaids) of Vṛndāvana, his magical feats, his resplendent personality epitomizing the Divine lover who summons human souls to the golden notes of his eternal flute, are part of the great heritage of Hinduism. Both Tulsīdāsa and Suradāsa, along with a number of other devotional saints including the Pathan Raskhan, another devotee of Śrī Kṛṣṇa gave a tremendous boost to popular Hinduism. At a time when Muslim rule was being established over most of India, and the older, classical orthodoxy was losing its hold upon the people's minds, the Bhakti movement once again demonstrated the resilience of Hinduism and its capacity to enable its followers to restate and reinterpret the eternal verities in the light of changed circumstances.

In Karnataka, the great saint Purandaradāsa (1480–1564) sang of the glory of God and won a vast following. Eastern India, particularly Bengal, has always been an important centre of Hinduism. The great eleventh-century poet-devotee Jayadeva, who composed one of the post-classical Sanskrit masterpieces in his poem the *Gīta-Govinda* relating the story of Śrī Kṛṣṇa, had given a great fillip to Vaiṣṇava worship in Bengal and Orissa. An extraordinary saint called Caitanya (1485–1534), popularly known as Mahāprabhu (the Great Lord) and considered by his devotees to be an incarnation of Śrī Kṛṣṇa himself, founded the Vaiṣṇava movement in Bengal. A special feature of his ministry was the *kīrtanas*, choral singing and chanting by groups of devotees wandering from village to village and from town to town. Often the men involved in chanting would be carried away by a religious frenzy, and Śrī Caitanya himself would be thrown into a trance or fit of ecstasy as he contemplated the glory of Kṛṣṇa. Although he did not write extensively, he exerted a profound influence on the subsequent development of Bengali and Oriya literature. Further east in the Brahmaputra valley, another great teacher and reformer Śaṅkaradeva (1449–1568) writing in Assamese greatly influenced the Hindus of that region. The same is true of Tukārāma (1607–1649) in Maharashtra, which had earlier produced the young saint Jñāneśvara (1275–1296) whose Marathi work, the *Jñāneśvarī*, is one of the great classics of Hinduism.

No survey of the Bhakti movement, howsoever brief, can omit the names of two remarkable women who have left the impress of their attainment upon future generations. Lalleśvarī (1317–1372) was a Kashmiri saint who attained God-realization at an early age, and whose life is full of legends and stories of miracles. Her utterances teach the direct path of realization through intense love of the divine, renouncing attachment to worldly possessions and family ties, and rising above the dualities of caste and creed. She writes:

> Shiva abides in all that is everywhere;
> Then do not discriminate
> Between a Hindu and a Mussalman.
> If thou art wise, know thyself;
> That is the true knowledge of the Lord.
> I renounced fraud, untruth, deceit;
> I taught my mind to see the One
> In all my fellowmen.
> How could I then discriminate
> Between man and man
> And not accept the food
> Offered to me by brother man?

The other great woman figure of the Bhakti movement was Mīrābāi (1450–1512), a Rajput princess who was married at an early age to the Rāṇā of Udaipur. She was a childhood devotee of Śri Kṛṣṇa, and had dedicated her life to him. After her marriage, she continued to devote her entire time to the worship of Kṛṣṇa, incurring the displeasure of her husband who even tried to poison her. By Kṛṣṇa's grace, however, the cup of poison turned into honey as she danced in ecstasy before the image of the god. Mīrā subsequently renounced her worldly life, and wandered through India singing her beautiful compositions, which are among the most moving devotional songs of Hinduism. One of her best loved hymns goes thus:

> Tying anklets upon her feet, Mira dances in ecstasy.
> People say Mira has gone mad,
> Her mother-in-law says she has disgraced the clan,
> The Rana sent her a cup of poison
> Which Mira, laughingly, drank.
> I have myself become the eternal maid-servant of
> My Narayana.
> Mira's God is Giridhar, lifter of the mountain.
> O Indestructible One, meet me swiftly in your
> Eternal embrace.

Thus we see that in its most difficult period Hinduism produced a glittering galaxy of saint-singers drawn from all corners of the country, who inspired millions by their devotion and poetry, presented in an idiom readily understood by the masses. They were re-stating the great Vedāntic truths—the unity of Ātman and Brahman, of the human and the divine—in a new phraseology which took the message down to the most humble villages where the majority of Hindus have always lived. Their songs remain to this day a major source of inspiration for Hindus, and while the sonorous Sanskrit chanting of the magnificent Vedic hymns can still be heard on special occasions, specially in South India, it is the songs of the medieval saints which echo and re-echo in fields and forests, in villages and towns. Truly has it been said that music has the unique capacity to carry the human consciousness out of its narrow confines towards the brimming ocean of the divine.

The Modern Renaissance

The entire history of Hinduism, looked at from a certain angle, can be seen as a constant process of challenge and response. To each major crisis, Hinduism reacted, first by briefly withdrawing into a shell and then, with its unparalleled capacity for assimilation and regeneration, by a new resurgence. This happened with the Jain and Buddhist movements, with the early Christian missionaries and, to a lesser extent, with the Muslim advent. But with the arrival of the British, first as traders and finally as imperial rulers, Hinduism was confronted with the most critical of all the challenges it had faced in its long and eventful history.

By the time the British arrived in India, Hinduism had reached perhaps its lowest ebb. All sorts of superstitions and undesirable practices flourished in the name of religion. Caste taboos had become so rigid that Hindu society, which a thousand years earlier had sent its great missionaries to the four corners of Asia, had begun to insist on anyone returning from abroad having to undergo purificatory rites. Women, who once enjoyed an honoured position and are found in the Upaniṣads conversing freely with men upon the highest philosophical topics, had become virtual slaves in the joint family. Widows were treated with great cruelty, female infanticide was rife in some castes, and compulsory immolation of widows was often enforced. Theologically also, the great Vedāntic truths that lay behind Hindu thought had been obscured by the jungle growth of superstition and corruption. The inspiration of the medieval saint-singers, while still prevalent, had begun to fade in the face of the political turmoil and widespread anarchy that followed the collapse of Mughal power. Indeed, it was one of the darkest periods in Indian history, and it seemed that Hinduism had at last exhausted its spiritual reserves and would gradually fade away in the face of the new onslaught.

However, once again the miracle of regeneration was witnessed, and Hindu society produced a series of remarkable men who, by the sheer power of their spiritual illumination, rekindled the dying spark. In 1857, after what is commonly known as the Great Indian Mutiny, but which many now prefer to call India's First War of Independence, India lay crushed and prostrate at the feet of her foreign conquerors, broken not only in body but also in spirit. People began to lose faith in their cultural and religious heritage, and a miasma of spiritual darkness pervaded the land. And yet, within a short span of ninety years, India not only rose phoenix-like from the ashes but swept to a triumphant freedom which marked the beginning of a global process of decolonization. This achievement can to a large extent be traced to a resurgence of

Hinduism. This is not to deprecate in any way the role of the other communities in India's national revival, but to highlight the fact that the majority of Indians have always been Hindus, and it is Hinduism, therefore, that predominantly set the tone of a national culture in India and provided the ethos, the cultural milieu, the great backdrop, as it were, against which the drama of her history was enacted.

It was in the great movement for social reform in Hinduism that the first creative reaction to British rule manifested itself, and it was Bengal, the first province in India to feel the brunt of British conquest, that spearheaded this cultural revival. It was here that the first of a long line of great leaders of thought and action arose, a man who has often been described as the 'path finder' of modern India. Raja Rammohun Roy (1772–1833) was a man of unusual intellectual ability, a profound scholar of Sanskrit and Persian as well as a deep admirer of British culture. He took a leading part in starting English-medium schools in Bengal, and in 1828 founded the Brahmo Sabha, later to develop under his successor Devendranath Tagore into the Brahmo Samaj. This was the first deliberate attempt in modern India to reform Hinduism and to cleanse it of the undesirable encrustation that had developed around it over the centuries.

The Brahmo Samaj, as well as its offshoots the Adi Brahmo Samaj led by Devendranath Tagore, the Brahmo Samaj of India founded by Keshub Chunder Sen in 1868, and the Sadharan Brahmo Samaj founded by some of his followers in 1878, all based themselves upon the pristine authority of the Vedas, and strongly attacked idol worship and undesirable social customs such as compulsory *satī*, immolation of widows upon their husbands' funeral pyres. The leaders of the movement, specially Sen, were considerably influenced by the style of Christian missionaries who had become active under British rule, and many of their prayer meetings were modelled upon Christian church services.

Under the influence of the Brahmo Samaj, several such movements started in other parts of India, notably the Prarthana Samaj founded in Bombay in 1867 by the great scholars M. G. Ranade and R. D. Bhandarkar. These societies, while influencing mainly the English-educated fringe of society, did play an important part in bringing a new intellectual awareness into Hindu society, and encouraged educated Hindus to re-examine their religious heritage in the light of changing conditions. The same is true of the Theosophical Society which was founded by Madame Blavatsky and Colonel Olcott in New York in 1875 and gained considerable popularity in India, largely through the work of Mrs. Annie Besant. Simultaneously, the rediscovery of the ancient Indian texts by European scholars such as Max Müller, Ferguson and Cunningham, and the work of Western archaeologists and linguists which brought to light the remarkable achievements of the Hindu past that had virtually been lost during centuries of Muslim rule, helped to give the nineteenth-century Hindu a new awareness of his rich cultural heritage and a renewed pride in his ancient religion.

All this, however, remained largely confined to the small, educated classes, awaiting a movement that would touch the heart of traditional Hinduism. This was not long in coming. A major figure in the Hindu revival was Swami Dayananda Saraswati (1824–1883) who founded the Arya Samaj in 1875. Unlike the Brahmo and its offshoots, which were considerably influenced by Christianity, the Arya Samaj was militantly Hindu. Swami Dayananda passionately advocated a return to the pristine purity of Vedic Hinduism, and denounced with intolerant indignation the post-Vedic Hindu scriptures such as the Purāṇas. He also condemned idol worship and caste distinctions, advocated full equality for women, initiated a widespread educational campaign with special emphasis on female eduation, and launched a crusade against untouchability. Rightly described as a human dynamo, Swami Dayananda shook the structure of established Hinduism to its foundations and infused into it new blood and fresh vigour.

Numerous other reformist and educational movements in Hinduism developed in the second half of the nineteenth century. For purposes of this review, however, we shall confine ourselves to a mention of five outstanding figures who have left their indelible impress upon modern Hinduism, and whose tremendous personalities have gone a long way in shaping the contours of the Hindu mind in our own century. These are Sri Ramakrishna, Swami Vivekananda, Sri Ramana Maharshi, Sri Aurobindo and Mahatma Gandhi. Each of these men, drawn from the very heart of the Hindu tradition, reinterpreted its eternal truths in the light of their own extraordinary attainment. Between them they achieved nothing less than a comprehensive revival of the best in the Hindu tradition, and collectively represent a major force in the contemporary religious thought of the world.

Sri Ramakrishna (1836–1886)

Born in a poor Brāhmaṇā family in Hooghly district, West Bengal, Gadadhar Chatterjee began showing unusual signs of religious ecstasy at a very early age. When he was nineteen, he came to Calcutta to live with his elder brother who had been appointed priest of a newly built temple at Dakshineshwar on the banks of the river Ganges. The main shrine is dedicated to the great goddess. Kālī, from which Calcutta derives its name, and it was as a devotee of the goddess that Sri Ramakrishna, as he came to be called, began his astounding career of spiritual discipline and attainments. Visions, trances and ecstasies crowded in upon him, and most of his time was spent in intense spiritual rhapsodies. His agonized craving to see the Divine face to face was fulfilled, and he then proceeded under various spiritual guides to experience the whole gamut of mystical relationships described in the Hindu scriptures, ranging from intense emotional raptures to the supreme beatitude of the *nirvikalpa samādhi*—contact with the all-pervasive, formless Brahman which is the highest goal of Vedānta. Not content with this, he proceeded to adopt the spiritual practices of Christianity and Islam, and in both cases he has recorded that they culminated in sublime spiritual experiences connected with the founders of these two great faiths.

The cumulative effect of these extraordinary phenomena was immense. By the sheer force of his spiritual attainment, Sri Ramakrishna became a beacon-light in the encircling gloom of his time. Gradually, the fame of this unlettered young priest began to spread far and wide throughout Bengal. The villager and the city dweller, the scholar and the poet, the educated and the illiterate people from all walks of life began finding their way to Dakshineshwar. Among them were some of the great luminaries from different walks of life in contemporary Bengal, men like Girish Ghose, Dr. M. L. Sircar, Keshub Chunder Sen, Bijoy Krishna Goswami, Pandit Sasadhar Tarkachuramani, etc. On his own part, Sri Ramakrishna paid visit to illustrious persons like Devendranath Tagore, Iswar Chandra Vidyasagar and Bankim Chandra Chatterjee.

To all who came Sri Ramakrishna gave the same message. He

exhorted them not to waste their time squabbling over this or that creed or religion, but to seek God with a pure and dedicated heart. He reaffirmed on the basis of his own spiritual experiences that all creeds and religions led ultimately to the same goal, and he expressed his teachings in a series of homely and telling parables that made them intelligible to even the most unsophisticated villager. His sayings and the story of his life remain to this day a major source of religious inspiration.

Sri Ramakrishna showed that, far from being a dying religion as some of the newly educated intelligentsia had begun to believe, Hinduism was an inexhaustible fount of spiritual inspiration. Though he lived quietly in Dakshineshwar and seldom ventured outside the temple compound, his very presence generated a powerful current of fresh light into Hindu society. And the Bengalis, with their unusual emotional and intellectual capacities, responded eloquently to this saint. Sri Ramakrishna was, indeed, an apostle of divine realization, one of those rare souls whose coming heralds a spiritual revolution.

Swami Vivekananda (1863–1902)

Apart from his influence upon those who occasionally visited Dakshineshwar, Sri Ramakrishna attracted to his feet a group of brilliant young disciples, several of them products of the new English schools and colleges that had been recently established in Bengal. Many of these young men had lost faith in their traditional religion and were wallowing in a sea of cynicism and spiritual despair. They found in Sri Ramakrishna a source of tremendous inspiration, a man who could banish their spiritual gloom and transform their very personalities. Outstanding among these disciples was young Narendranath Dutta, later to be famous the world over as Swami Vivekananda.

One has to go all the way back to Socrates and Plato to find a parallel for the Ramakrishna-Vivekananda relationship. Though apparently poles apart from the master, it was the student who spread his teachings far and wide until they encompassed almost the entire world. Vivekananda was a man of remarkable qualities, gifted both with a powerful physique and outstanding intellect. Just before his death, Sri Ramakrishna designated Vivekananda his spiritual heir, and after his master's passing he took upon himself the task of knitting the disciples into a dedicated band. After wandering the entire length of India as a penniless ascetic seeking a way to propagate the ideals of his beloved master, Vivekananda heard of the Parliament of Religions that was to be held in Chicago in 1893 in connection with the World Fair. With considerable difficulty he succeeded in getting a passage to America, and after facing further hardships finally reached Chicago and enrolled himself as a delegate to the conference. His advent at the gathering had all the elements of high drama. An obscure and unknown Hindu monk, he succeeded by the very force of his personality in dominating the whole concourse which today is remembered mainly because of him. A powerful speaker with a sonorous voice and a fine command of English, Vivekananda's famous address on the first day of the Parliament created a sensation, and his subsequent speeches established him as an outstanding preacher.

In his short life of thirty-nine years, Swami Vivekananda undertook what was in effect a restatement of Hinduism in the light of the new situation that had developed during the nineteenth century. He travelled extensively in India and abroad, lecturing on the basic Vedāntic principles that underlay Hinduism. He thundered against the 'Kitchen religion', the ridiculous taboos and restrictive customs that had overlaid the tremendous Vedāntic truths. He reaffirmed not only the divinity of God but also the inherent divinity of man. A special feature of his teachings was his keen social conscience and his intense emphasis on service to the poor and the down-trodden, the sick and the hungry. He often quoted the Ṛgvedic dictum of the human life having a two-fold aim—*ātmano mokṣārthaṁ jagat hitāya ca*—for the welfare of the world and the salvation of one's soul. One of his celebrated remarks is that it was an insult to preach religion to a man with a hungry stomach, and that the only way God could appear before the masses of India was in the form of bread. He stressed the primacy of spiritual life, preached a doctrine of inner strength and spiritual power which alone could free India from her material, intellectual and spiritual bondage, and stressed the essential unity of all religions.

Two features of Vivekananda's ministry merit special mention, as they had an abiding influence upon the revival of contemporary Hinduism. In 1897 he founded the Ramakrishna Math and Mission with headquarters at Belur near Calcutta. Although Hinduism had a long and distinguished monastic tradition going back to

Ādi Śaṅkarācārya, the Ramakrishna Mission was a new order and its approach to the problems of contemporary India was based on a modern reinterpretation of the ancient doctrines. It had a special bias towards educational and medical work, and has over the decades distinguished itself in providing relief to the victims of natural calamities such as floods and famine. In this respect, Vivekananda clearly modelled his organization on the pattern of the Christian missionaries who had been active in India ever since the British advent. The Ramakrishna Mission today, with numerous branches in India and abroad, continues to play a significant role in spreading the gospel of Sri Ramakrishna and his great disciple.

The other feature of Swami Vivekananda's life was the contribution he made to the spread of Hindu thought abroad, specially in America. Prior to his advent, it was only a handful of Western Indologists and scholars who had any real insight into the Hindu ethos, while among the general public, there flourished all sorts of grotesque impressions regarding this great religion. Vivekananda pioneered a new awareness of Hinduism in the West. His eloquent and able presentation of the essential truths that underlie Hinduism, and his broad approach of the essential unity of religions, combined to make him a unique spokesman of the eternal East to the bustling technological culture of Western society.

Vivekananda had a deep conviction that India's goal was not only to achieve her own regeneration but also to give a new spiritual impetus and light to the world. Hinduism is not a proselytizing religion; therefore, Vivekananda was not seeking converts. Rather, he sought to state the basic principles of Vedānta and allow their inner power to work upon the minds and hearts of his listeners. Indeed, he was the torchbearer of a whole new religious movement, and the forerunner of numerous other Hindu teachers and yogis who continue to this day to work in the West. Thus, both in India and abroad, Vivekananda stands as a towering figure in modern Hinduism. His advocacy of 'neo-Vedānta', as it is sometimes called, gave a new direction to traditional Hinduism and continues to have a profound influence upon contemporary religion.

Sri Ramana Maharshi (1879–1950)

If Sri Ramakrishna was a *bhakta* par excellence and Swami Vivekananda a *Karma-yogī*, Sri Ramana was in the great Hindu tradition the *Jñāna-yogī*. Belonging to a middle-class Brāhmana family of

Tamil Nadu, Ramana at the age of seventeen had a series of powerful spiritual experiences that culminated in his taking up permanent residence at the holy Arunachala Hill with the town of Tiruvannamalai at its foot. Here he gradually started attracting a group of devotees, and lived for the rest of his life as a revered saint, or *maharshi*, recognized by all as a powerful figure on the spiritual firmament.

Sri Ramana's teachings expound the Vedāntic path of self-knowledge, and his original works as well as commentaries upon the Hindu classics all flow from the process of self-enquiry. The question 'Who am I?' is to be found in most religious traditions, because the quest for self-knowledge is at the heart of every spiritual endeavour. But Sri Ramana made this the cornerstone of his whole philosophy. To every question he would respond by asking a counter-question. 'Who is it that asks?' Thus when the body, the senses, the mind are all negated, the real 'I' begins to shine forth in all its glory.

This process of spiritual introspection was presented by Sri Ramana with great clarity, and he also taught a process of *prāṇāyāma* or breath control that would assist the seeker to still the modifications of the mind and focus the psychic energy upon asking that single question 'Who am I?' He likened this to the flaming brand that is used to light a great fire; it not only sets the entire material ablaze but also consumes itself in the process. Thus Sri Ramana taught that the question 'Who am I?' if properly and persistently asked has the capacity to destroy all delusion and ultimately itself disappear with the dawn of spiritual realization.

Unlike Vivekananda, Sri Ramana never concerned himself with social service or reform movements. He seldom ventured outside his abode at Arunachalam, and yet such was his spiritual presence that he commanded veneration from all sides. The thousands who trekked to see him were often content to do just that, because in the Hindu tradition even the sight of a holy person—*darśana*—has its own spiritual merit. Sri Ramana had an extraordinary presence. Quite unconcerned with outer events, he was as one permanently centred in the Brahman, and his words came not from intellectual brilliance but from a perfect inner assurance. Like Sri Ramakrishna before him, he was a living proof of the spiritual power of Hinduism. It is said that the night he passed away after undergoing a long and painful ailment with no sign of suffering or complaint, a bright comet moved across the sky and shone for a while in splendour above Arunachalam before disappearing behind the holy mountain.

Sri Aurobindo (1872–1950)

Born on 15 August 1872 in Calcutta, Aurobindo Ghosh was sent to school in England at the age of seven. There, first at the Manchester Grammar School, then at St. Paul's in London and finally at King's College, Cambridge, he underwent a full educational career covering fourteen years during which he passed the classics tripos in the first division and won college prizes for English and literary ability. He returned to India in 1893 at the age of twenty-one and entered Baroda State Service as Professor of English, then Vice-Principal and later Principal of Baroda College.

Aurobindo was gifted with a brilliant mind and a deep psychic power. While in England he read the writings on the Irish Sinn Fein movement and the Italian Risorgimento. This filled him with a fervent sense of patriotism, and back home he began taking keen interest in the freedom movement still in its infancy.

In 1885 an Englishman, Alen Octavian Hume, founded the Indian National Congress, and soon there developed two clear trends of thinking in this great organization, the 'moderates' who aimed at gradual transfer of power, and the 'extremists' whose ideal was full freedom at once. Sri Aurobindo soon became a leader of the extremists along with Lokmanya B. G. Tilak, and in 1905, when the British pushed through the highly controversial partition of Bengal, he quit his Baroda job and plunged into the national movement.

For five years, from 1905 to 1910, Aurobindo shone like a meteor on the political firmament. His brilliant editorials in the *Bande Mataram* and *Karmayogin*, patriotic journals he edited, are among the most outstanding of political writings in the English. His political philosophy was deeply rooted in the Hindu tradition of mother-worship, particularly pronounced in Bengal. Drawing his inspiration from the famous Bengali novel *Ananda Math* by Bankim Chandra Chatterjee, written half a century earlier, and in particular from the poem 'Bande Mataram' (Hail to Thee, Mother) contained therein, Aurobindo developed a comprehensive political philosophy. The key concept was the divinity of the motherland, which he idealized as the goddess Bhavanı Bharatı, and flowing from that the concept of nationalism not simply as a political credo but as a spiritual imperative. The spiritual nationalism expounded by him had an electrifying effect upon the youth of Bengal and other parts of India at that crucial juncture; and, though the movement did not meet with immediate success, it brought about for the first time a mass involvement and left an indelible impress upon the Indian freedom movement.

While at Baroda Sri Aurobindo had begun following some yogic practices, and during the Bengal agitation he was arrested in the celebrated Alipur Bomb Conspiracy Case and kept in jail for over a year. It was during this enforced solitude that the spiritual trend in his psyche gained predominance; and, though after his acquittal he continued for some time with political activities, he realized that his real life-work lay elsewhere. In 1910, on a sudden inner impulse, he left Bengal for the French possession of Chandernagore and from there moved on to the other French possession of Pondicherry where he lived for forty years until his death in 1950. In the course of his four decades at Pondicherry, Sri Aurobindo developed one of the most comprehensive and original systems of thought in modern times. He based himself upon the Hindu tradition, but gave creative interpretations to the ancient texts including the Vedas and the Upaniṣads. His masterly work, *Essays on the Gita*, is perhaps the most outstanding of the many commentaries that have been written upon this sacred text since Śaṅkarācārya, while his chief literary work, *The Life Divine*, the massive epic poem, *Savitri*, and numerous other works stand as a testimony to his gigantic intellect and deep intuition.

If his political philosophy can be called spiritual nationalism, Sri Aurobindo's general philosophy can well be called spiritual evolution. He rejects the traditional Hindu concept of individual salvation and stresses those aspects of the Hindu tradition that speak of raising the collective consciousness of the race. The key concept in his thought is that of spiritual evolution. According to Sri Aurobindo, man is the result of aeons of evolution from unicellular organisms up through mineral, vegetable and animal forms. However, he is by no means the end-product of evolution. Sri Aurobindo postulates a further evolutionary thrust from man with his mental faculties to superman with supramental faculties. Indeed , he holds that it is only with the next quantum leap in the evolutionary adventure that mankind will break out of its present impasse and fulfil its spiritual destiny.

Sri Aurobindo wrote at great length with regard to this leap, and presented for its fulfilment his own path which he called 'Integral Yoga' because it seeks to draw together the strands of the four traditional *yogas* into a single, multi-faceted spiritual endeavour. Sri Aurobindo's goal was not individual salvation, not even racial salvation, it was nothing less than a fundamental change in the texture of terrestrial consciousness itself, the creation of 'a new heaven and a new earth'. Often described as the pioneer of the supramental. Sri Aurobindo's 'Integral Yoga', worked out with the active collaboration of his companion Madame Alfassa, known as the Mother, has three broad movements: first, a complete and integral surrender to the divine; second, a raising of the human consciousness to the supramental level; and, third, a return to earth after absorbing the power and light of the supramental so that its influence can be directly brought to bear upon terrestrial life. This stress on evolution, though based essentially upon Hindu texts, marks a new development in contemporary Hinduism which has still not fully unfolded itself.

Mahatma Gandhi (1869–1948)

Mahatma Gandhi is known throughout the world for his unique leadership of the Indian freedom movement, for the concepts of *satya* and *ahiṁsa* (truth and non-violence) which were the cornerstones of his political philosophy, and for the manner in which he was able to shake the foundations of the great British Empire. Indeed, the Indian freedom movement marked the end of the colonial era that had dominated the world scene for the preceding three centuries, and India's independence in 1947 heralded the emergence into freedom of dozens of other nations that had for long been the victims of colonial subjugation. Mahatma Gandhi is today revered in India as the Father of the Nation, and remains a source of not only inspiration in India but wherever man is still struggling for freedom.

It is useful to remember, however, that Gandhi's approach to politics was broadly based on Hindu principles. He was himself a devout Hindu, and will go down in history as one of the greatest social reformers that Hinduism has produced. In a way he combined the two streams of thought—radical and moderate—in the freedom movement. While accepting the radicals' goal of *Purna Swaraj* or complete independence, he also breathed new life into the reform movements that the moderate leaders had espoused.

Gandhi's main contribution to Hinduism was the manner in which he took up the problem of untouchables, whose ill-treatment had been one of the most disgraceful features of Hindu society. By renaming them as Harijans, or children of god, he made a symbolic gesture of atonement, and thereafter, he pursued a policy of living in Harijan colonies wherever he went, personally cleaning latrines and giving depressed classes a sense of self-esteem and involvement in the mainstream of Hindu society. The special reservations in legislatures, services and educational institutions are a direct result of Gandhi's influence and the remarkable contribuition of Dr. B. R. Ambedkar, the Harijan leader.

Another major contribution made by Gandhi was the involvement of women in large numbers in the freedom movement and the stress he laid upon their social emancipation. His 'Constructive Programme', which included the propagation of handicrafts and cottage industries, also had an egalitarian effect upon Hindu society. All his prayer meetings began with *Rām Dhun*, chanting of the Lord's Name, and for his concept of the perfect government he went back to the *Rāma Rājya*, the ideal rule in the ancient days of Sri Rāma. He wrote a commentary on the *Bhagavad-Gītā* which he looked upon as a perennial source of inspiration. He encouraged the worship of the cow, not so much on religious grounds but as a symbol of the beneficent symbiosis between human and animal existence.

Gandhi's concept of 'truth' is deeply based on the Hindu tradition. The famous words of the *Muṇḍaka Upaniṣad—satyam eva jayate* (truth alone triumphs)—constituted his motto. This was adopted as India's national motto after independence. His insistence on *ahiṁsā* (non-violence) also had its roots in one aspect of Hinduism, although this was stressed more in the Buddhist and Jain traditions. His autobiography, *My Experiments with Truth*, is a remarkable document, and shows Gandhi's deep commitment to the fundamental ideals of Hinduism. While he never claimed to be a religious leader and always displayed the utmost humility in such matters, he was categorical in his assertion that for him religion had primacy over all other aspects, and that it was absurd to hold that politics had nothing to do with religion. He stressed the Hindu concept of the essential unity and harmony of all religions, and his prayer meetings would include readings from other religious scriptures in addition to those from Hinduism. He was greatly influenced by the saint-singers of medieval India, specially Kabīr and Mīrābāi, and shared their direct and simple approach to religion for the masses.

During his three decades of political pre-eminence in India, Gandhi's contribution to the regeneration of Hinduism and the reform of Hindu society was monumental. He must, therefore, be ranked not only as a unique political leader but also as one of the main formative influences in modern Hinduism, a man who left the indelible impress of his personality not only upon his country but upon his religion as well.

In addition to these five outstanding personalities of modern Hinduism, numerous other major figures on the contemporary Hindu scene have made their contribution to the regeneration and re-interpretation of Hinduism in our own century. Most of them have founded their own societies and religious organizations. These include such persons as Yogananda Paramhansa who preached in America and founded the Yogoda Society; Swami Nikhilananda and Swami Prabhavananda of the Ramakrishna Mission in the USA; Swami Sivananda of Rishikesh who founded the Divine Life Society; Swami Bhaktivedanta Prabhupāda, whose Kṛṣṇa Consciousness movement has made such a mark in the West, and Sri Krishna Prem, an Englishman who has written glowing commentaries on the *Bhagavad-Gītā* and the *Kaṭha Upaniṣad* and who, along with his *guru* Yashoda Mai, founded a Kṛṣṇa temple near Almora in the Himalayas.

Among those still active at the time of writing are the saintly Śaṅkarācārya of Kāñcī Kāmakoṭi Pīṭha in South India; the blind centenarian Swami Gangeshwarananda, who has done such remarkable work in the interpretation and popularization of the Vedas and is still alert; Maharshi Mahesh Yogi with his transcendental meditation; Swami Ranganathananda and other saints of the Ramakrishna Mission; Swami Chinmayananda, who has founded his own mission for the regeneration of Hinduism; Sai Baba of the miraculous materializations, and Sri Madhava Ashish, who carries on the tradition of his *guru*, Sri Krishna Prem, at Mirtola. A special word may be said about J. Krishnamurti who, though he would not have accepted the description, was deeply rooted in the great tradition of Hindu teachers, and Pandit Gopi Krishna, who wrote remarkable books on the *kuṇḍalinī*. In addition, of course, there are numerous heads of the traditional monastic orders including those established in the country by Śaṅkarācārya.

This list is by no means exhaustive, but is enough to show that Hinduism is in one of its important phases of creative resurgence. The rise of science and technology, on the one hand, and of communism with its atheistic implications, on the other, is a profound challenge to established religions throughout the world. To survive, a mere reiteration of old orthodoxies is not enough. What is required is a reinterpretation of ancient truths in the light of contemporary compulsions, and this Hinduism has done time and again in its long and eventful history.

The Future

Mankind faces a complex dilemma at this stage of its evolution. Science and technolgoy, if wisely used, have given him for the first time the capacity to abolish deprivation and poverty, illiteracy and disease, unemployment and inequality from the face of the earth. On the other hand, the same science has also given him the power to destory not only the human race but perhaps all life. There is a great churning of the collective consciousness of humanity, and a tremendous urge for new certitudes to take the place of the old bulwarks that are collapsing. In such a situation, all religions face a fundamental challenge. Hinduism, with its tremendous capacity for regeneration and reinterpretation, should not have anything to fear. Indeed, India, with its rich and varied religious heritage as well as the most distinguished pool of scientific talent in the developing world, should be able to give the right lead to humanity at this crucial juncture.

The contribution of Hinduism, in the past, to world civilization has been many-faceted. It covers, to mention just a few fields, mathematics (the discovery of zero or *Śunnya* which was the prerequisite for any advance in this highly abstract science); medicine (through *Āyur-Veda*, one of the most ancient and integrated systems of medicine known to man); architecture (which produced such wonders as the rockcut caves of Ellora and the great temple cities of South India); dance (with the Bharata Nāṭyam and other classical dance forms based upon Bharata's great treatise, the *Nāṭya Śastra*); music (both in the Karnataka tradition and the Hindustani mode which has had such an impact in recent years upon the West); psychology (through *yoga*, which represents the most profound enquiry into the mysteries of the human mind and psyche yet developed by man); linguistics and literature (through the vehicle of Sanskrit, unparalleled in its power and majesty, and other great languages including Tamil); and, of course, philosophy (from the luminous utterance of the Upaniṣads to Swami Vivekananda and Sri Aurobindo in this century). In these and other fields too numerous to catalogue, the Hindu mind has contributed to the corpus of human knowledge and attainment in a manner of which few religions can boast.

Hinduism retains an inner dynamism and presents certain key concepts that are particularly relevant in this nuclear age, not only for Hindus but also for the entire human race. The five seminal ideas that follow have been chosen for the width of their outlook that transcends religious and denominational barriers, and gives them universal relevance.

The Unity of Mankind

Every country has developed a love for its own nationhood, but there are few that have had the capacity to rise above the imposing mansion of nationalism and conceptualize the unity of the entire human race. It has been the Hindu genius that, although it has accepted and reiterated nationalism in the modern sense, particularly after the great renaissance in the nineteenth century, its best minds have always held up the concept of mankind as a single family, *vasudhaiva kuṭumbakam*, as the *Ṛg-Veda* has it. The relevance of this to the present human predicament is obvious. Science and technology have now converted what was once only a vision in the minds of seers into a concrete reality. Time and space are shrinking before our eyes, and the extraordinary photograph of earth taken from the moon shows our planet, as it really is, a tiny spaceship hurtling through the endless vastnesses of space, so beautiful and yet so fragile. The essential unity of the race that inhabits this planet, based upon the fact of 'humanness' itself, is thus a concept that is growing increasingly relevant as this century draws to its close and mankind struggles desperately to survive its own technological ingenuity.

The Harmony of Religions

The second great concept that Hinduism has developed through the ages is that of the harmony of religions. The yearning of the human for the divine, which is at the heart of the religious quest, has in practice often been translated into hideous strife between the followers of different religions, each convinced of its own righteousness and of cruel persecution within various religions themsleves. The Hindu ethos, however, has always accepted different paths to the divine—*ekaṁ sad viprāḥ bahudā vadanti* (Truth is one, the wise call it by many names) as the *Ṛg-Veda* has it. Apart from Hinduism, which has always been the predominant religion of India, there are millions of Muslims, Buddhists, Jains, Sikhs, Parsis, Christians (of several denominations) and Jews who have lived peacefully in this country for centuries. There are also famous shrines and pilgrimage-centres sacred to all these religions.

The unique synthesis achieved in Kashmir between the Śaiva tradition and the Sufi influx, resulting in the *ṛṣi* cult equally sacred to Hindus and Muslims, is only one of the more dramatic manifestations of the Hindu tradition of religious harmony. Tolerating another religion is at best a negative approach, but accepting all religions positively and gladly is a peculiarly Hindu contribution. Its message of the harmony of religions, of the essential unity of mystical experiences, of accepting the divine as so opulent and all-embracing that any effort to move towards it is to be welcomed regardless of its style or idiom, is thus extremely relevant in the modern age.

The Divinity of the Individual

Flowing from the concept of the unity of mankind and the harmony of religions is the third aspect of the Hindu message which reiterates the divinity and dignity of the individual. It is true that Hindu society often appears to be so highly hierarchical and stratified and places so much emphasis upon social duty and status that individual freedom seems to be at a discount. However, it must be remembered that parallel to and, ultimately, overriding these social stratifications runs the basic concept of the divinity of the human individual. Every person born into the human race, regardless of sex or religion, colour or caste, language or geographical location, partakes of the essential mystery of divine potential. Every Ātman, in the Hindu view, contains the seeds of spiritual growth and ultimate realization.

Howsoever diverse the circumstances, howsoever hostile the environment, Hinduism believes that there is within the human psyche the unquenchable spark of divinity that can, sooner or later, be fanned into the blazing fire of spiritual realization. This concept endows every individual with a dignity that immediately places him, in essence, above and beyond social customs and traditions. Today, when human dignity is at a discount with various collectivities imposing their domination over the individual in a hundred different ways, this aspect of Hinduism's message is of no mean significance. It provides the counterpoint to the concept of human unity, reasserting the unique significance of each individual while stressing the unity of the entire race.

The Quality of Creative Synthesis

The fourth facet of the Hindu ethos flows from its unusual synthesizing and syncretizing capacity. Against the rigid dichotomy between action in the world and withdrawn meditation, it places the great ideal of the *Gītā*, wherein the way of *karma* (action) and the way of *jñāna* (knowledge) are fused in the crucible of dedication to the divine; against the cruel dichotomy between matter and energy (which has only recently been breached in the West by Einstein and his successors), the Indian mind has postulated the essential oneness behind all existence—*īśā vāsyam idaṁ sarvaṁ yat kiñca jagatyāṁ jagat*—as the *Īśā Upaniṣad* has it, the same energy pulsating in the heart of the atom as in the depths of the farthest galaxy; against the dogmatic confrontation between science and religion, there is the vision of both these great disciplines as two different approaches towards essentially the same truth, one reaching outwards into the very structure of the cosmos and the other inwards into the very essence of the human psyche. This capacity to balance, to harmonize disparate concepts and apparently contradictory movements, has been the hallmark of the greatest Hindu minds, and carries within it the ideological seeds of a world civilization in the future which, ideally, would weld together the best traditions of national cultures into a glowing and harmonious synthesis.

Cosmic Values

Finally, in the context of our newly achieved capacity to break away from the confines of this planet and begin a tentative advance into the vastnesses of outer space, Hinduism has provided a scheme of cosmic values which are startling in their contemporary relevance. The concept of vast aeons of time through which the world passes (four ages or *yugas* totalling 4.32 billion years, each adding up to only a single day of Brahmā) more closely approximates to the age of this earth than any other scheme of classical calculation. The concept of millions upon millions of galaxies, *koṭi koṭi brahmāṇḍa*, once considered to be merely an absurd flight of fancy, is now beginning to come alive as the boundless universe unfolds itself before our startled gaze. The vision of the cosmic dance of Śīva, where millions of galaxies spring into being every moment and millions are extinguished in the unending cycle of eternity, is only now beginning to reflect the knowledge that we are receiving from our initial probings into the universe around us.

And yet, within this incomprehensible vastness, perhaps because of it, remains the eternal mystery of the human personality. Among billions of galaxies in the universe, one is ours; among billions of stars in this galaxy one is ours; among billions of human beings in this solar system one of them is ourselves, but such is the grandeur and mystery of the Ātman that it can move towards a comprehension of the unutterable mystery of existence. We, who are children of the past and the future, of earth and heaven, of light and darkness, of the human and the divine, at once evanescent and eternal, of the world and beyond it, within time and in eternity, yet have the capacity to comprehend our condition, to rise above our terrestrial limitations, and, finally, to transcend the throbbing abyss of space and time itself. This, in essence, is the message of Hinduism.

2

Vedānta in the Nuclear Age

Mankind today is in an epoch of transition, as significant if not more so as the earlier ones from nomadic to agricultural society, from agricultural to industrial and from industrial to post-industrial society. We may be too close to the event to grasp its full significance, but it is now quite clear that we are in the throes of a major change. Whether it is in the field of politics or economics, communications or culture, a powerful new globalism is developing. With the impact of post-Einsteinian physics, quantum mechanics, Heisenberg's uncertainty principle and many other conceptual revolutions, the old structures have begun to crumble. 'Solid matter' dissolves into 'waves of probability', and the new physics seems to be approaching the mystic vision of which seers and sages of all traditions have spoken.

The predominant consciousness of the human race reflects its evolutionary situation, and it would be true to say that at this crucial crossroads mankind is groping for a new philosophy, a new paradigm, a new consciousness to replace the old. And it is no coincidence that this is happening at a juncture when humanity is in supreme peril, not from another species, not from outer space, but from itself. There has been a tragic divergence between knowledge and wisdom, and from deep within the human psyche there has developed a terrible poison that threatens not only our own generation but countless generations yet unborn; not only our own race but all life on this planet.

Ancient myths often illuminate the human predicament, and there is the powerful Paurānic myth of the Churning of the Milky Ocean (the *Samudra-Manthana*) which speaks to us from across the millenia, symbolizing, as it does, the long and tortuous evolution of consciousness on Planet Earth. The myth vividly illustrates the human predicament today. Prolonged churnings have given man the great gifts of science and technology. There have been incredible breakthroughs in medicine and communications, agriculture and electronics, space travel and cybernetics. We now have enough resources and technology to ensure, for every human being on earth, the physical, intellectual, material and spiritual inputs necessary for a full and healthy life. And yet, surely the poison is also upon us. Billions are spent every day on the manufacture of monstrous weapons with unprecedented powers of destruction. It is estimated that there are now well over fifty thousand nuclear warheads on Planet Earth, each a thousand times more powerful than the bombs that devastated Hiroshima and Nagasaki at the dawn of the nuclear age; some with more explosive force than used by both sides in the entire Second World War.

It is in this chilling context that the necessity for an alternative philosophy of life becomes so intense, and, because of the universal values that it enshrines, the Vedānta represents precisely such an integrated and universal philosophy. Based upon the collective wisdom of generations of seers and sages, the Upaniṣads and the *Bhagavad-Gītā* stand as testimony to the magnificent spiritual endeavour and achievement of ancient India. This vast corpus of wisdom, collectively known as the Vedānta, provides insights which can be of crucial value for the survival of the human race in this nuclear age. While the field is extremely broad and rich, I have abstracted five major principles of the Vedānta that collectively can provide the framework for a philosophy to sustain the emerging global consciousness on our planet.

The first and most basic concept is that of the all-pervasive Brahman—*īśā vāsyam idaṁ sarvaṁ yat kiñca jagatyāṁ jagat* (whatever exists and wherever it exists is permeated by the same divine power and force). Indeed, there *can* be no manifestation without the divinity behind it, and this in a way parallels the realization of modern science. Previously, in the classical science of Newton, there was the incurable dichotomy between matter and energy; but in the post-Einsteinian situation there is now the realization that whatever exists is really the same energy, although it may appear as matter, as a particle or as a wave. So the unified-field theory towards which the scientists are desperately probing already has its spiritual counterpart in the concept of the all-pervasive

Brahman of the Upaniṣads. This is the first important concept of the Vedāntic knowledge.

The second is that this Brahman resides within each individual's consciousness, in the Ātman. The Ātman, as it were, is the reflection of this all-pervasive Brahman in individual consciousness; but the Ātman is not ultimately separate from the Brahman, it is a reflection of that Brahman, it is a part of it. One of the examples given in the Upaniṣads is that as, when a great fire is lighted, millions of sparks fly up out of the fire and then fall back into it, so from the Brahman arise all these millions of individual selves and into the Brahman again they all ultimately disappear. The concept of *Īśvaraḥ sarvabhūtānāṁ hṛddeśe 'rjuna tiṣṭhati*, of the Lord residing within the heart of each individual, is the second great insight of the Upaniṣads, and the relationship between the Ātman and the Brahman is the keynote point upon which the entire Vedāntic teaching revolves. All the four *yogas* are directed towards bringing about a union between the Ātman and the Brahman—*Jñāna-yoga*, the way of wisdom; *Bhakti-yoga*, the way of emotional rapport; *Karma-yoga*, the way of dedicated action; and *Rāja-yoga*, the way of ecstasy.

Flowing from this is another important Vedāntic concept: all human beings, because of their shared spirituality, are members of a single, extended family. The Upaniṣads have a beautiful word for the human race, *amṛtasya putrāḥ* (children of immortality), because we carry within our consciousness the light and the power of the Brahman, regardless of our race or colour, our creed or sex, or any other differentiation. That is the basis of the concept of human beings as an extended family: *vasudhaiva kuṭumbakam*. A famous verse points out that the division between 'mine' and 'yours' is a small and narrow way of looking at reality, indulged in by people with immature minds. For those of the greater consciousness, the entire world is a family. This is another great insight of the Upaniṣads peculiarly relevant at this juncture in human history.

We come now to a fourth major Vedāntic concept, the essential unity of all religions, of all spiritual paths—*ekaṁ sad viprāḥ bahudhā vadanti*, the truth is one, the wise call it by many names—as the *Ṛg-Veda* has it. The *Muṇḍaka Upaniṣad* has a beautiful verse which says: as streams and rivulets arise in different parts of the world but ultimately flow into the same ocean, so do all these creeds and religious formulations arise in different times and areas, but if they have a true aspiration, ultimately reach the same goal. Here is a philosophy which cuts across barriers of hatred and fanaticism that have been built in the name of religion. The Vedānta is a universal religion; it accepts the infinite possibilities of movements towards the divine, it does not seek to limit or confine us to any particular formulation, it not only accepts but welcomes a multiplicity of paths to the divine. It is like climbing a mountain. There are several different starting places, and if we keep arguing at these points we will remain miles apart. But when we start to climb and actually move upwards, then as we approach the summit our paths will begin to converge, and ultimately when we get to the top we will all meet there, because there is only one summit. Similarly, once we really start moving upwards in the field of spiritual endeavour, we will find our denominational and intellectual differences gradually losing their importance, and as we rise to the summit we will realize the spiritual oneness of humanity.

The fifth Vedāntic concept is that of the welfare of all beings: *Bahujana sukhāya bahujana hitāya ca.* The Vedānta seeks the welfare of all creation, not only of human beings but also of what we call the lower creatures. In our arrogance and ignorance we have destroyed the environment of this planet. We have polluted the oceans, we have made the air unbreathable, we have desecrated nature and decimated wildlife. But the Vedāntic seers knew that man was not something apart from nature, and, therefore, they had compassion for all living beings. That is why the Vedānta constantly exhorts us that, while we are working for our own salvation, we must also shun the path of violence and hatred. We must seek to develop both elements of our psyche, the inner and the outer, the quietist and the activist. Indeed, these are two sides of the same coin, so that while working out our own destiny we have also to work for the welfare of all beings.

These five concepts from the Vedānta—the all-pervasive Brahman; the Ātman which resides in all beings; the concept of the human race as members of a family; the idea that all religions are essentially different paths to the same goal; and the concept that we must work for the welfare of society as a whole and not only for ourselves—when taken together provide us with a comprehensive world-view which will greatly help in the process of globalization upon which we have embarked.

Gradually a world civilization is being born, and it *has* to be born if mankind is to survive in this nuclear age. Science and technology have given us tremendous power, and that power, if used for benign purposes, can abolish poverty and hunger, malnutrition and misery, illiteracy and unemployment from the face of this earth by the end of this century. On the other hand, we now have enough nuclear power to destroy the human race forty times over, to commit not only racial suicide but terricide, the destruction of Planet Earth.

We must never forget that power by itself is neither good nor evil; there is the *daivi śakti* and there is the *āsurī śakti*, the benign power and the malign power. The worship of power, of science, is not enough, we also need to recapture wisdom, compassion and understanding. We can now survive only if we have an alternative ideology to the one which has led mankind to this position, and if we boldly act in harmony with that ideology. The Vedānta provides such an alternative world-view; and if even at this late hour we can imbibe some of its universal truths, we can perhaps reverse the mad rush towards destruction and begin the long, slow climb-back to sanity. Let us close then with that immortal Vedic prayer that seeks to lead us from the untruth of ignorance into the truth of knowledge; from the darkness within into the light above; and from the cycle of birth and death into immortality:

Asato mā sad gamaya!
Tamaso mā jyotir gamaya!
Mṛityor mā amṛtaṁ gamaya!

3

The Message of the Upaniṣads

In this age of turmoil and transition, it sometimes appears as if the human psyche itself is adrift on a vast and turbulent ocean, without any sense of direction, without any landmarks or lighthouses to show the way, buffeted by winds seen and unseen. There is turmoil in the outer world, there is violence and hatred, killing and suffering all around us, and there is also turmoil in the inner world; the deep psychological currents that rule human consciousness also seem to be disturbed. The old is dying and the new is struggling to be born, and our generation finds itself precariously poised between the past and future.

At a time like this we look towards our great spiritual traditions not to go back in time, for that is not possible; it is a common mistake for many civilizations to look back in yearning and to long for a so-called golden age that may have existed at one time but which is no longer within the realm of possibility. Within this present space-time continuum time flows only in one direction and, therefore, there is no advantage in trying to recapture the outer structures of a bygone age. But there is great importance in trying to understand the inner spirit of a tradition.

What was it that kept India alive down through the long centuries? What was it that enabled Hinduism to survive even when it was subjected to the most cruel persecutions and invasions age after age, century after century? Why is it that whereas other great world civilizations, some of them even older than the Indian—the Egyptian, for example, Mesopotamia and Babylon, or the great contemporary civilizations of Greece and Rome—have disappeared and live today only in the minds of research scholars or in the four walls of museums. Indian civilization remains vibrant down to the present moment? That is what we have got to try and discover, because perhaps in the recapturing of the inner spirit of the Indian civilization we will be able to derive the inspiration, the strength and the light that we require to face the problems that lie ahead; to cross this dark and stormy ocean which is before us.

When we look at the great landscape of Indian culture, we find that like the mighty Himalayas themselves from whence our culture originated stands the mighty structure of the Vedas. In flight from Delhi to Calcutta one travels parallel to the Himalayas, it is amazing to recall those great words of Kālidāsa with which he opens his *Kumārasambhava: Astyuttarasyam diśidevatātma himālayonāma nāgādhi-rajaḥ, paurvaparau toyanidhi vāgahya, sthitaḥ prithivyaiva mānadandaḥ* (The Himalaya is a great *devatātmā*, a great spiritual presence, stretching from the west to the eastern sea like a measuring rod to gauge the world's greatness). Kālidāsa could not possibly have flown and yet such is the creativity of genius that he was able to see as a single unity this overwhelmingly powerful image of the Himalayan range.

Similarly, the Vedas stand in all their might and majesty as the very source and bedrock of Hindu civilization. The Vedas are the inspired utterances of a whole galaxy of realized souls, of spiritual geniuses, of people not merely well versed intellectually but with spiritual enlightenment. They are unique, both because of the timespan over which they were composed—the whole Vedic tradition which has come down to us must have been composed over a period of at least 1000 to 1500 years—and because of the scope and diversity of the people who received these great spiritual messages. And if you look upon the Vedas as the Himalayas of our cultural traditions, the Upaniṣads can well be described as those great peaks which are so prominent when you view the Himalayas from the air. The peaks are only a part of the entire mountain range, and yet it is they with the eternal snow upon them that draw our minds and our admiration.

The Upaniṣads are known as the Vedānta, both because chronologically they come at the end of the Vedas and also because philosophically they represent the noblest upshot, the highest watermark of the Vedic civilization and genius. One meaning of the word Upaniṣad is to sit nearby. In the Indian tradition, the *guru* would be seated under a tree, near a river or a lake, and one or more disciples would cluster around him to *learn the wisdom*.

This is interesting, because it is in juxtaposition to the Greek tradition where Socrates and his disciples, including Plato, would walk up and down the corridors of their academy. Indeed, the Socratic dialogues and the Upaniṣads have a great deal in common; they are all dialogues between the *guru* and *śiṣya*. But the Greeks used to walk; perhaps because of climatic factors they found that the processes of thinking were stimulated by walking; hence they came to be known as the 'peripetatic' or walking philosophers.

In Sanskrit, a single word or phrase can have many shades of meaning, and they are not mutually exclusive. We do not accept the rigid dyarchy whereby one word can have only one meaning. Another meaning of Upaniṣad is the 'secret doctrine'. In the *Muṇḍaka Upaniṣad* the great householder Śaunaka goes to the sage Aṅgiras and asks him the famous question: *Kasmin nu bhagavo vijñāte sarvam idaṁ vijñātaṁ bhavati iti* (Venerable Sir, what is that by knowing which everything becomes known)? And in reply to that question the teacher expounds the theory of the two types of knowledge, the higher and the lower, the *parāvidyā* and the *aparāvidyā*.

The Upaniṣads deal with the higher knowledge, which is suprarational knowledge. It does not negate rationality, it transcends it, because, while the mind is a brilliant and multifaceted instrument, it is nonetheless limited by its very structure. There are ranges of knowledge and experience which do not come within the ambit of so-called rational thinking. At some point in our adventure of consciousness the mind has to be transcended, and the Upaniṣads deal with the higher knowledge, the suprarational realization which comes not by intellectual gymnastics but by spiritual realization. The ultimate goal of knowledge, spiritual realization, is the basis of all Upaniṣadic teaching.

Again, in the *Muṇḍaka*, there are two memorable verses which describe what the Upaniṣads are really supposed to do. They are likened to a great bow upon which the arrow must be fastened, sharpened by meditation and *sādhanā*. The arrow is the Ātman; the target is the Brahman and the bow is *Aum*, the sacred word. The bow has to be drawn with great attention and single-mindedness, then only do we become one with the Brahman in the same way as an arrow becomes one with its target. That is the central point of the teaching; it is a vehicle whereby the Ātman becomes one with the Brahman, or, in theological terms, where the soul becomes one with God. The words, 'God' and 'soul' are not really part of the Vedāntic tradition, and have certain connotations in the Semitic religions which are not entirely parallel to Hinduism. The key Vedāntic concepts are the Ātman and the Brahman, and the merging of these two. The Upaniṣads as the great bow become the vehicle for this merger.

Traditionally, there are said to be 108 Upaniṣads, which is a sacred number. But the major Upaniṣads number about fourteen. Ādi Śaṅkarācarya wrote his luminous commentaries upon eleven of these Upaniṣads—the *Iśā*, the *Kena*, the *Kaṭha*, the *Praśna*, the *Muṇḍaka, the Māṇḍūkya*, the *Aitareya*, the *Taittirīya*, the *Chāndogya*, the *Bṛhadāraṇyaka*, and the *Śvetāśvatara*. The texts vary considerably in length. The *Iśā Upaniṣad*, for example, has only eighteen *mantras*, whereas the *Bṛhadāraṇyaka*, the Upaniṣad of the great forest, runs into many hundreds of verses. Despite their diversity and the fact that they were composed over a vast period of time, there is an inner unity among the Upaniṣads which is quite extraordinary. All of the great seers seem to be talking about the same basic experience, that is, the experience of the divine, of the Brahman. So the Upaniṣads can be said to be essentially the *Jñāna-mārga*, the way of knowledge, and for that there are only two qualifications laid down for the teacher; he must be *srotriya* and *brahmaniṣṭha*, well versed in the scriptures but also founded upon spiritual realization. It is important to remember that the Upaniṣadic teaching is not a mere academic exercise; it is a teaching for spiritual quest.

The cardinal concepts of the Upaniṣads can perhaps be expressed in a brief compass as being five. The first and most basic concept is the concept of the all-pervasive Brahman— *īśā vāsyam idaṁ sarvaṁ yat kiñca jagatyāṁ jagat* (whatever exists and wherever it exists is permeated by the same divine power and force). This is an important realization, because many philosophies have postulated dichotomies between God and the world, between matter and spirit, between good and evil, between the divine and the devil, and so on. But the Upaniṣadic view is that in the ultimate analysis all that exists is a manifestation of the divine. Indeed, there can be no manifestation without divinity behind it, and this, in a way, is the realizaton of the new science. Previously, in the classical science of Newton, there was the dichotomy between matter and spirit, matter and energy; but in the post-Einsteinian situation you find now a realization that whatever exists is really the same energy. It may appear as matter, it may appear as energy; it may appear as a particle or as a wave, it is essentially the same energy. So the unified-force theory towards which the scientists are desperately probing has its spiritual counterpart in the concept of the all-pervasive Brahman of the Upaniṣads. The greatest realization is to see the Brahman everywhere, wherever you look above or below, to the right or to the left, within or without. This is the first important concept of Vedāntic knowledge, the all-pervasive Brahman.

The second is that this Brahman resides within each individual consciousness, in the Ātman. The Ātman, as it were, is the reflection of this all-pervasive Brahman in individual consciousness; but the Ātman is not ultimately separate from the Brahman, it is a reflection of that Brahman, it is a part of it. One of the examples given in the Upaniṣads is that as, when a great fire is lighted, millions of sparks fly up out of the fire and then fall back into it, so from the Brahman arise all these millions of galaxies and into Brahman again they all ultimately disappear. The concept of *īśvaraḥ sarvabhūtānāṁ hṛddeśe 'rjuna tiṣṭhati*, of the Lord residing within the heart of each individual, is the second great insight of the Upaniṣads, and the relationship between the Ātman and the Brahman is the keynote upon which the whole of Vedāntic teaching revolves. All the four *yogas* are directed towards bringing about the union between the Ātman and the Brahman. The word *yoga* comes from the same root as the English word 'yoke', to join. *Yoga* is that which joins the Ātman and the Brahman. There are in our tradition four major paths of *yoga*—*Jñāna-yoga*, the way of wisdom, *Bhakti-yoga*, the way of emotional rapport; *Karma-yoga*, the way of dedicated action, and *Rāja-yoga*, the way of psychic discipline. All of them are directed towards bringing about the union between the all-pervasive Brahman without and the immortal Ātman within.

Flowing from this, we come now to another important Vedāntic concept, that all human beings because of their shared spirituality are members of a single, extended family. The Upaniṣads have an extraordinary phrase for human beings, *amṛtasya putraḥ* (children of immortality). We do not look upon human beings as essentially sinners, weak and cringing, begging and supplicating some unseen being hidden in some seventh heaven. Rather, we are children of immortality, because we carry the light and the power of the Brahman within our consciousness. This is within the consciousness of every human being regardless of race or colour, creed or sex, or any other differentiation. That is the basis of the concept of human beings as an extended family: *Vasudhaiva kuṭumbakam*. A famous *śloka*, not from the Upaniṣads but from a later text, points out that the decision between 'mine' and 'yours' is the small and narrow way of looking at reality, indulged in by people with small minds. But for those of the greater consciousness, the entire world is a family. This is another great insight of the Upaniṣad, peculiarly relevant at this juncture in human history as I will point out later.

We come now to a fourth major philosophical concept of the Upaniṣads, the essential unity of all religions, of all spiritual paths—*ekaṁ sad viprāḥ bahudhā vadanti* (truth is one, the wise call it by many names)—as the *Ṛg-Veda* has it. The *Muṇḍaka* has a beautiful *mantra* which says that as streams and rivulets arise in different parts of the world but ultimately flow into the same ocean, so do all these creeds and castes and religious formulations arise in different times and areas, but, if they have a true aspiration, ultimately reach the same goal.

Here is a philosophy which cuts across barriers of hatred and fanaticism that have been built in the name of religion. The Vedānta is a universal religion; it accepts the infinite possibilities of movements towards the divine, it does not seek to limit or confine us to any particular formulation. After all each one of us is different. Whether you believe in reincarnation or in genetic configuration, the fact remains that there are no two human beings who are exactly alike, and so all have to seek their own path to the divine. The Vedānta welcomes and accepts the multiplicity of paths to the divine, provided those paths are true paths towards divine realization, not merely intellectual gymnastics and disputations. It is a little like climbing a mountain. There are several different starting points, and if we keep arguing at those starting points we are miles apart. But when we start climbing and are actually moving upwards then, as we come nearer and nearer to the summit, our paths will begin to converge and ultimately when we get to the top we will all meet there. Similarly, once you really start moving upwards in the field of spiritual endeavour, you will find these denominational differences gradually losing their importance, and as you rise to the summit you will realize the spiritual oneness of divinity.

A fifth Vedāntic concept is the concept of the welfare of all beings: *Bahujana sukhāya bahujana hitāya ca*. The Vedānta does not seek to throw one class against another class, one caste against another caste, or one group against another group. The Vedānta seeks the welfare of all creation, not only of human beings but also of what we call the lower creatures. In our arrogance we have destroyed the environment of this planet, we have polluted the oceans, we have made the air unbreathable, we have desecrated nature and decimated wildlife. So many species have become extinct because of our *ahaṁkāra* as human beings. But the Vedāntic seers knew that man was not something apart from nature, that human consciousness grew out of the entirety of the world situation, and, therefore, they had compassion for all living beings. That is why the Vedānta constantly exhorts that, while we are working for our own salvation, we must also shun the path of violence, shun the path of hatred, try and develop both elements of inner and outer work: *Ātmano mokṣārthaṁ jagat hitaya ca*. Indeed, these are two sides of the same coin; we must work for our own salvation, but also for the welfare of the world. We also have a social responsibility, and as long as we are embodied we have to continue to work for the welfare of all beings.

These five concepts from the Vedānta—the all-pervasive Brahman; the Ātman which resides in all beings; the concept of the human race as members of a family regardless of all differences; the idea that all religions are essentially different paths to the same goal, and the concept that we must work for the welfare of society as a whole and for the welfare of this entire ecosystem and not only for ourselves—if taken together provide us a comprehensive world-view which will greatly help us in these troubled times. We are living in a very difficult age, but it is an exciting age to be alive, particularly for the younger generations. People today are often upset and worried as to why everything is so turbulent, but that is inevitable, because we are in a period of major transition. It is my belief, strengthened over the last few years by travelling extensively throughout the world, that mankind today is at a transition as important as the one many thousands of years ago from nomadic to pastoral civilization, then from pastoral to agricultural, agricultural to industrial and to post-industrial civilization. Each transition is now coming quicker because of the accelerated pace of growth and development, and what is happening is that a global consciousness is beginning to emerge despite all our discords and problems.

We are too close to the event to really grasp what is happening, but what I can see is a paradigm shift, a total shift of emphasis. Whether in dress or in music, in language or in food habits or any other sphere, gradually a world civilization is being born. And it has to be born if mankind is to survive in this nuclear age. Science and technology have given us tremendous power, but that power can be used for benign or malignant purpose. We can abolish poverty and hunger, malnutrition and misery, illiteracy and unemployment from the face of this earth by the end of this century. It can be done quite easily—seven days' expenditure on world armaments can abolish hunger in Africa, ten days' expenditure on world armaments can abolish the debt of Latin America. But, instead, thousands of billions of dollars and roubles and pounds and rupees and other currencies are going into the manufacture of weapons of mass destruction every year. We must never forget that power by itself is neither good nor evil; there is the *daivī śakti* and there is the *āsurī śakti*—the benign power and the malignant power. The worship of power, of science, is not enough. Hitler's gas chambers were an example of science and technology; the Hiroshima and Nagasaki atom bombs were an example of science and technology. We now have a single nuclear warhead packing the power of 1,000 Hiroshima bombs, and there are 50,000 such nuclear warheads on earth today. Are we not standing on the threshold of a major disaster? Are we not on the verge of the *mahāpralaya*, great deluge, or *mahāgnī*, great fire or whatever mode of destruction will finally develop? At such a time we can survive only if we have an alternative ideology to the present one which has led mankind to this position. I claim that the Vedānta in fact provides such an alternative ideology. Even at this stage, even at this late hour, if we can imbibe some of the universal truths of the Vedānta we can perhaps reverse the processes of destruction.

It is a tragedy that in India today, more than forty years after we have been free, our educational system is totally devoid of any exposure to the great truths of the Vedānta. Ask young students today to name two Upaniṣads, they will not be able to do so because they have never been exposed to them. Here we have a great heritage towards which the entire mankind is now beginning to turn, and we in India are deliberately and cold-bloodedly neglecting this heritage. Whenever one talks of the Upaniṣads, people think that they are something strange and bizarre, not realizing that, in fact, they provide the very foundation of the entire Indian civilization. If the whole of Western philosophy has been described as a series of footnotes to Plato, the whole of Eastern philosophy can be described as a series of footnotes to the Upaniṣads.

I would, therefore, urge you to go to these great and beautiful texts; do not allow yourselves to be frightened away by them, do not think that they deal with matters which you cannot grasp; open yourself to them, try and understand them. In the *Śvetaśvatara Upaniṣad* the seer says: *Vedāham etaṁ puruṣaṁ mahāntam āditya varṇaṁ tamasaḥ parstāt* (I know that great being, shining like the sun beyond the darkness; it is only by such knowing that you can overcome death, there is no other way to immortality). The immortality of the Upaniṣads is not survival after death, that is already taken for granted, it is the transcending of birth and death. The immortality of the Upaniṣads means that our consiousness is raised to a state where we are not obliged to be born and reborn again and again in the cycle of *saṁsāra*. It does not mean that we must run away. The great *ṛṣis* and their power is still there. In the Buddhist tradition we have the *bodhisattvas* who had attained Buddhahood but turned back in order to help the suffering humanity. In the Upaniṣadic tradition we have the *siddhas*, people who can materialize anywhere at will in order to help suffering humanity.

So it is not a question of being selfish but of being able to break the bonds in which we are caught. Can you imagine what it is like when a caterpillar, an ugly, land-bound worm, goes into a chrysalis and a miraculous metamorphosis takes place so that it emerges as a beautiful, radiantly coloured butterfly? That is the sort of metamorphosis that the Upaniṣads envisage for human consciousness. We change from our earth-bound consciousness into this bright, multi-coloured consciousness which can still alight upon the ground like a caterpillar but can also fly into the air which the caterpillar could not. That, as I see it, is the true message of the Upaniṣads, and I will end with that great and immortal Vedic prayer that seeks to lead us from the untruth of ignorance into the truth of knowledge; from the darkness within us into the light above us, and from the cycle of birth and death into immortality:

Asato mā sad gamaya!
Tamaso mā jyotir gamaya!
Mṛ tyor mā amṛtaṁ gamaya!

That is the highest achievement of the Upaniṣads; and that is the goal towards which we all must strive.

4

The Message of the Bhagavad-Gītā

Human consciousness as we see it today is the result of billions of years of evolution on this plane: three billion years of pre-biological evolution; a billion years of biological evolution; perhaps five hundred thousand years of human evolution; ten or fifteen thousand years of human civilization. The juncture at which we have now arrived brings to our mind the great myth of the *Samudra-Manthana*, (the Churning of the Milky Ocean). In this great myth—and I use the term in the deeper sense of the word meaning a powerful story which is suprarational—the Devas and the Asuras co-operated without any reservation. They churned for aeons, and ultimately the ocean began to throw up great gifts: Uccaiḥśravā, the divine horse; Kāmadhenu, the divine cow, Kalpavṛkṣa the wish-fulfilling tree; Airāvata, the six-tusked elephant and so on. These great *ratnas* emerged from the churning, and the Devas and Asuras distributed them amongst each other, happy and secure in the assumption that the churning was going to continue with benign results.

Suddenly, the occan began to boil with a totally unexpected factor, the *garala* (the terrible poison) that was hidden in the heart of this consciousness began to emerge. And when the poison emerged, the Devas and the Asuras fled in terror, because they had not expected this. They had assumed that they could continue to exploit and to churn *ad infinitum* without being forced to face the terrible reality. The poison rapidly spread through the three worlds—the Earth, the Water and the Skies—and it was only when the great primal-divinity, Śiva Mahādeva, appeared and drank the *garala*, integrating that poison into his own being, that the danger passed; the Devas and the Asuras returned. The churning continued and ultimately the *amṛta kalasa*, the vessel of nectar appeared.

This myth seems to me to illuminate the human predicament today. Science and technolgy have given us tremendous gifts, unprecedented power to ameliorate the human condition. And yet at the same time it has thrown up this terrible poison of destruction, the destructive power that is built into the very texture of matter in the splitting of the atom. And so here we are today; after all the great gifts, the poison has begun to emerge. And there is another story, this one from Western civilization, the story of Atlantis which we came across first in the writings of the great Greek philosopher, Plato. This great and glorious civilization flourished where the Atlantic ocean now holds its sway. It was unprecedented in its glory and its splendour, in its wealth and its technology. But we are told that one day it sank below the waves, unable to survive its own technological ingenuity.

It seems to me, as I travel from land to land, and as I talk with people of different faiths and ideologies, that perhaps we are the neo-Atlantis, perhaps human civilization today stands on the verge of a mighty *pralaya*. And, therefore, we are compelled to turn to our scriptural tradition, our cultural tradition, not to go backward, for there can be no going back for man, but to go forward into the future, to derive the courage, the strength and the wisdom to see the path ahead. The reason our Indian cultural tradition has come down unbroken for thousands of years is that it has the capacity for spiritual renewal from age to age. No philosophy or religion that does not have the capacity for renewal and renaissance can really meet the requirements of a changing society. It has to have the inner elasticity and breadth to cover the new developments, and there also have to be men and women who, in their own lives, live and illuminate these great truths.

When we look at the Indian civilization, particularly the great Hindu tradition, we have the Vedas stretching back into the very dawn of history, the great inspired utterances of *ṛṣis* in thousand upon thousands of beautiful *mantras*. We have the Upaniṣads, the Vedānta, representing the culmination of the Vedas both philosophically and chronologically. We have the Brahma-Sūtras, which give us an intellectual guide and key to the understanding of the Vedas. We have the Purāṇas, we have the epics, the *Rāmāyaṇa* and the *Mahābhārata.* I have spoken of the great Himalayan range of the Vedas, and of the Upaniṣads as the mountain peaks. Now I will change the metaphor, and talk of the starry sky at night. Nothing is more magnificent and beautiful than looking up at the sky on a moonless night, when you see thousands upon thousands of celestial bodies all glowing with inner power and light. But among these you will notice that there is one star that shines brighter than the others. It may not be bigger, it may not be closer, but it is the brightest star—what we know as the 'morning star' or as Venus. And as we look at this great galaxy of Hindu texts and scriptures, there is one star that shines brighter than the rest, and that is the *Bhagavad-Gītā*.

The *Gītā* occupies a unique place, even though it is Smṛti whereas the Vedas and the Upaniṣads are Śruti, and the latter are considered superior in their authenticity and chronology. But the *Gītā* has a very special position. Adi Śaṅkarācārya, in one of his memorable *ślokas*, says that anyone who has tasted even a drop of *amṛta* or who has understood even a little of the *Bhagavad-Gītā*, need not have any fear of death. It has been commented upon by all the great philosophers, by Śaṅkara and Madhva, by Rāmānuja and Vallabhācārya, by Jñāneśvara, and, in our own century, by Balgangadhar Tilak and Sri Aurobindo, by Mahatma Gandhi and Vinoba Bhave. In my view, after Śaṅkarācārya's commentary, Sri Aurobindo's *Essays on the Gita* is the most luminous and magnificent of modern commentaries. The whole galaxy of leaders of our freedom movement were influenced by the *Gītā*.

What is the reason for this extraordinary popularity of the *Gītā* and its relevance to modern times. As I see it, there are four main reasons why the *Gītā* is so tremendously significant and relevant in this age, and why it is the best known of the Hindu scriptures—along with the Bible and the Quran one of the three most influential religious texts in the history of mankind. The first reason is that the *Gītā* is born in a situation of conflict—in the very midst of the great Kurukṣetra war. Both the armies are drawn up, the flight of missiles has begun, the conchshells have sounded, the clamour of war is tumultuous and the hearts of the participants are torn by the conflict. It is then that the *Gītā* teaching comes to us, it is there that Śrī Kṛṣṇa calls upon Arjuna to arise, to get ready for battle. The *Gītā* is a scripture of conflict, whereas the Upaniṣads are set in a very calm and peaceful atmosphere.

Let us remember that Kurukṣetra is not only a plain in Haryana. The outer Kurukṣetra is still there, of course, but the inner Kurukṣetra is within each one of us. It is within our psyche that the āsurī and *daivī* powers are drawn up in array against each other, and it is within the heart of our consciousness that this battle has constantly to be fought. Today, with the world poised on the brink of a mighty conflagration, it is a Kurukṣetra situation and the *Gītā*, a *saṅgharṣa śāstra* (scripture of conflict), is what mankind requires, a stirring call to arms, not for personal aggrandizement, not even for national glory, but for the deeper, more difficult task of becoming an instrument of the divine will, a warrior for the divine cause, a fighter for the divine consciousness. That is the battle to which Śrī Kṛṣṇa calls us, and that is why man today, torn as he is in a situation of conflict, responds to the message of the *Gītā*.

The second reason for the importance and relevance of the *Gītā* lies in the divine personality of the teacher. Every scripture has its *guru*, its *ācārya*. The *Muṇḍaka Upaniṣad* has Aṅgiras, the *Bṛhadāraṇyaka Upaniṣad* has Yajñavalkya, and other seers and *ṛṣis* are there. But in the *Bhagavad-Gītā* it is the divine Lord Himself disguised in a human form who is talking to us. Śrī Kṛṣṇa can be looked upon in many different ways. In one view, he is the personification of the Brahman, the great power which, shining, causes everything else to shine, which illuminates everything that exists— *tam eva bhāntam anubhāti sarvaṁ, tasya bhāsā sarvam idaṁ vibhāti* (everything shines only after that shining light, his shining illumines all this world). In the Eleventh Chapter of the *Gītā*, he appears in his great *virātasvarupa* in which everything that exists is to be found, and by the glory of which Arjuna is dazzled, as if a thousand suns had risen together upon the horizon.

And yet this very Kṛṣṇa comes before us in the *Gītā* as a charioteer, as a guide, as one holding the reins of the chariot. We have God himself descended in the forms of the divine charioteer, and that is why when Śrī Kṛṣṇa speaks he does so with absolute and overriding authority, not simply from the human standpoint but from the divine. That is why the *Gītā* is so significant, because it personalizes the Parabrahman (the highest god-consciousness of the Upanisads). The Upaniṣads say: *Sarvaṁ khalv idaṁ brahma* (all this is Brahman); the *Gītā* says: *Vāsudevaḥ sarvam iti* (all this is *Vāsudevaḥ*, the supreme). So in the *Gītā* the figure of Śrī Kṛṣṇa personifies that divine splendour and power which is described so beautifully in the Upaniṣads, and that is why it has a unique impact upon our minds and hearts.

The third reason for the *Gītā's* special importance lies in the relationship between the *guru* and the *śiṣya*. In the Hindu tradition this is a very intimate relationship. In the Upaniṣads the *guru* uses the term *saumaya* for disciple, meaning 'dearly beloved'; he looks upon the disciples as even more close to him than his own sons, because whereas the father only gives physical life the *guru* makes real spiritual birth possible. But in the *Bhagavad-Gītā* there is a closeness between Arjuna and Kṛṣṇa which is not, as far as I am aware, to be found in any other scripture. One of the most moving verses of the *Bhagavad-Gītā* is when Arjuna, after he sees the *virāta-svarupa*, says to Śrī Kṛṣṇa: 'I bow to you, I prostrate myself before you, and I demand grace from you. Like a father to his son, like a friend to his dear friend, like a lover to his beloved, do thou bear with me.' Where else in the scriptures of the world would you get this composite relationship; the love between a father and a son, between a friend and a dear friend, between a lover and the beloved, all combined in the relationship between Kṛṣṇa and Arjuna. That is what makes it so significant. It is a relationship of trust, faith and devotion. Kṛṣṇa is urging his friend, not threatening him. At the end of his entire teachings, Kṛṣṇa says to Arjuna: *yathe 'cchasi tathā kuru* (do as you please). He says, in effect: 'I am not forcing you, I am not threatening you, I am not cajoling you. You asked me a question and I have shown you the path. It is now your decision, you have to do what you like.'

It is this aspect of the *Gītā* which makes the teaching so significant and attractive, specially for the younger generations, because the youth, not only in India but throughout the world, is not prepared to be bullied or badgered by the older generation, or to accept their claim to superior wisdom or knowledge or morality. However, if we guide them with love, if we are friends with them, then perhaps we can influence them more effectively.

A fourth reason for the importance of the *Gītā* is its universal applicability. The *Gītā* as a doctrine does not confine itself to any particular creed. In the Tenth Chapter, Śrī Kṛṣṇa is very clear: 'In whichever way people approach me, as long as they do it with faith, I make that resolve firm.' What an amazing assertion this is! Hinduism does not generally wish to make converts, because it is aware that the divine Ātman is residing in all beings. Who is it ultimately that it will convert? The universal applicability of the *Gītā* and its wide, all-embracing doctrine is extremely important. It is not a narrow creed. Again and again Śri Kṛṣṇa in the *Gītā* says that, whatever faith one may have, ultimately that worship will come to him. That is why the *Gītā* has such a great appeal not only to Hindus but to genuine spiritual seekers whatever religion they may belong to.

Let us turn now to the content of the *Gītā*. It is multifaceted and many-dimensional; a single *śloka* can be taken up and developed for days as has been done by many commentators. But, briefly, I will place before you four major aspects of the teachings of the *Gītā* which I consider to be particularly significant. The first is the theory of correct action. I have said that the *Gītā* is a *saṅgharṣa śāstra* and the problem in war is: what is to be done? Indeed, at any given point of time in our lives, whether we are students or in business or in politics or in any other field of life, the question always is: what is to be done, what is our *kartavyaṁ karma*?

This is the most difficult of all questions. The *Gītā* itself realizes this, and at one point Śri Kṛṣṇa says: *Gahanā karmaṅo gatiḥ* (Thick and tangled is the way of action). The theory of correct action in the *Gītā* revolves around a single concept; that action should not be purely for selfish purposes, although the self is obviously involved; it should not be simply as a necessary evil, because we have to act. Action must be a positive, joyous, affirmative action, it must be an offering to the divine. This is the important point. It does not really matter what it is we are doing; what is important is the psychological and spiritual input into that action. In the Eighteenth Chapter there is a very important *śloka* which says that by worshipping through one's action the divinity that pervades the entire cosmos man moves toward perfection.

So there you have the answer. It has to be an action which is skilful, which is efficient, but which tries to avoid obsession, because obsessive action can easily become self-negating. If the action is detached, there is an inner freedom and inner dedication and you do not become obsessed. I have met so many people in my life, particularly in politics, people of great gifts; but they become so obsessed with their action and the result of the actions that ultimately they destroy themselves as human beings. We must have involvement without attachment and commitment without obsession. It is a very difficult path. Involvement we need, but without attachment. If you do not get involved, then you are evading your responsibility; but if you get attached, you are distorting your consciousness. Similarly commitment without obsession, that is the special type of action that the *Gītā* gives us.

There is a story about the building of the great Bṛhadīsvara temple a thousand years ago by Rajaraja Chola in Tanjavur, probably the most beautiful temple in India. The king one day decided to go and inspect the work; so he drove to the temple site, got out of his chariot and walked towards where this temple was being built. He came across a man who was cutting stones, and he asked him: 'What are you doing?' The man said: 'Sir, I am cutting stones.' He went a little further, and there was another man who was doing the same thing. He said: 'What are you doing?' The man answered: 'Sir, I am earning a living.' He went further and came to a third person who was doing exactly the same thing. He asked: 'What are you doing?' He said: 'Sir, I am building a great temple.' Now you will see the difference in attitude. They were doing exactly the same thing, they were getting exactly the same wages. But the first man was mechanically performing a task, he had no greater consciousness. The second one had a slightly broader vision, he had the problem of his family and was earning for them. The third one was earning for his family certainly, but he had the broad vision that he was building a great temple to Lord Śiva. That illustrates what I mean by the theory of correct action. Whatever you may be doing, it does not really matter as long as you are doing it with inner dedication and devotion, and as long as you are using action itself as a powerful means of spiritual development. This is the first major teaching of the *Gītā*, the theory of correct action.

Secondly, there is the theory of an integrated *yoga* that the *Gītā* places before us. I spoke yesterday of the four *yogas*, the four paths to divine union—*Jñāna-yoga*, the way of wisdom, of intellectual discrimination; *Bhakti-yoga*, the way of emotional outpouring towards a personalized image of the divine; *Karma-yoga*, the way of dedicated action; and *Rāja-yoga*, the way of psychic discipline, of Prāṇāyāma, the discipline of breathing control, and the development of the *kuṇḍalinī śakti* (serpent power) within us. These are the four main types of *yogas* that we have in our tradition, and for each there are scriptures which deal with various aspects. Thus, for the *Jñāna-yoga* we have the Upaniṣads; for the *Karma-yoga* we have the *Karma-kāṇḍa*; for the *Bhakti-yoga* we have the *Śrīmad-*

Bhāgavatam, the *Siva Purāṇa* and other Purāṇas; and for the *Rāja-yoga* we have Patañjali's *Yoga-Sūtras* and other texts. But the *Gītā* is unique in that, in the short compass of 700 *ślokas*, it integrates these four *yogas* into a single, unified path.

The *Gītā* points out that it is no longer enough for us to follow only one of these paths. In the old days, if you were a *jñānī* you could go off into the mountains in Kashmir and sit there for the rest of your life meditating, but that is not good enough for the *Kali-yuga*. In the old days, if you were a *bhakta*, you could spend the whole of your life going around doing *kīrtan*. If you were a *Rāja-yogī*, you could sit in your own *āśrama* and develop your powers. If you were a *Karma-yogī*, you could wander around doing good deed. But it is not enough now for us to be one of these; we have to be all four. Every individual has to develop his mind, his heart, his physical capacity and his inner spiritual power, and that is the important message of the *Gītā*. It brings us to what Sri Aurobindo calls *pūrṇayoga*, an integrated *yoga*. I am often asked about caste, and I say that whatever importance caste may have had at one time, today everyone of us has to have the *guṇas* (qualities) of all the four castes. We need the knowledge and learning of the Brāhmaṇa; the valour and patriotism of the Kṣatriya; the commercial acumen and ability of the Vaiśya; and the capacity for physical service and work of the Sūdra. Each one of us has to combine these four qualities, if we are really to be able to move forward in this age of iron, the *Kali-yuga*.

Thirdly, there is in the *Gītā* a repeated reassurance of divine intervention. You are familiar with the popular *śloka* where Śrī Kṛṣṇa says that from age to age, whenever unrighteousness flourishes and *dharma* is about to disappear, he will assume human form for the destruction of the evil-doers and re-establishment of the *dharma*. This is an assurance given to all humanity, and, if we read the *Gītā* with an open mind and have faith in it and Śrī Kṛṣṇa, we must accept this assurance at its face value. It is not simply a bit of hyperbole in which he was indulging. Somebody introducing me to someone mentioned that I have been a minister. As you know, when a minister makes an assurance in the House, everybody holds him to it. I think today the time has come when we have got to ask Śri Kṛṣṇa why he is not fulfilling the assurance that he gave us. Surely, if we need the divine, the divine also in some way needs us. Śrī Kṛṣṇa had the *Sūdarśana Cakra* (thousand-spoked discus), he could have used it and finished the war himself.

Why did he not do it? He also needed Arjuna, may be *nimittamātraṁ* but he needed the *nimitta*; otherwise, he could not have won the war of *Mahābhārata*, at least not in the way it was won.

Perhaps this is a new thought that I am putting into your mind. If we need the divine, does the divine not need us? Does the supramental power, does the greater consciousness that is seeking to descend or to emerge not need active co-operation from us? I think it does, and I make bold to say that, as Sri Aurobindo puts it, without an aspiration from below there will not be an answering call from above. And that is why it is so important that we shun the attitudes of dejection, despair and negativism that one finds so often in India; people constantly bemoaning and bewailing their lot and saying that the country is going to the dogs and that everything is breaking down. It is no use moaning and groaning like that, it will get us nowhere. We have to arise and be ready to fight the battle of existence. If our lives end before it is completed, so what? We had had thousands of lives before, and we will have thousands more. The Ātman, as the *Gītā* says, cannot be burnt, cannot be cut, cannot be drowned, cannot be cleaved. But we must have faith; faith in our own inner capacity and in the assurance of no less a person than Śrī Kṛṣṇa.

I have spoken of the theory of correct action, of the integration of the four *yogas*, the four paths to spiritual development, of the repeated assurance of divine intervention. Finally, we come to the *Gītā's* gospel of total surrender to the divine. Ultimately, at the end of the entire discourse, after Śrī Kṛṣṇa has said *yathe 'cchhasi tathā kuru*, once again he speaks; without a question this time, he speaks on his own. All the rest of his speeches were in response to questions from Arjuna, but the last statement of Śrī Kṛṣṇa is *suo moto*. And he says: *Sarvadharmān parityajya mām ekaṁ śaraṇaṁ vraja, ahaṁ tvā sarvapāpebhyo mokṣaiṣyāmi ma sucaḥ*. What a beautiful *śloka* this is!

What is *dharma? Dharma* comes from the root *dhṛ*, that which supports. In the final analysis, what is it that supports human consciousness? It is not wealth, it is not position, it is not political power, howsoever important these may appear to us. Ultimately, it is the divine consciousness that supports us, that supports our very existence. Therefore, Srī Kṛṣṇa urges us to give up all other supports and come alone to him. Śrī Kṛṣṇa speaking as the divine himself says... 'I will free you from all sins. Do not fear'—*mā sucaḥ*. How much love there is in those two words 'fear not'. When a child is to go into a dark room with the parent behind, the parent says: 'Do not be afraid, I am here; go ahead.' These words *mā sucaḥ* in a way sum up the entire message of the *Gītā*. Let us not be afraid, and let us give up all lesser supports so that ultimately we get the one true support, the only thing that can support the growth and development of the higher consciousness, the grace of the divine.

Śrī Kṛṣṇa's flute is still playing in Vṛndāvana. We may not be able to hear it because our ears are so full of the clamour and noise of daily living, and the conflicts and the tensions around us, but it is still playing. And Śrī Kṛṣṇa is still there as the charioteer riding with us in our own higher consciousness. We do not have to go back to Kurukṣetra, we do not have to go back to Arjuna. Śrī Kṛṣṇa is with us always, provided we have ears to listen, provided we have eyes to see, provided we do not get totally blinded and deafened by the outer material conflicts which surround us. The outer is also important, but ultimately it is he whose inner consciousness is firmly centred in the divine alone will be able to meet the conflicts that lie ahead.

The conflicts are there. There is no easy path to greatness or to spiritual realization, either individual or collective. We must always remember the Vedic exhortation: *Caraiveti, Caraiveti* (Move on, Move on). Imagine human consciousness as a great current that is flowing down through the dark channels of time. If we do not swim upwards against the stream, we will be carried down to the rapids and the waterfalls below. There can be no standing still for man. Man is a transitional being, half way between the animal and the divine. Man's destiny is to move onwards to the next stage of evolution, for then only can our divine nature be fully developed. But, in order to move upwards, we have to struggle. If we have faith and reverence, then, with the sound of the divine flute echoing in our ears and the voice of the divine charioteer resounding in our hearts, we can move resolutely onwards towards the divine destiny that awaits us. That, in essence, is the message of the *Gītā*.

5

The Insight of the Mystics

The outstanding feature of the last quarter of the twentieth century is the final collapse of the materialistic paradigm that had dominated the world for many centuries. The Cartesian-Newtonian-Marxist paradigm has finally collapsed, and in the post-Einsteinian period, with quantum mechanics and Heisenberg's Uncertainty Principle, with Stan Grof's Extended Cartography of the Psyche, and so many other exciting and interesting developments, we find that the ancient vision of the mystics is again being recaptured. This too solid matter dissolves into waves of probability, and all materialistic philosophies, whether Marxist or capitalistic or of any other brand, have failed. Humanity gropes for a new model, a new philosophy and a new paradigm to replace the old: in fact, for a new consciousness. Mankind is at a revolutionary crossroads, and it is no coincidence that this has happened when it is in supreme peril, not from another species, not from so-called 'natural' changes in the weather, not from some other world, but from itself. Deep within the human psyche has developed a terrible power that threatens not only our generation, but all species of life on this planet.

Ancient myths can often illuminate the human predicament, and I want to start my presentation with a brief description of a powerful Hindu myth the *Samudra-Manthana* or the Churning of the Milky Ocean. In this great myth the Devas and the Asuras, the bright and the dark powers, both combined to churn the milky ocean. We do not have the absolute dichotomy of good and evil that is there in the semitic tradition; the bright and the dark powers, the Devas and the Asuras, are, in fact, related within the whole theory of duality.

Both of these combine to churn the milky ocean for aeons and then great gifts begin to appear. Kāmadhenu, the all-giving cow; Kalpavṛkṣa, the wish-fulfilling tree; Uccaiśravā, the divine horse; Airāvata, the divine elephant; Mahālakṣmi, the goddess of wealth and prosperity. These and other great gifts appeared and were happily divided between the Asuras and Devas. The ultimate objective was the pot of ambrosia, the elixir of immortality, the *amṛta kalaśa*.

Suddenly, and without warning, the ocean started to boil with a terrible poison, the *garala*, a new and malign dimension, of which neither the Devas nor the Asuras had any knowledge. The poison spread throughout the three worlds, the ocean, the land and the sky. The Devas and the Asuras ran helter-skelter in panic in a vain attempt to escape this terrible poison, forgetting all the gifts that they had divided, because it appeared as if the whole process of creation was coming to an end. And it was then that Śiva, the great primal divinity, aloof from the avarice and materialism of the Devas and Asuras, appeared. He collected the poison in a cup, and as he drank it his throat turned blue, hence one of the names of Śiva is *nīlakaṇtha*, the blue-throated one. And it was only when he had absorbed the poison that order was restored, the Devas and the Asuras returned, the churning was resumed until finally the ambrosial pot appeared.

This is a myth of great significance. The human condition now seems to me to be very similar. Prolonged churning has given us incredible gifts. Science and technology, medicine, communications, space, the extraordinary adventure into outer space. The tremendous development of science has brought material benefits and comforts to millions upon millions of people. It gives us the capacity to abolish poverty and hunger, illiteracy and unemployment, by the end of this century. We can ensure for every human being born upon this planet the necessary physical, intellectual and material inputs for a full life.

And yet surely the poison is also now upon us. Thousands of billions of dollars and roubles, pounds and francs, and other currencies are spent every year on monstrous weapons of unprecedented destruction. The planet today is bristling with 50,000 nuclear warheads, each a thousand times more powerful than the ones that demolished Hiroshima and Nagasaki, each having more than the entire explosive power used by both sides in the Second

World War. With all our knowledge, with all the gifts, we have come to a single *mantra*—Mutually Assured Destruction—MAD. Five thousand years ago, there was another three-letter word which was the epitome of the Vedic knowledge—*AUM*. In five thousand years the human race has come from *AUM* to MAD.

It is not necessary to go into details of the effect of even a so-called 'limited' nuclear war which itself is a myth. *The Day After* is a film that has had a tremendous impact, though it is a gross understatement of the situation. Jonathan Schell's marvellous book *The Fate of the Earth* and its follow-up *The Abolition* give some idea of what would happen in the event of a nuclear war. The new report, *The Cold and the Dark*, by Carl Sagan and others also gives overwhelming evidence to show that any sort of nuclear war would end human civilization as we know it, poison the air and the oceans and render the planet uninhabitable.

No bomb has so far been invented that would destroy only the Russians and the Americans. All of us, whether we live in Asia or Africa, in the Arctic areas or at the ends of the Earth, will be effectively eliminated. In fact, those people on whom the bombs fall may be luckier because they would go instantaneously, whereas millions of others would die lingering deaths longing to be released from their torture. And this can happen not necessarily through a political decision. A miscalculation, an accident, a flock of geese, an earthquake, a malfunctioning computer—anything can now do it.

Do we realize that we are a privileged generation, that we may be the last generation of human beings to inhabit this earth? Can we as thinking beings accept this situation without striving for a solution? Can we acquiesce in a situation where one-quarter of the world is overfed and three-quarters underfed? Can we live in a global village where millions die of malnutrition, stunted in body and mind, and other millions suffer from obesity and over-eating? Can we live in an age where millions lack elementary medical care and other millions are overmedicated? Can we fail to heed the cry of the oppressed and the deprived and yet claim that we are on the inner path?

If the answer to these questions is in the negative, as it must be, then we must move towards a new transition. It is going to be painful as are all transitions, but they are essential for human survival. We have got to move towards complementarity in place of competition, and convergence in place of conflict. We must heal the split in the human psyche. We must gather the shattered fragments of human consciousness and weld them into a glowing whole. We must affect the transition to a new global consciousness to replace the present fractured and fragmented condition of the human race.

But can this be done? Many thinkers have pointed out that, whenever there is a major transition, there is a period of reaction and crystallization. Can we afford that type of crystallization in a world bristling with nuclear weapons? Will there be a substantial enough transformation of consciousness on Planet Earth in time to prevent its destruction? Or is this particular adventure in consciousness, as Arthur Koestler has pointed out, doomed to failure? Is man a creature programmed for self-destruction, and not even a graceful exit like the dinosaurs but a malignant one, taking all life with it, not only collective suicide but terricide?

No one knows the answers. But the *Bhagavad-Gītā* teaches that we must act in the manner we feel right, and not worry about consequences. 'By worshipping through our actions that great power that permeates the universe, man moves towards perfection.' We must act not from our inflated or deflated egos, but from the depths of our inner being. Indeed, at this juncture in planetary history, creative action is a spiritual imperative; we simply cannot accept the negative option.

And yet with the world apparently rushing towards its doom, what is it that we can do to help the favourable resolution of this terrible conflict, to encourage a transition to the new consciousness? I have a five-point programme which could help in this process.

The first point is to work out the conceptual, and theoretical philosophical underpinning of the new global consciousness. We can draw from many traditions, from science and from religion. We have inherited some astounding insights from the *ṛṣis*, the great seers who lived in the Himalayas thousands of years ago. One is the unity of all existence: the fact that there is no ultimate duality, whether on this planet or on the billions upon billions of galaxies. It is all the expression of a single power, of a single energy, of a single divine force. Then there is the divinity inherent in every human being. If God exists, He is divine by definition; but the concept that the human being is potentially divine, that the divine resides in every human being regardless of race or religion, caste or creed, language or ideology is of signal importance. Again there is the vision of mankind as a family. We are all related by the fact of our humanness, we are members of the human family. Yet another Hindu concept is the harmony of religions. Religion has been a source of great art and inspiration, and also of unprecedented destruction. Even today thousands lie dead on the battlefield in the name of religion. We have got to understand that all these great religious traditions draw their sustenance from the same centre. We have got to move towards the concept of the unity of all religions. Finally, there is the concept of the welfare of all mankind, regardless of whether they live in the East or the West, the North or the South. These were some of the insights which we find in the Hindu tradition. We can go to other religious traditions and also non-religious traditions in order to develop a coherent philosophy.

Having developed this new philosophy, it should be widely spread through the media. The media today are full of violence; of negative vibrations. Why can we not use the media for something positive for a change? Why not use the tremendous power of communications, television? Television does not have to be an 'idiot box'. It can be a box of enlightenment, but only if there are enlightened people behind it. If you have compassion and understanding behind it, this can become one of the most powerful instruments for mass enlightenment that has ever been produced. We had a Spiritual Summit in New York in October 1983 where the Dalai Lama, and Archbishop Helda Camara of Brazil spoke. I also had the privilege of speaking. We adopted a Declaration of the Spiritual Summit, but nobody has ever heard of it because the media are not interested in anything of a philosophical nature. Disaster, murder, anything that fractures the human psyche and fragments it, yes. But where is the healing? Where is that power that can bring about a new development in the humam psyche? The media are not with us, and, therefore, we have to utilize our resources to get our message across. There must be an inter-religious dialogue, a science-spirituality dialogue. Human survival is too important to be left to military or political leaders. Those of us who are in this field, who are working towards the new consciousness, have got to assert ourselves and get into the mind of the world.

Thirdly, we must work immediately and urgently to set up a

worldwide network. There are hundreds of groups today all over the world, there are millions of people on all continents feeling the great pressure of the future. But they are disparate, not properly knit together or co-ordinated. They can have a symbiotic relationship with each other, if there is a pooling of all this energy. Time is rushing by very fast, and we seem to be moving towards some traumatic event in human history. I commend the image of a great philharmonic orchestra in which all the creative, positive movements of the world are knit together into one tremendous power and force which has overwhelming influence upon mankind. Into the United Nations is built an incurable dichotomy which prevents it from becoming an effective organ. Why should we not set up a new United Nations of the New Consciousness to take upon itself the task of spearheading this new movement. This might sound presumptuous, but then no great task is ever accomplished without a certain element of presumption. We must be humble, and yet our humility should not lead us into a sort of passivity, nor should we end up by hypnotizing ourselves into an inability to act.

The fourth point is an immediate involvement in peace and disarmament movements. I am aware that there are political implications in this, and yet I do feel that we have to get involved in the broader anti-nuclear movements. We do not necessarily have to demonstrate on the streets, but in our own way we have to do this, first in the open societies and then in the closed societies, because no society can today remain closed howsoever much they may want to. The winds of change, the winds of awareness are blowing across the frontiers of the world. Howsoever much the United States may feel that the Soviet Union is closed, and the Soviets may feel that the United States is not open to conviction, the fact of the matter is that there is now a new awareness, a new permeability in both these great blocs. We can see that from our third vantage point, as it were.

Finally, it is not enough to be involved in a movement for outer peace; there has to be a parallel movement for inner peace within each one of us. In our own lives, we must move towards a realization of the truth at the core of our being, the higher consciousness that is the birthright of each individual born on this planet, 'the light that lighteth every man that cometh into this world'. In the crucible of our individual consciousness alone can the poison be contained, transformed into nectar and released into society and the world. In this age, it is not realistic to expect the great Lord Śiva to appear once again and drink the poison for us. We have now passed that stage in evolution. Now that we have reached the stage of self-individuation, we have got to drink the poison ourselves. Each one of us has to integrate the poison within our psyches, and convert it by the power of our spiritual striving into nectar.

The last point that I wish to make is that we must co-operate with the spiritual power of the earth. Every ancient tradition has known that Planet Earth is not just a ball of mud, stone and lava, but a living spiritual presence. The dramatic photograph of Planet Earth taken from the moon shows our earth as it really is: a tiny, glowing jewel against the unending vastnesses of outer space, so fragile and yet so beautiful. In the *Atharva-Veda*, composed five-thousand years ago by the *ṛṣis*, there is a Hymn to the Earth known as *Bhūmī-Sūkta*. It has sixty-three verses which speak to us today with a new urgency and a new resonance. I would like to read a translation of twelve of these verses to show you that the insight of the mystics is again becoming viable and important:

> Truth, eternal order that is great and stern,
> Consecration, Austerity, Prayer and Ritual—
> these uphold the Earth.
> May She, Queen of what has been and will be,
> make a wide world for us.
> Earth which has many heights, and slopes
> and the unconfined plain that bind men together,
> Earth that bears plants of various healing powers,
> may she spread wide for us and thrive.
> Earth, in which lie the sea, the river and other waters,
> in which food and cornfields have come to be,
> in which lives all that breathes and that moves,
> may she confer on us the finest of her yield.
> Earth, which at first was in the water of the ocean,
> and which sages sought with wondrous powers,
> Earth whose heart was in eternal heaven,
> wrapped in Truth, immortal,
> may she give us lustre and strength
> in a most exalted state.

Earth, in which the waters, common to all,
moving on all sides, flow unfailingly, day and night,
may she pour on us milk in many streams,
and endow us with lustre.
Pleasant be thy hills, O Earth,
thy snow-clad mountains and thy woods!
O Earth—brown, black, red and multi-coloured
the firm Earth protected by Indra,
on this Earth may I stand—
unvanquished, unhurt, unslain.
I call to earth; the purifier,
the patient Earth, growing strong through spiritual might.
May we recline on thee, O Earth, who
bearest power and plenty,
and enjoy our share of food and molten butter.
May those that are thy eastern regions, O Earth,
and the northern and the southern and the western
be pleasant for me to tread upon.
May I not stumble while I live in the world.
Whatever I dig from thee, Earth,
may that have quick growth again.
O purifier, may we not injure thy vitals
or thy heart.
May Earth with people who speak various tongues
and those who have various religious rites
according to their places of abode,
pour for me treasure in a thousand streams
like a constant cow that never fails.
May those born of thee, O Earth,
be, for our welfare, free from sickness and waste.
Wakeful through a long life, we shall
become bearers of tribute to thee.
Earth, my mother, set me securely with bliss
in full accord with heaven.
O wise one,
uphold me in grace and splendour.

This earth, our mother, has nurtured consciousness from the slime of the primeval ocean billions of years ago and has sustained the human race for countless centuries. Will we repay our debt to our mother by converting her into a burntout cinder circling the sun into eternity? Or will we so marshal our inner and outer resources that even at this late hour we succeed in making the crucial transition to the new consciousness? The answer will depend upon many factors, not the least of which is whether each one of us lives up to our ideals and our humanity, whether the transpersonal vision is translated into creative action individually and collectively.

Do we remain mired into the old consciousness, or are we able to make the transition to the new? This is truly an absorbing, exciting and exhilarating challenge. Let us pray then for courage and wisdom at this crucial hour, pray to the great power that permeates the cosmos, the earth and the sky, the mountains and the rivers, the forests and the oceans, the humans and the beasts. The great power that, shining, causes everything else to shine; the great power that blazes like a thousand suns on the other shore beyond the darkness. The great power so beautifully symbolized by the figure of Śiva Naṭarāja—the dancing Śiva holding in one hand the drum, the creative sound, by which millions of galaxies spring into being, and in the other hand the eternal fire in which the cycle of regeneration is completed. Let us pray to the divine power to give mankind courage at this critical phase, so that we are able to make the transition to the new consciousness.

May that great divine power give us the strength and the courage that we need to make the transition!

6

Hinduism and Humanity

Ninety-one years ago, when Swami Vivekananda arose to address the Parliament of Religions in Chicago, he was the only Hindu present. Today, as a result of the great work done by Swami Vivekananda, many of his followers and Swamis of the Ramakrishna Mission and a number of other great Hindu teachers—Paramahansa Yogananda who came here and who founded his own society; Prabhupāda who has founded one of the most remarkable movements that we have seen in recent times; Swami Muktananda who passed away very recently but who was a source of great inspiration to thousands of people; and a large number of others including the inaugurator of today's conference, Swami Chinmayanandaji, who has founded his mission here—there are hundreds of thousands of Hindus living in the North American continent, making a vibrant and valuable contribution to the country of their adoption and residence.

As was rightly said this morning, we have made a proud contribution; we have produced Nobel Laureates, we have produced technicians, entrepreneurs and businessmen of the very highest standard; and we can be proud that wherever the Hindus are they are not parasites, they are making a major contribution to the countries in which they live. And this is so particularly in America, this great land of freedom and democracy which, as you will remember, was discovered by chance by Columbus when he was actually looking for us! We have a very special link, as it was a psychic link, with the United States and its great leaders, particularly thinkers like Abraham Lincoln whose words have inspired the leaders of our own freedom movement.

We can be proud to be Hindus, because Hinduism is unique in

world history, it is the oldest continuing religion which comes down to us from the very dawn of human civilization. There were other religions at that time; there was a great religion in Egypt, in Babylon, in Mesopotamia, and there were other creeds unknown today; but they have all disappeared and survive only in the minds of research scholars or the four walls of museums. It is Hinduism alone that has retained its dynamic and vibrant presence down through the corridors of time. It is not as if Hinduism has not been persecuted. In fact, if you look at the history of Hinduism for the last thousand years, you will see that we have been through the most severe persecution that any religion in the world has ever undergone. Yet, despite that we have retained not only our identity but our vibrancy and our power as well.

Today hundreds of millions of Hindus live not only in India but in many countries of the world. Let us remember that all Indians are not Hindus, and all Hindus are not Indians. Hinduism is not the monopoly of India. If I were to say that Hinduism was the monopoly of India, I would have a lot of problems in my own family, because my wife comes from Nepal which is the only Hindu State in the world today. Similarly, there are many other countries with large Hindu populations; there are Bangladesh and Pakistan, Sri Lanka and Mauritius, and countries far away from India such as Fiji and Surinam, Guyana and Trinidad. All over the world, in all the major continents, Hindus live and are proud to be Hindus.

What are the reasons for this vitality of Hinduism, for this unique capacity to retain its inner strength and dynamism? As I see it, there are two main factors. The first is that Hinduism is based not upon the teaching of any single individual, or upon any single text, but upon the collective wisdom of a whole spectrum of great men and women who, by dint of their spiritual power and realization, laid down certain eternal and permanent truths which will never change. Conditions change, customs change as they must, dress changes; but the eternal principles upon which Hinduism is based remain valid for ever. Secondly, Hinduism has produced a series of remarkable men and women down through the ages who, by dint of their renunciation and power of wisdom, have reilluminated the flame whenever it was in danger of being extinguished. Let us not forget that for any religion to be valid in the nuclear age it must have both these aspects; it must have the eternal truths and it must also have the capacity for creative reinterpretation and regeneration.

We cannot go back to some mythical past, however great it might have been. But at the same time we cannot go forwards into the twenty-first century with a moral and spiritual vacuum in our hearts. The most dangerous of all the black holes that exist in the cosmos is that vacuum within the heart of twentieth-century man. If this continues, man himself will not survive into the twenty-first century. Mankind today is at crucial crossroads of destiny. After millions of years of evolution man has reached the point where science and technology have given him tremendous power which, if used with wisdom and compassion, can eradicate poverty, illiteracy, disease and ignorance from the face of this earth by the end of this century. And yet the same power can be misused. We saw what happened in Hitler's gas chambers; that was also an application of technology. Remember that the demoniac forces are there deeply embedded in the human psyche, and today, with the possibility of nuclear destruction staring us all in the face, we find ourselves precariously poised between a past that is collapsing and a future that refuses to be born. We find ourselves in a position of extreme danger.

You have no doubt seen the film *The Day After*. My criticism of it is that it is a gross understatement. What, in fact, will happen is going to be very much worse than that. Jonathan Schell in his book *The Fate of the Earth* describes what may happen more accurately than does the film. This brings to my mind two ancient myths, one of the Western world and the other in our own tradition. There is a myth of Atlantis—you came across it first in the writings of Plato—that great and glorious civilization, glittering with all the achievements of science and technology, that flourished where the Atlantic Ocean now holds its sway. It was a fabulously rich and wealthy civilization, but one day we are told that Atlantis sank below the waves, unable to survive its own technological ingenuity. It seems to me that we may be the neo-Atlantis, standing on the verge of another major catastrophe.

And then there is from the Hindu tradition the myth of the *Samudra-Manthana* (the Churning of the Milky Ocean). It seems to me that science and technology have similarly caused this great churning of human consciousness. We have remarkable gifts; we can fly beyond the moon to the planets, beyond the plantes to the stars. There are marvellous miracles of technology; as I speak here I can be seen at the other end of the earth. There are fabulous gifts in medicine and in many fields of science. But at the same time the poison is there and it is beginning to emerge, and the question that everybody has to face is what our attitude towards this should be. In the final analysis, the power of the atom and the power of the Ātman are pitted against each other. If in the heart of the atom such tremendous destructive power can be found, cannot we find in the heart of the Ātman an equally great and beneficent power which would help us to meet this tremendous challenge?

What is the Hindu response to the human crisis in the nuclear age? We must confront the crisis. There can be no running away, there can be no retreat into individual salvation. If we call ourselves Hindu, we must boldly face the challenges that confront us. 'Therefore arise, O Arjuna, determined to battle for *dharma*', as Śri Kṛṣṇa says in the *Gītā*. I would say that our response lies in a restatement of five fundamental concepts that are embedded in the Hindu tradition, the eternal principles of Vedānta, and these flow logically from each other.

The first great concept is the fact that this entire cosmos, whether it is this tiny planet or the billions upon billions of galaxies which are in the universe, are all pervaded by the same divine power. There is no ultimate duality in human existence or in consciousness. This is a truth which in the West is only recently being understood after Einstein and Heisenberg and quantum mechanics. The Newtonian-Cartesian-Marxist paradigm of a materialistic universe has now been finally abolished, it has collapsed in the face of the new physics. We must remember that our ancient seers had a deeper insight into the nature of reality than people had even until very recently. Even today the new physics and the new science has not fully grasped what the ancients knew. That is the first principle embedded in the Vedānta.

The second is that this divine which permeates the entire universe is found in the heart of every human being regardless of race or culture, religion or nationality. Every single human being, every person who is born with human consciousness, partakes of this great divine potential. This is the second great principle of the Vedānta. Flowing from that is the principle that, if the divine is in each one of us, then we are all members of a single family, and, for those of the greater consciousness, the world is a family. Is it not remarkable that thousands of years ago, when man could not travel more than ten or fifteen miles a day, our seers should have realized the essential unity of the entire human race?

And then, flowing logically therefrom, is the concept of the unity of all religious faiths. The truth is one, the wise may call it by many names. Our Śāstras teach us to respect all religions; all we expect in return is equal respect from the followers of other religions. One thing has to be made clear, and that is that Hinduism is no longer prepared to be on the receiving end of aggressive proselytization. There is no longer going to be a one-way traffic. We owe no ill-will to any religion. I personally come from a Muslim majority state in India. I have worshipped at the great shrines of all the religions of the world, whether it is the Darbar Sahib, Saint Peter's Cathedral or the Mohammad Ali Mosque. But one thing is clear; we revere other religions and we expect equal reverence and respect from them. The day has gone when Hinduism was like some helpless whale being constantly bitten into by aggressive sharks.

The fifth concept is the welfare of the many, the happiness of the many. Hinduism does not throw one class against another class as some of the materialistic philosophies do. Hinduism seeks to look after the welfare of the entire humanity, particularly the weak, the neglected, the exploited. And the first responsibility that Hinduism has is to look after the welfare of the weaker sections within Hindu society itself, particularly the Harijans and the Adivasis. If we talk about looking after the welfare of the world, and are not able to safeguard the welfare of members of our own community and religion, our word will not carry conviction.

These five principles provide a basic philosophical framework which even today can knit the people of the world together, and can save mankind from great disaster. Always remember that Hinduism has never been content simply with serving Hindus, it has always sought to serve humanity. Swami Vivekananda, Sri Aurobindo, Mahatma Gandhi—they all had a message for mankind, not just for Hindus. And today what we need is the vitality of a Vivekananda, the profundity of an Aurobindo and the humanity of a Gandhi combined together to create the higher consciousness for Hinduism.

Before we can save the world, however, we have got to set our own house in order. Many organizations in India and abroad are now trying to do this; and in 1981 I also founded an organization called the Virat Hindu Samaj for this very purpose, so that we can get together people of different denominations within Hinduism. When we talk of the new Hinduism, it is no denominational thing. We have on our stage Jain *munis* and people belonging to other sects and communities all of which have flowed from the great matrix of Hinduism. Ours is a philosophy which is broad enough and bold enough to embrace a wide spectrum of views and ideas. We have two immediate tasks before us. One is eradicating the last vestiges of undesirable social customs that have developed due to centuries of servitude and have overlaid our glorious philosophical heritage. In particular, untouchability is the antithesis of Vedānta, and as long as a single drop of this poison remains in Hinduism all our talk of saving humanity or of raising the level of consciousness is totally meaningless.

Similarly, we have got to work against other undesirable customs. Dowry is now beginning to raise its head higher. I do not know whether it has hit the Hindus of America or not, but from the way people in the audience are laughing I can guess that it has extended its ugly tentacles here also. What a disgrace it is! We look upon women as the embodiment of the mother, look upon them as the Śakti; and yet when it comes to marriage we enter into these sort of commercial transactions. It is a shame and a disgrace, and I would like to say to all of you here that, while you may have become very rich and your boys may command better dowry now that you are living in America, as true Hindus you should under no circumstances demand a dowry. Everybody loves their daughters and they give what they can; but any person who demands dowry as part of the marriage contract, or who mistreats a bride because she has not brought adequate dowry, is a shame and a blot on the face of Hinduism.

On the one hand is the task of getting rid of these undesirable social customs, and on the other is getting together on one common platform the broad spectrum of Hindu organizations and sects. I do not accept the theory that the multiplicity of sects in Hinduism is a cause of weakness. On the contrary, I think that this is the reason that we have been able to survive. Our very diversity, the fact that we appreciate different paths to the divine, different *gurus*, different *mantras*, is a source of strength. And yet there must be a common platform. All the different instruments, as it were, must be brought together in a vast philharmonic orchestra and they must play in harmony. Let us all, all the sects of Hinduism, be one great orchestra playing in harmony; then and then alone will we be able to pull our weight. As Swami Chinmayanandaji said: 'Whether it is in America or in India, it is only if the Hindus are united that they will be able to get a fair deal and to see that their interests are properly safeguarded.' This is where the overseas Hindus can blaze a new trail, whether they are living in North America, in the Caribbean or anywhere else in the world.

I am very happy to see this great conference beautifully organized, and I bring warm fraternal greetings on behalf of the six hundred million Hindus of India. I would like to make a few suggestions for your consideration. The first would be to strengthen organizational links between various Hindu groups functioning in North America. I know a large number are present here, but I also know a large number are unrepresented, and I would like to see a more comprehensive representation. It would be useful if an information office is set up where all the Hindu sects and societies on the American continent—be it Canada or the United States, the Caribbean or South America—are listed. There should also be a directory and a journal and meetings from time to time, so that you can consolidate your thought and your actions.

Secondly, many new temples are being constructed here. This is a matter of great pride. I come from a family of temple builders, and have built some temples myself. Our temple traditionally has four doors, and it is my conception that these should symbolize the four *yogas* of Hinduism. *Bhakti*: there must be proper devotion, prayers, festivals, *bhajanas, kīrtanas* and *satsaṅga*, these represent one aspect, the emotional aspect of the human psyche. *Jñāna*: there must be classes on the Upaniṣads and the *Bhagavad-Gītā*, not only for children but also for adults; there must be the teaching of Sanskrit, the *devavāṇī*, the great language that is the repository of Hindu texts and Hindu wisdom; that also must form a part of every temple, that is the second gate. Then *karma*, social work, looking after the weak in your own community and in your own society, organizing social functions, weddings and so on, serving the community; that is the third aspect. And, finally, *rāja*; *prāṇāyāma* spiritual practices must be taught. In my conception, our temples should not only be a focus of devotion, they must combine devotion, wisdom, service and *prāṇāyāma*, then only will they be able to play their rightful role in the community. I would urge upon those of you who are involved in these temples to keep this concept in mind when you plan your activities.

Thirdly, in the educational sphere there is a great problem. Even in India, where eighty-two per cent are Hindus, there is a deplorable erosion of moral and spiritual values. And here, when young children are growing up in an alien environment, there is no way in which they can make contact with their cultural heritage. The Bharatiya Vidya Bhavan, I understand, is opening a school in the United States. I would like to see more Hindu missions open schools, and not only for the Hindus. After all, the convents in India are patronized largely by non-Christians; I went to a convent school myself. Your schools should be of such a standard that you are able to attract American children also. But you must go in for education, and you must also go in for a programme of audio-visual aids. What is required is a series of video films, professionally produced, dealing with Hindu pilgrimages, Hindu festivals, Hindu rituals, Hindu saints, Hindu philosophy and so on. These should be of the highest technical standard and must be professionally marketed, so that Hindus living abroad and their children can imbibe some of these values. If Indians can market jeans successfully, I see no reason why you cannot market video films. I am prepared on behalf of the Virat Hindu Samaj to help you with the preparation of these films in India.

Apart from serving Hindus in North America or wherever, we must also be able to present the universal teachings of Hinduism to the wider public. There is tremendous interest now growing in Eastern regions. With the collapse of the materialistic philosophies of the West, people are turning more and more to Hinduism for the answers of life. Here I would quote what Sri Aurobindo said in his message on 15 August 1947:

> The spiritual gift of India to the world has already begun. India's spirituality is entering Europe and America in an ever increasing measure. That movement will grow amidst the disasters of the time, more and more eyes are turning towards her with hope, and there is even an increasing resort not only to her teachings, but to her psychic and spiritual practice.

This was 15 August 1947, our Independence Day and Sri Aurobindo's own birthday. And to the extent that we can fulfil that hope, we will be fulfilling our personal and collective destiny. With the dawn of the nuclear age we have entered qualitatively a new situation and Hinduism has to spearhead this great new consciousness that is required, because Hinduism alone, of the religions of the world, has this capacity to synthesize science and spirituality.

I would like particularly to appeal to the younger generation here. The youth today has a challenge and an opportunity. You have the idealism, you have the strength, the resilience. Above all, you must reiterate in your own life the glowing ideals enshrined in Hinduism. Living outside India you must retain your Hindu identity and yet must become citizens of the world. You must discover within yourself the core of spiritual power with which you can show a new light to humanity.

Friends, Planet Earth, embattled, endangered, polluted, is yet the mother that has nurtured and nourished our race for millions of years from the slime of the primeval ocean up to the *ṛṣis* and the saints. The most remarkable photograph ever taken is the photograph of earth taken from the moon. It shows us as we really are, a tiny speck of life and light against the unending vastnesses of outer space. Will we convert this beautiful jewel into a burnt-out cinder, or will we cherish it as the cradle of the higher consciousness? We are a minor planet of middling star of an average galaxy, and yet it is here that human consciousness has arisen. And Hindu thought believes that the light of the Ātman, the light of the divine, is working through every human being and is shining in glory beyond the world of men. As our *Ṛṣis* say: 'I know that great being shining like the sun on the other shore beyond the darkness. It is only by knowing it that we can pass beyond death, there is no other way to immortality.'

We must strive towards that light. Its symbol is the sun, and that is why our great prayer—the *gāyatrī mantra*—is dedicated to the sun. We must soar towards the sun like an eagle, so that we can find our individual destiny and our collective destiny. Let this great conference mark a new thrust towards that light, not only for Hindus but for the entire human race. And let the keynote of this great conference be that prayer that has echoed and re-echoed since ancient times the eternal prayer on the lips of every Hindu:

> From the unreal lead me to the real,
> From the darkness, lead me to the light,
> From death, lead me to immortality!

7

Yoga: An Integrated Philosophy of Life

Yoga represents a central and pivotal concept in Indian culture, and some understanding of this is essential for those who wish to grasp the deeper significance behind Hinduism. The relationship between the Brahman and the Ātman, between the all-pervasive divinity and its reflection within individual consciousness, is the main concept behind Vedāntic philosophy. Spiritual realization involves in some way a joining of the Ātman and the Brahman in its broadest sense. *Yoga* represents both the process as well as the goal of this union. It brings experiential and holistic dimensions into religious quest, without which the whole exercise remains one of intellectual disputation without any real spiritual progress.

Theoretically, there can be an infinite number of different ways to approach the divine; indeed, as many paths as there are individuals. However, in the Hindu tradition, these approaches can largely be said to fall into four major categories—*Jñāna-yoga, Bhakti-yoga, Karma-yoga* and *Rāja-yoga*. While the path is essentially an integrated one, each of these *yogas* lays special emphasis upon different human faculties.

Let us start with *Jñāna-yoga*, the *yoga* of wisdom or intellectual discrimination. This is a path particularly suited for those whose intellects are highly developed. The discipline consists in developing the ability to discriminate between the real and the unreal, the ephemeral and the eternal, until finally spiritual realization is achieved. The classical texts of the *Jñāna-yoga* are the Upaniṣads, which are based on the collective realization of a whole galaxy of realized seers or *ṛṣis* over at least a thousand years. They present in memorable language the great Vedāntic truths which stand behind the tradition of *Jñāna-yoga*.

While the Upaniṣads have been the spiritual source for all the schools of Indian philosophy, it is Ādi Śaṅkara, the great eighth-century reformer and exponent of monism, with whom the *Jñāna-mārga* is specially associated. He interpreted Vedānta, as leading to *Brahma-jñāna* or knowledge of the Absolute. It is to his glowing commentaries on the Upaniṣads, the *Brahma-Sūtras* and the *Bhagavad-Gītā* that we owe a great deal of our understanding of this path. The *Jñāna-yoga* can perhaps be compared to the wisdom of Solomon, or to the great Socratic dialogues so beautifully recorded by Plato. In this path, it is the intellect that has to be increasingly illuminated by the divine truth, so that ultimately it is transcended when spiritual realization is achieved.

While *Jñāna-yoga* deals essentially with the intellect, *Bhakti-yoga* is based upon a spiritualizing of the other great human faculty, that of the emotions. The mind and the heart are two predominant aspects of the human personality, and if the *Jñāna-yoga* revolves around a progressive spiritualizing of the mind, the *Bhakti-yoga* does the same for the emotions. The concept that the emotions are necessarily a hindrance to the spiritual path is not justified. They certainly can be, if they are misdirected or indisciplined; but when directed towards the divine they can be a potent source of spiritual realization.

Bhakti-yoga involves the turning of the emotions towards the divine envisaged in a human form, whether it is Śiva or Viṣṇu, Rāma or Kṛṣṇa, the goddess or Subrahmaṇya or any other. It involves the passionate outpouring of the emotions, culminating in a spiritual rapture of union with the chosen divine form, and is, therefore, characteristic of theism, with its emphasis on personal divinity, surrender and grace. The history of all religions is replete with instances of such devotion. Śrī Caitanya who was born 500 years ago, re-established the great cult of Krsna worship throughout the country, while Sri Ramakrishna worshipped the Goddess Kālī as the divine mother. South India has producced a whole series of saints devoted to Śiva and Viṣṇu. In the Christian tradition, we have saints like St. Theresa of Avila, St. John of the Cross, St. Francis of Assisi and many others. In Hinduism, there are numerous texts on the *Bhakti-yoga*, predominant of which is the *Śrimad-Bhāgavatam* which deals with the incarnation of Viṣṇu, specially as Śrī Kṛṣṇa, the *Śiva Purāṇa* and the Śaiva texts of South India. The great mystic poetry of medieval India represents the anguish and ecstasy of the *bhakta* in a most lyrical and profound way.

Karma-yoga is the way of right action. In the *Bhagvad-Gītā*, one of the greatest religious texts of the world, the theory of *karma* is expounded to encompass all actions done as an offering to the divine. *Yogaḥ karmasu kauśalam* (*Yoga* is skill in actions), says Śrī Kṛṣṇa to Arjuna on the battlefield of life, and adds: 'Thou hast the right only to the deeds, not to the fruit thereof.'

The theory of *Karma-yoga* is complex and subtle. We all *have* to work, not only for our sheer material existence but also for our intellectual and emotional welfare. But if all action is bondage, as some philosophers seem to claim, then it would appear that we are all doomed to eternal suffering on the constantly revolving wheel of *saṁsāra*. However, Śrī Kṛṣṇa points out that it is not the action itself which is the cause of bondage, but rather the psychological attitude behind that action. Therefore, if action is done as an offering to the divine, if it is performed with devotion and dedication, but without an obsessive attachment to its consequences, then that action itself becomes a potent instrument for spiritual development. Indeed, Śrī Kṛṣṇa expressly points out in the *Gītā* that many persons, including the great King Janaka, achieved realization through *Karma-yoga*. Perhaps Kant's ethical standpoint in the West may, to some degree, correspond with this view of action.

The *Bhagavad-Gītā* is considered to be the prime text for *Karma-yoga*, although it deals with all the four *yogas*, and, as Sri Aurobindo points out in his glowing *Essays on the Gita*, presents before us an integrated philosophy of life. In the Western tradition, it can be said that the Christian denominations which have specially taken upon themselves the work of spreading education and medical services throughout the world are in the tradition of the *Karma-yoga*. Several Christian and other groups exist today, who dedicate their lives to service and the alleviation of suffering, both physical and psychic. In our own generation, Mother Teresa is an unparalleled example of this Christian commitment to service of suffering humanity as a dedication to the divine.

We come now to the fourth path which is known as *Rāja-yoga*, the royal path. Whether this term is used because the path is considered to be particularly effective, or because it was, in fact, preferred by the ruling classes in ancient India, is a debatable point. It is true, however, that this is in some ways the most potent and dramatic way of achieving union between the human and the divine. It revolves around techniques to modify our normal waking consciousness and thereby bring about a dramatic encounter with the unlimited power of the divine. It is here that Patañjali's *Yoga-Sūtras* have such an important role to play.

Because the yogic *āsanas* involve manipulation of the body, an erroneous impression seems to be prevalent that *yoga* is simply some kind of complicated physical exercises. This is a very restricted view of *yoga*. While certainly *yoga-āsanas* can have a dramatic impact upon our bodily condition and can significantly improve our general health, it would be wrong to limit their effects only to the body. It will be recalled that Patañjali's eight steps start with *yamas* and *niyamas*, which involve certain psychological restraints and disciplines, and bring in *āsanas, prāṇāyāma* and *pratyāhāra* only as the third, fourth and fifth steps. The remaining three steps again are essentially psychological. We must always remember, therefore, that *yoga* is very much more than simply the capacity to perform difficult physical postures. Indeed, the interior or *antaraṅga-yoga* is the more significant achievement when compared to the outer, the *bahiraṅga* aspects.

Another point needs to be made, and that relates to the whole question of the *kuṇḍalinī* and its awakening. The *yoga* tradition postulates the existence of a divine power—the *kuṇḍalinī*—located at the base of the spine and often called the serpent power, because it is coiled like a snake three and a half times when at rest. Under certain conditions, and by various practices including *āsanas* and *prāṇāyāma*—regulation of the breathing process—it is possible to stimulate this *kuṇḍalinī* into movement. When it uncoils and starts rising, it progressively penetrates seven *cakras* or centres along the spinal system until it finally bursts in ecstasy into the thousand-petalled lotus in the cerebral cortex and the *yogī* is flooded with the *brahma-saṁsparsa*, the contact with the Brahman.

A whole science, known as the Tantra, has developed around the *kuṇḍalinī-yoga*. After Patañjali's seminal work there have been many other texts in the Hindu and Buddhist traditions, as well as commentaries upon them. A century ago, a remarkable Englishman, Sir John Woodroffe, wrote a series of pioneering books on various Tāntrik texts under the pseudonym of Arthur Avalon, and in our own times Pandit Gopi Krishna, whom I last met in Switzerland in 1979, has written a memorable series of books on this astounding phenomenon. This is an aspect that must be kept in mind by all serious practitioners of *yoga*, so that if the *kuṇḍalinī* starts moving they are prepared to absorb the experience in a positive and creative manner. This is a matter with which the *guru* has to deal, because of its tremendous potential both for progress and, if mishandled, for disaster.

While on this question of *Rāja-yoga* and changed states of consciousness, it needs to be pointed out that, with all its aberrations, the drug phenomenon, specially LSD, has opened the minds of many in the West who previously had decisively dismissed the whole *kuṇḍalinī* phenomenon as either a fraud or a self-imposed hallucination. The work of Stanislav Grof on LSD therapy, and the amazing series of books by Carlos Castaneda, are only two of the numerous indications that the conceptual revolution, begun by Aldous Huxley in his small but seminal book *The Doors of Perception* (1954), has, in fact, gathered tremendous momentum and shows no signs of declining. The gross misuse and exploitation of drugs, which have become an international menace, has most unfortunately distorted the possibility of their creative use by serious spiritual teachers as a trigger to break into higher states of consciousness. Of course, this issue is still very controversial—and the discipline required to achieve psychic wholeness wihout the use of external stimuli is still far more desirbale. C. G. Jung, with his tremendous insights in this field, has contributed enormously to knowledge of the self in the modern context.

I have broadly described the four major paths to the divine—the path of wisdom, the path of devotion, the path of dedicated action and the path of psychic discipline. It remains for me to point out that these four can, in fact, be combined into an integrated philosophy of life. Humankind today is living in a unique situation. Science and technology are transforming human civilization before our very eyes, and in our own lifetimes we have witnessed incredible breakthroughs in numerous fields. Man has broken away from the confines of earth, reached the moon and begun his exploration into the planets and even the stars far beyond. Agriculture and industry, medicine and communications, all have benefited tremendously from the efflorescence of human creativity expressed through science and technology. And yet the destructive potential of humankind also grows apace, with tens of thousands of nuclear warheads of such potency that even a fraction of them can destroy not only the human race but probably all life on this planet. This is the dilemma of man in the nuclear age.

At such a juncture we can no longer be content with following a single path; what is needed is an integrated, multifaceted endeavour. We need the mind to be illuminated by *jñāna* (wisdom); the heart to be flooded by *bhakti* (devotion); the will to be disciplined by *karma* (action); and the psyche to be spiritualized by *rāja* (practice). It is only if we are able to develop all these four elements of our personality that we will achieve the capacity to function as integrated and harmonious human beings, capable of building a new, global civilization on planet earth. And, surely, we can today accept no lesser goal than to be pioneers of the global consciousness that is painfully struggling to be born on our beautiful planet, on Mother Earth that has nurtured the human race up from the slime of the primeval ocean to where we stand today, poised on the threshold of a new leap forward.

The path ahead is difficult and dangerous, but that is inevitable in any great undertaking; and, as long as we have courage and faith, we need fear no evil. The goal of individual salvation and collective transformation may be far away, and may need many generations to achieve. But we must press on undeterred, summoning all our material, moral, intellectual and spiritual resources to this most important of all undertakings. Let us recall that immortal verse from the *Kaṭha Upaniṣad* which exhorts us to arise, awake and move onwards across the sharp and difficult razor-edged path laid out by the great spiritual beings of past ages:

Uttiṣṭhata jāgrata prāpya varān nibodhata,
Kṣurasya dhārā niśitā duratyayā
Durgaṁ pathas tat kavayo vadanti.

8

Moral and Spiritual Values in New India

The erosion of values in our country now is something that has been virtually accepted, and I say this with a sense of sorrow; because wherever one goes, not only is corruption virtually accepted as a way of life, it has virtually become a philosophy of life. It is rampant in all spheres of activity, not just in politics. May be in politics it is a little worse than most, for obvious reasons. But in all spheres of activity there has been this widespread erosion of moral and spiritual values. To some extent this is true the world over, but it is specially tragic for a country like India, which has from the beginning of its civilization sought to base itself upon certain spiritual and moral values.

I do not claim that India has always lived up to these values. I do not claim that Indians are necessarily more moral than any other poeple. But I do claim that the conceptual and ideological foundations of Indian culture have been on the basis of certain moral and spiritual principles. I think this is undeniable, and this, in fact, is the reason why, despite tremendous upheavals and long centuries of foreign aggression and subjugation, India has retained some vitality and dynamism. If it had not been based upon certain fundamental principles, I do not think that Indian civilization could have withstood the sort of repression which it had had to undergo.

Our freedom movement also sought to base itself upon certain ideals. Whether it was the beginning of the Hindu renaissance with reformers such as Raja Rammohun Roy with the Brahmo Samaj and Devendra Nath Tagore with the Adi Brahmo Samaj, or R. K. Bhandarkar and M. G. Ranade in Maharashtra with the

Prarthana Samaj, or Swami Dayanand Saraswati with the Arya Samaj, or whether it were great men in the mainstream of the Hindu tradition like Sri Ramakrishna and Swami Vivekananda, Sri Aurobindo and Lokmanya Tilak who enthused the Indian national movement, in each of these cases you will find a clear attempt to re-establish and recreate the spiritual foundation of India. And then when Gandhiji came on the scene. His whole life is clear evidence of his attempt to re-establish *dharma* in India, *dharma* in the broadest sense of term, not excluding anybody, in fact including everybody.

Gandhiji was very clear about this in his mind, and said that people who say that there is no relationship between politics and religion understand neither. And his whole life—his talks, his prayer meetings, his entire thrust—was based upon certain values. Apart from the freedom movement, the major and the outstanding contribution of Gandhiji was in the sphere of Harijans, that terrible karmic burden that Hindu Society has been carrying for so many centuries. When we became free, we adopted as our national motto these words from the *Muṇḍaka Upaniṣad: Satyam eva jayate* (Truth alone triumphs).

That a country based upon this should today be sinking in a morass of corruption is a tragedy too deep for tears, not only for India but for humanity, because India has always claimed to have a message for humanity. I was in south-east Asia recently. If you go to Java or to Bali, or to Bangkok or Cambodia, you will see there the influence of Indian culture. The story of Śrī Rāma is probably better known in Indonesia, which is eighty-five per cent Muslim, than even in parts of India. And we carried the message not through conquest, not through atomic bombs, not through force of arms, but through moral and spiritual power. Therefore, the claim that India has some message for the world is not simply a chauvinistic claim, it is based upon our achievements over the last three thousand years and more.

Today mankind needs this message more than ever before. Sri Aurobindo wrote that India is rising, not only so that it itself should be free but so that it can bring the message of spiritual realization and spiritual power to the whole of humanity. Today there is this tremendous crisis of technology and science of divergence between knowledge and wisdom. Science is one of the great achievements of the human race, perhaps unparalleled in human history. And yet that very science has given us the means of destruction, not only of the human race but perhaps of all life on this planet.

How are we going to bridge the gap between science and philosophy? I think it can now be done, because in post-Einstenian science, with the development of quantum mechanics and extra-galactic physics, the old rigidities of Newtonian science have collapsed and many of the approaches inherent in the mystical tradition are again becoming relevant. Science and religion started together; whether it was with *Āyur-Veda* in India or with Alchemy in the West. Then there was this tremendous divergence. Now, I think, we have come full circle, and the salvation of the human race lies in the possibility of a convergence of science and philosophy. And India is the only country that can bring this about, because we alone, of all the nations of the world, have a philosophical background as well as a scientific temper and also the third largest pool of scientists in the world. There is a fledgling 'new consciousness' movement throughout the world now, with which I am in touch, where great scientists and philosophers are trying to get together.

So the point I am making is that the tragedy of our erosion of values is much larger than simply an Indian tragedy. It is a tragedy for humanity, because if India does not do it nobody else can do it. But how can India bring any light to the world, if it is itself sinking in a morass of corruption? Therefore, the re-establishment of moral and spiritual values in India is now not only an imperative for India but for the human race. There have been some welcome indications recently that the silent majority in India is beginning to assert itself, that the widespread revulsion against corruption is beginning to come to the surface, that people are no longer prepared to tolerate this nonsense that is going on in the name of politics. But that is a political process which will take some time to come to maturity. Meanwhile, the question is: what can we in the Virat Hindu Samaj do?

The whole philosophy of the Virat Hindu Samaj revolves around what may be called the neo-Vedānta, the reinterpretation of Vedāntic principles for the twentieth and the twenty-first century. There is a sharp divergence between the sort of fundamentalism that is going on in Iran and the sort of movement that we are trying to develop here. Ours is not a revivalist movement, it is a renaissance. There is a very important difference between these two words. A revivalist movement would be, for example, if one were to demand scrapping of the Indian Constitution and going back to the *Manu-Smṛti* where different castes have different types of punishment. But if we are interpreting the great concepts and principles of Vedānta for the twenty-first century, how can that be called a revivalist movement? Swami Vivekananda did the same thing at the end of the nineteenth century when he reinterpreted religion for the need of that time. Almost hundred years have elapsed since then and, I think, the time has come when there must be a fresh reinterpretation on the basis of our spiritual and intellectual structure which lies in the *Bhagavad-Gītā* and the Upaniṣads.

The Virat Hindu Samaj is functioning on two levels. On one level, we are trying to create public opinion with regard to the importance of social reform within Hinduism, and of solidarity and of a reassertion of our spiritual principles. For that purpose, we had a series of *sammelanas*, beginning with the historic Virat Hindu Sammelana in Delhi in October 1981 which was attended by a million people. But apart from the mass *sammelanas*, what we need is something substantial in the educational system. Unfortunately, as a result of a wrong interpretation of secularism, our education today has become totally devoid of values. Is it not a tragedy that in the land of the Vedānta the study of Upaniṣads and the *Bhagavad-Gītā* have been virtually banned in our schools? I do not understand what sort of secularism this is in which we deprive millions of children in India of their right to be acquainted with their own cultural heritage. We have, in effect, thrown the baby out along with the bath water. Perhaps it was the result of an over-reaction to partition. The country was partitioned in the name of religion, and the leaders at that time were so shocked by the development that they over-reacted. Whatever may be the reason, today, four decades after independence, the time has come when we must sit down and think about this problem.

What sort of cultural and spiritual ideals are we giving to our younger generation? The joint family is breaking up because of socio-economic causes. So the major value-inculcating instrument is no longer in operation. The other major instrument is the school, where, because of our wrong interpretation of secularism, we are not allowed to teach any values. The third is example. The sort of example that our leaders are giving, the less said the better. So the three ways in which the younger generation can be influenced have all collapsed. Where, then, is the value orientation going to come from? Is this not a matter of the greatest concern for all Indian intellectuals, whether they are Hindus or Muslims, Sikhs or Buddhists?

I would like to stress a few points which need careful consideration. First, there is the problem of the educational curriculum. Can something be done to introduce textbooks which have some spiritual basis for the primary, secondary and higher classes, which reflect to some extent our spiritual and cultural heritage? How are the textbooks to be produced, and how do we get them prescribed? The second point is supplementary literature. Apart from textbooks, there must be an adequate flow of tastefully produced supplementary literature, so that the students feel like reading it. At present, the only religious education our children are getting is through comics, and they deserve all our thanks.

Finally, there is the possibility of setting up schools in India based upon our spiritual tradition. There are certain schools already functioning—Guru Shikha, Vidya Bharati, the Krishnamurti schools, Ramakrishna Mission and Chinmaya Mission schools, and so on. The Bharatiya Vidya Bhavan is setting up three international schools, one in Kodaikanal, one in London and one in the USA. These are the sort of institutions which could specifically be utilized as models for the development of this new education that we want. The Virat Hindu Samaj is a platform upon which we want to bring together various elements of Hindu society. That is what we did in our Virat Hindu Sammelans, that is what we now want to do in the educational field. We could set up a working group where people who have this experience can act and interact upon each other. We can also take advantage of the experience of Christian Missionaries, who have done a lot of educational work and have made a major contribution.

Jawaharlal Nehru used to often quote from *Alice in Wonderland*: 'We have to run as fast as we can to stay where we are.' Unfortunately, we are not staying where we are; we are going backwards in many spheres. And, therefore, let there be a sense of urgency, let there be a sense of commitment. I am sure that, if people apply their minds in this direction, something concrete can emerge which would conduce to the welfare not only of Hindu society but of the whole of India and even of mankind.

9

Religion Today

Every great world religon today is facing a major crisis, and this arises not from persecution by some other religion, nor even from the threat of communism which has itself developed many characteristics of a religion with its own scripture and rival high priests claiming infallibility. It arises, rather, from the impact on modern life of science and technology that is transforming the world before our very eyes. The old is collapsing, the new is struggling to be born, and we find ourselves poised precariously between the past and future.

In the West, religious values have largely ceased to exercise any sovereignty over the hearts of the younger generation, and yet the growth of material prosperity by itself has proved woefully inadequate to meet the deeper aspirations of the young. The alienation between generations, which is steadily growing with the growing speed of technological change, is making it increasingly difficult for any sort of accepted values to be passed on from one generation to the other. The poverty barrier in the affluent countries has been broken, but this does not seem to have brought about any substantial increase in human happiness. Millennia ago, the seers of the Upaniṣads said: *Na vittena tarpaṇīyo manuṣyo* (Wealth does not bring contentment to man), and today, when an increasing section of mankind is at last breaking out of the poverty that has encased it for centuries, the validity of this view is being established.

In a country like ours there are still millions who live below the poverty line, for whom the basic necessities of civilized life are lacking, and we must bend every effort to see that by the end of this century every Indian is assured of at least a minimum standard of living. And yet the problem of religious values in a developing society remains, and cannot be postponed until our economic breakthrough occurs. In fact, the problem is potentially more acute in a largely traditional society like ours, which will increasingly feel the traumatic impact of science and technology over the next decade. It is, therefore, necessary that we clarify our approach to this crucial problem, especially when the voices which are loudest today either advocate a wholesale jettisoning of religion or propound views whose blatant obscurantism is matched only by their pathetic anachronism.

Ever since Vedic times, the religion that is now popularly known as Hinduism has played a decisive role in the destiny of this nation. This is not in any way to depreciate the role of the other great world religions that continue to flourish in this country, but to stress the fact that it is Hinduism that has predominantly moulded the contours of our national consciousness through the ages, that has, indeed, been largely responsible for the very subsistence of India as an entity, despite centuries of despotic rule and incredible political fragmentation. Today, after numerous alternations of shadows and sunlight, of triumph and tragedy, of hope and despair, India has at last emerged as a sovereign independent republic containing within its boundaries one-seventh of the entire human race. Our constitution lays down that India is to be a secular nation in the sense that the state is not to be partial towards any religion, and every citizen is to enjoy complete equality in the eyes of the law, and this despite the trauma of partition and recurring tension.

Secularism, however, cannot and does not mean that the people of India should forget their religious heritage. And as the vast majority of Indians are Hindus, the restatement of Hinduism in the context of the nuclear age assumes tremendous importance. A great strength of Hinduism has been that, based as it ultimately is upon direct spiritual realization rather than scripture and dogma, and lacking as it does any rigid ecclesiastical structure, it has always been open to creative reinterpretation. From the time of the Vedas, thousands of years ago right down to the present century, there have been constant restatements of Hinduism which, basing themselves upon the fundamental verities of the Upaniṣads, have reinterpreted these principles to meet the requirements of the changing times. In our century, savants such as Swami Vivekananda and Ramana Maharshi, Sri Aurobindo and Mahatma Gandhi have given a new impetus to society by dynamic reinterpretations of the eternal truths underlying Hinduism.

Today the phenomenal progress of science and technology will no longer brook the continuance of outmoded superstitions and dogmas. And yet science itself has been forced to give up the arrogance that characterized it earlier when scientists proclaimed that they had finally found the solution to all the mysteries of life. Indeed, the deeper science probes into the heart of the matter and the farther it soars into the unending vastnesses of outer space, the more clearly does it recognize that it is still only on the threshold of understanding the cosmos in which we exist. And, at its greatest, science seems to converge towards an almost religious attitude before the infinite and unending mysteries of existence. Therefore, while on the surface it may appear that there is a sharp polarization between science and religion, a deeper view shows that there is for the first time a convergence between the two great approaches to life: by science into outer space and the structure of matter, and by religion into inner space and the nature of the human spirit.

In this broad context, there are some fundamental concepts that we must accept, if religion is not to become increasingly, peripheral to the vast majority of human beings but, on the contrary, develop into a dynamic force for a new integration without which, in this age of thermonuclear weapons, the continued existence of the human race itself has become uncertain. The first is the concept of the unity of the human race. The Ṛg-Vedic concept of *vasudhaiva kuṭumbakam* (the world as a family) is now becoming a reality. With supersonic travel and the extraordinary growth of global telecommunications, the world, in fact, is shrinking before our eyes, and a concept which came to our *ṛṣis* in a flash of inspiration has now assumed tremendous relevance. The growing gap between man's destructive ability and his capacity for constructive co-operation poses a serious threat to our continued existence, and unless we can look upon mankind as a single family, cutting across divisions of race and nation, religion and belief, it will not be possible for man to survive much longer.

The second concept is the divinity of man. The Upaniṣads have a marvellous phrase for the human race, *amṛtasya putraḥ* (children of immortality). This means that every human being born into this world, regardless of where he lives or what beliefs he professes, enshrines a spark of the divinity that pervades and permeates the cosmos. In this view, man is not merely a fortuitous conglomeration of atoms, but embodies a divine principle which makes the enjoyment of human dignity his birthright. The divinity of God is now no longer a sufficient slogan. If God exists, He is by definition divine, and this divinity hardly needs reiteration. Today we must move on towards the concept of the divinity of man and, flowing therefrom, the inalienable dignity of the human individual.

Thirdly, we come to the essential unity of all religions, 'unity' rather than 'tolerance', because tolerance is a negative concept implying a somewhat grudging agreement to let religions other than one's own continue to exist. This is not enough; what is required is an active acceptance of the doctrine put forward in the Ṛg-Vedic dictum: *Ekaṁ sad viprāḥ bahudhā vadanti* (Truth is one, the wise call it by various names). An unequivocal acceptance of the fact that all religions are different paths leading to the same goal forms the true foundation for an enlightened secularism. Religions provide the broad framework and the psychological motivation within which can develop the eternal mystery of communion between man and the divine or, to put it differently, between our outer and our deeper reality. Viewed thus, religion can become a great unifying force in a world torn by suspicion and hatred, rather than a source of conflict which it is increasingly becoming.

Finally, there is the reconstruction of society. It is our duty to work for the betterment of society, *bahujana sukhāya bahujana hitāya ca* (for the happiness of the many and for the welfare of the many) as the Upaniṣad has it. We must realize that as long as millions in this country go without adequate food and clothing, shelter and education, our theoretical postulations regarding the divinity of man have little relevance as far as they are concerned. Swami Vivekananda used to say that it was a sin to preach religion to one who is hungry or naked, and today in free India it must be our active endeavour to alleviate the suffering of our countrymen and to build for them a new socio-economic order which would ensure that every Indian receives at least the basic requirements for a decent human existence. In this context, such absurd irrelevancies as untouchability must be swept aside once and for all. No longer can we afford to indulge in spurious intellectual gymnastics to justify a practice that for centuries has been a black mark upon the face of our nation, and constitutes the very antithesis of the deeper principles of Hindu thought.

These principles, based upon the deep spiritual experience of seers and mystics, not only in Hinduism but in other great world religions, are crucially relevant to the present predicament of man. It is my belief that only by a generous and unqualified acceptance of these can religion become truly significant in this nuclear age, and provide that firm bedrock of inner values upon which alone can an integrated and coherent superstructure of material welfare and intellectual emancipaton be raised. If religion remains bound within the shackles of narrow orthodoxy, it will become increasingly irrelevant to the coming generations; and mankind will be left with an inner void that no amount of material progress will be able to fill.

10

American Gurus

From the time Swami Vivekanada made his historic debut in Chicago almost a century ago, a whole host of Hindu *gurus* and teachers have visited the United States, and today their followers must run into hundreds of thousands. In the last twenty years, there has been a dramatic increase in Western receptivity to Hindu and Buddhist teachings, and this is specially marked in the State of California where I had occasion to spend some time recently. The extent of Hindu-Buddhist influence in the USA is now substantial enough to sustain a major study. Being non-proselytizing religions, their impact is not to be measured in terms of the number of people who have formally adopted them. Rather, it is the general influence of *yoga* and meditation that has become so widespread, and that constitutes one of the saving features in Western civilization which, despite its spectacular economic and material success, seems to be groping for a new inner certitude.

While this is generally well known, it is not often realized in India that many of the leaders of Hindu and Buddhist missonary work in the United States are of American or European origin. We still seem to hold the quaint notion that India has a monopoly on Hinduism, and tend to be somewhat condescending towards Western Hindus. As one travels, however, it becomes increasingly clear that Hinduism is now developing as a world religion; and, although India will always enjoy a special position as the birthplace of Hinduism and the home of the largest number of Hindus, she will have to remember that the Hindu teachings have now become very much the property of the world.

This was brought home strongly to me through two meetings that I had during a recent visit to the United States. The first was on Hawaii, that group of islands in the Pacific Ocean which are the American version of our Lakshadweep. The four main islands in the archipelago are Hawaii (the big Island), Ohai (where Honolulu is situated), Mavi and Kuai. It is on the island of Kuai that the American-born Swami Sivaya Subramaniya has built a beautiful Naṭarāja temple on a fifty-acre estate at a place called Kapaa.

I had read some of the excellent pamphlets that he has written on various aspects of Hinduism over the last few years, and also seen issues of the *āśrama* journal, *The New Shaivite World*. But what particularly attracted me was the Naṭarāja. This great figure, surely one of the supreme artistic achievements of the human race, has always fascinated me since I read Ananda Coomaraswami's *The Dance of Shiva* and visited the great temples of South India several decades ago. Being the first person, as far as I am aware, to have built a Naṭarāja temple in North India (at Jammu) I was interested to meet the man who built the first Naṭarāja temple outside India.

The flight from Honolulu to Kuai takes just over twenty minutes, and three of the Swami's monks were at the airport to meet me. They wore chocolate-brown, short-sleeved jackets (their 'working clothes', as they described them) which they don when they go outside the *āśrama*. They all seemed to be in their early thirties, were robust and alert, and had Hindu Śaiva names. The most impressive among them was Palani Swami who was my guide for that memorable day. There was also a young Tamil priest who had been in Kuai with the *āśrama* for a few months.

The Hawaiian islands can really be seen in all their beauty only from the air, and Sivaya Swamiji had thoughtfully arranged for me to fly from the airport to his *āśrama* in a helicopter. The view of the ocean, the sharp ravines and the stark canyons from the air were spectacular, and, after circumambulating the island and flying into its largest volcanic crater, our craft landed in the *āśrama* grounds. As I stepped out of the helicopter, I felt as if I were witnessing a scene from *Lost Horizon*. About a dozen ochre-clad monks were standing in the compound playing on South Indian drums and pipes, and in their midst was a bearded man with snow-white hair who emanated power and vitality.

Swami Sivaya Subramaniya greeted me warmly, and we walked further up to the temple a few yards away. At the entrance was a huge stone Nandī bull, the largest ever to leave India's shores, made by the master craftsmen of Mahabalipuram. The temple itself is a simple structure, beautifully finished and decorated, which was constructed in the early sixties. According to the South Indian tradition, the first *kumbhābhiṣekam* had recently been performed at a function attended by devotees from many parts of the world.

The image of Naṭarāja is extremely graceful, about a metre high and beautifully decorated. In front is a *Śiva-liṅgam* of black stone, while on the right and left are shrines with large images of Gaṇeśa and Subrahmaṇya. A special *pūjā* had been arranged for me and for an hour there was an *archanā* performed by the Swamis so perfectly that if I closed my eyes I could have been in any South Indian temple. The enunciation of the Sanskrit texts by the American monks could put many of our Paṇditas to shame.

Sitting in the hall after the *pūjā* with Swamiji, I learnt that he belonged to the Śaiva Siddhānta tradition of South India which produced the sixty-three Śaiva saints known as the Nayaṇārs. This is a tradition parallel to the better known Advaita Vedañta associated with the name of Ādi Śaṅkarācārya, and has links with the Siddha Nāth Sampradāya of North India. The Swami was very interested to learn about the present position of Kashmir Śaivism and was surprised when I told him that this particular tradition had virtually disappeared and that its last surviving *guru* Swami Lakshmanju, who lives in Gupt Gaṅgā near Srinagar, is over eighty.

If someone had told me that I would have a full, traditional South Indian meal served on leaves in a Hawaiian island, I would not have believed it possible. But that is exactly what I enjoyed that day at Kapaa, served with great devotion by the younger novices. The temple is built on a small hill, and about a hundred metres below is a stream-fed pool bubbling with energy and filling the afternoon with a rich sound. This was a sacred pool in the days when the Hawaiians worshipped their ancient gods, and the *āśrama* had, indeed, sought to identify some of those deities with the Śaiva pantheon.

Appropriately enough, the main source of income for the *āśrama* is honey. There are several hymns in the Vedas extolling the properties of honey (*madhu*), and bee-keeping has developed as a major avocation for the monks. Almost all the honey consumed on the island of Kuai comes from the *āśrama*, and some is exported. Another impressive feature is the press, managed entirely by the monks, which brings out the excellent quarterly journal as well as books and pamphlets on Hinduism. Swami Sivaya Subramaniya's *guru* was a Śaiva Ācārya from Sri Lanka, and the *āśrama* is specializing in bringing out meticulously edited books covering the Śaiva Āgamas that are not as widely known as the Vedañtic texts. An American-born Swami, with all his monks also non-Indian, interacting creatively with Indian-origin families living in the United States as well as in South Asia, is a perfect illustration of the fact that Hinduism is now a global and not only an India-based phenomenon.

A second example of this is found in Śri Dayā Mātā, the gracious lady who for thirty years had presided over the self-realization fellowship set up in the forties by Paramahansa Yogananda whose remarkable *Autobiography of a Yogi* is one of the most widely read of contemporary religious classics. I first met Dayā Mātā when she visited Srinagar in the sixties and called upon my mother. She is now over seventy, but exudes an aura of love and compassion which is almost palpable. Indeed, she could be described as a sort of American version of Anandamayee Ma, and it was a joy to see her at the Mount Washington headquarters of the SRF in Los Angeles. Later my wife and I spent a marvellous weekend at their retreat in Encinitas, commanding a spectacular view of the Pacific ocean.

The SRF has branches and centres in many countries of the world; and its Swamis and Brahmacāris are mainly American, though the followers include a large number of Indians. We have here again an interesting reversal of roles. On the one hand, there are Indian *gurus* with large Western followings who are well known, and, on the other, we now have American *gurus* with growing Indian followings. This is a healthy development, because it highlights the important fact that in the realm of spiritual endeavour the barriers of race and nationality are inconsequential. It so happens that my own *guru* was born an Englishman as was his.

As mankind now sweeps frantically towards the end of this century, it faces unprecedented challenges. The breathtaking advances in science and technology have literally turned the world into a global village over the last few decades. There is a tremendous explosion of vitality and energy, but there is also the dark side of the picture. Millions starve in Africa while farmers in the United States are paid vast sums of money *not* to grow foodgrains. Billions are spent every year in manufacturing increasingly destructive nuclear weapons, when there is already enough fissionable material on earth to destroy the entire human race and probably all life on this planet many times over. In such a situation, anything that builds bridges between peoples and cultures, cutting across barriers of race and language, ideology and nationality, is to be welcomed. This dialogue needs to be strengthened at various levels—within religions, between religions, between religious and non-religious societies, and between philosophers and scientists. The phenomenon of American *gurus* is a hopeful sign, and a shape in the direction of structuring a global culture which must emerge if man is to move into the next millennium.

11

Secularism: A New Approach

The classical concept of secularism which we adopted soon after freedom is now subject to immense pressure and seems to be rapidly disintegrating. There are three main reasons for this. Firstly, the Western concept of secularism originated in Europe several centuries ago when the question of separation of the church and the state had become a major concern and a subject of fierce political controversy. India has never had an organized church, so the European concept of secularism was not really relevant to our requirements. The term *sarva-dharma-sambhāva* which is sometimes used in place of secularism is, in fact, a far more meaningful formulation, and certainly much closer to the views of Mahatma Gandhi, who was deeply imbued with the Vedantic concept of the essential unity of all religions.

Secondly, our secularism was based upon the assumption, which has proved to be erroneous, that religion is a purely private affair with which the state is not concerned. This may be true as far as individual prayer and spiritual practice is concerned, but quite clearly the collective impact of religion upon society and the state is something which is far from personal. That millions of Indian citizens should flock regularly to the Kumbha Melās and numerous places of worship, whether Hindu, Muslim or any other, is itself an indication that the state has necessarily to take cognizance of religion as a social force. When we add the conflicts within and between religious groups which create serious law and order problems, it becomes quite clear that the myth of religion being a purely personal matter can no longer be sustained. Indeed, that view is often put forward by a section of our intelligentsia who, for all practical purposes, are not believers and who, therefore, tend to look upon all religions as being equally irrelevant hangovers from the past. It is obvious that such a view is shared only by a miniscule percentage of India's vast population.

The third assumption upon which classical secularism is based revolves around the belief that, as education increases and living standards improve, religion will steadily lose its hold over the minds of people and become increasingly peripheral in its impact upon the human psyche. This assumption, too, has been repeatedly disproved in our own lifetimes. Not only in India but in other developing countries it has become clear that there is little relation between economic progress and the decline of religion. On the contrary, there is evidence to show that with increasing affluence in hitherto poor nations the interest in religion shows a marked upsurge. One has only to travel in the more affluent parts of India to see the tremendous burgeoning of new temples and gurdwaras, mosques and churches, while a survey of rural India will show that a place of worship is one of the first demands of a new affluent area. The upsurge of Islam in the oil-rich countries of West Asia proves the case convincingly.

If these three points are accepted, it becomes quite clear that we have to move on to an entirely new concept of secularism if it is to have relevance in the years and decades to come. In the Indian context, secularism cannot mean an anti-religious attitude or even an attitude of indifference towards religion on the part of the state. What it should mean is that, while there is no state religion, all religions are given respect and freedom of activity, provided they do not impinge upon each other and provided again that foreign funds are not allowed to be channelled through ostensibly religious organizations for political purposes.

It is also essential that we overcome the religion-phobia in our educational system. At present we are getting the worst of both worlds. On the one hand, we refuse to take a positive attitude of presenting our rich, multireligious heritage to our students, thus depriving them of contact with much that is noble and great in our civilization. On the other, we leave religious education entirely in the hands of bodies which are seldom adequately equipped to undertake the task, and usually offer narrow and obscurantist interpretations of the living truths that permeate religious traditions. While the new education policy talks of 'value education', it is clear that without an understanding of our religious heritage it will be extremely difficult to develop a coherent and widely accepted value system.

The multireligious situation in India is a reality which will not go away. Instead of approaching the whole problem from a negative viewpoint, it would be far better to take the bull by the horns and convert what is sometimes looked upon as a major 'problem' into a positive asset for the new India that is struggling to be born. This can only be done, if our educational system gladly accepts the multiplicity of our religious tradition. I have before me an admirable textbook brought out in London last year entitled *Worlds of Difference*, which presents a variety of cultural traditions in a simple, positive and appreciative manner. Sponsored by the World Wildlife Fund and with a foreword by His Holiness the Dalai Lama, the book published by Blackie has separate chapters on the Chinese world, the humanist world, the Jewish world and the Muslim world. Attractively illustrated with photographs from the various religious traditions, it is accompanied by a guide which provides the teacher with an interpretative framework for the classroom. The book is meant for the age group 9–13, but much of it is useful for older children also.

I doubt if in our educational system, whether at the primary, secondary or higher levels, there is a single book which presents the rich diversity of the Indian cultural tradition in this manner. Even at the post-graduate level there is hardly any significant work being done in the field of religious studies and comparative religion, which is so popular an area in the West. Inter-religious dialogue is also virtually non-existent in our country. All this is a reflection of the fact that among our elite religion seems to have become unfashionable. This is a sad commentary upon our intellectual capabilities. India is by far the richest area for multireligious studies anywhere in the world, and should attract some of our best scholars. Hinduism itself, the religion of over four-fifths of Indians, is a vast treasure house of philosophy and mythology, sociology and worldly wisdom. Yet, in the last four decades, more work on Hinduism has been done by foreign scholars than by our own. Evidently *their* 'secularism' is not affected by working on one of mankind's oldest religious traditions.

If we are really serious in our efforts to build a strong and integrated India, it is incumbent upon us to ensure that the younger generation understands and appreciates not only its own religious traditions but also those of the other religions in the country. How many Muslims in India are able even remotely to appreciate the depth of feeling among the Hindus regarding the sanctity of Lord Rāma's birthplace? Conversely, how many Hindus understand the emotional trauma among Muslims when they see idols being worshipped in what they consider to be a mosque? I do not want to comment on this deeply divisive issue, which is still *sub judice*, except to say that in Kashmir we do have places of worship which are common both to the Hindus and the Muslims, where *ārati* and *namāz* are done at the same time. But my point is that the gulf of incomprehension between the Hindus and the Muslims on this issue is fraught with grave danger for the nation, and is a reflection of our failure over the last forty years to tackle the religious issues adequately.

No nation can continue to grow if its central concepts become fossilized and it loses the capacity for creative reinterpreation of its philosophical roots. The great secret of Indian civilization, which has survived so long lies precisely in its capacity for such periodic reformulations. It is no longer good enough for us to try and hide behind an outmoded concept of secularism. What is needed is a deeper understanding of the importance of religion in the life of our people, and the formulation of a new and dynamic interpretation of secularism which would ensure the creative co-existence of our many religions, all making a positive contribution to the rich and varied mosaic that is India.

12

Restructuring Education

India today is on the threshold of a major transition, the foundations of which have been laid by fundamental changes in our demographic structure and the cumulative effect of various economic and developmental policies pursued since Independence. These have begun to manifest themselves in the form of a new awareness and self-confidence among the younger generation. Unperceived by many who are unable to shake off the modes of thinking developed during the pre-Independence era, a remarkable change is becoming evident among the young men and women whom one encounters both in urban and rural areas. It is a joy to see the light in their eyes, often enough tinged with anger but always reflecting an irrepressible desire to do well, to build a better future for themselves and their country.

In a world rushing headlong into the twenty-first century we are now called upon to make a major effort to shed the shackles of corruption, superstition and obscurantism that have bound us for long, and to mobilize our inner and outer resources for a decisive leap into the future. The main instrument for this process will inevitably be the educational system and it is only appropriate that a youthful Prime Minister has laid great emphasis upon restructuring education. But in order to begin this tremendous task we will have to be quite clear as to what exactly it is that we wish to achieve. Simply tinkering with the whole system without any clear objectives will be a negative and self-defeating exercise.

The task lies in the universalization of primary education, vocationalization of secondary education and rationalization of university education, and in binding all three sectors and thus making a coherent and desirable value system. In view of the vast numbers involved and the limitation of resources, the undertaking will by no means be easy. But unless tackled with vigour and imagination we will be losing a unique opportunity to mould the future destiny of our nation.

First, the problem of resources. It is clear from the Seventh Plan document that health and education are still looked upon as 'soft' sectors, and are being given low financial priority. This is most unfortunate, because it is really these two sectors that represent a direct investment in the individual. We spend thousands of crores of rupees upon putting up buildings, bridges, hotels and other structures that are to be used by our citizens, but we are not prepared to spend even a quarter of that amount directly upon the health and consciousness of these citizens. As a result, we are getting into a situation where the gap between inner and outer development is rapidly widening. We will never be able to match the living standards of the West. On the other hand, we will lose our inner capacity and integrity unless we can give our educational system a new value orientation. For this a drastic reordering of plan priorities is necessary, so that the investment in man is at least commensurate, if not higher, with the investment in steel.

The universalization of primary education is a constitutional imperative upon which we have defaulted and which must be fulfilled at all costs. We simply cannot have a situation in which India goes into twenty-first century with millions of its citizens not able to read or write. The constitution envisaged the provision of free and compulsory education up to the age of fourteen within ten years of its adoption, but even forty years later we are still far from attaining this. Any restructuring of education will have to begin by fulfilling this moral and constitutional obligation, and the resources necessary for this will have to be provided in the Seventh Plan, even if it means cutting back on other sectors.

In the secondary sector, the concept of vocationalization has already been introduced at the plus-two level, but it is now widely admitted that it has not really worked satisfactorily. The idea was that it would siphon off a large percentage of young people into various vocations, thus reducing the aimless drift into college which constitutes such an appalling waste of human resources. This has not happened for a variety of reasons, one of them being that a two-year period is really not adequate to teach a vocation properly. Perhaps it should seriously be considered whether one more year from the college curriculum should not be added to the higher secondary level, thus resurrecting in a new form what in earlier times used to be called junior colleges. These would cover three years after the tenth standard, would be predominantly vocation oriented, and would cater to the rapidly growing technical requirements which will flow increasingly from a modernization of the economy.

It is ironical today that while lakhs of graduates and post-graduates are unemployed, it is becoming impossible to get a well-trained plumber, electrician or TV mechanic even in big cities. Similarly, the growing rural and self-employed sector needs a whole army of vocationally trained young men and women who should be motivated to work in the rural and semi-rural areas rather than rush into the already overcrowded cities with their cancerous slums growing every day. There is a whole spectrum of ancillary and supportive activities for which our present college education is entirely unsuited, and which could be catered to by carefully planned three-year higher secondary vocational courses.

If this is done, admission to colleges can be on a much stricter and more selective basis than at present. The tragic waste of human and material resources that we now find in the aimless drift from school to college is a luxury that a nation like ours cannot afford. College admission will have to be restructured on a competitive basis, so that only those young people who have the talent for higher studies are able to undertake them. If this could be achieved, it would amount to a virtual revolution in the education process. The overcrowding and dilution of standards in colleges would begin to disappear, while at the apex the universities would once again be able to concentrate on higher studies rather than get endlessly entangled in educational administration at the lower levels. The degree colleges would develop as self-contained institutions up to the graduation level, leaving universities free to undertake post-graduate teaching and research for which they have been set up.

What is envisaged, in effect, is a five-tier education structure, beginning with the primary school up to the fifth standard, the lower secondary sector from the sixth to the tenth, the higher secondary vocational sector from the eleventh to the thirteenth, the college or lower tertiary sector from the fourteenth to the sixteenth, and the university or higher tertiary sector for postgraduation and research. Medical, engineering and other professional streams would start from the eleventh standard onwards. Quite clearly, the implications of such a proposal are wide-ranging. The transition from the matric to the higher secondary system itself required several years of painful adjustment, particularly as far as textbooks and teacher training were concerned. However, this time it should be easier, because what is being suggested is a logical progression from the earlier situation.

Apart from the structure, however, what is even more important is the content of education. One of the great tragedies of our time has been that, although we are heir to one of the most distinguished and powerful intellectual traditions of all mankind, our educational system suffers from a lack of direction and purpose. As a result of the traumatic circumstances in which we achieved freedom at the price of partition, we reacted to such an extent that our education is entirely devoid of any moral or spiritual orientation. So afraid were we of being accused of a Hindu bias that we refrained from introducing any value orientation in the system at all despite the fact that whole series of committees and commissions of the Government of India, starting from the Radhakrishnan Commission in the sixties, have strongly recommended the introduction of moral education.

A restructuring of the curriculum will enable us to undertake a thorough revision of courses and educational methodology, keeping in view the necessity for imparting a desirable value system to our citizens. I am not making a plea for the introduction of religious education, which, in our constitutional structure, is something which must be left to private and religious institutions. However, it is surely our responsibility to see that the younger generation of India grow up with some knowledge of our rich spiritual and intellectual heritage. The study of Socrates and Plato in the West by no means implies the propagation of paganism any more than that of the Upaniṣads would involve the propagation of Hinduism as such. Similarly, a socially oriented work ethic directed toward individual and collective growth can only become operative, if the concept of selfless and dedicated work found in the *Gītā* and other religious texts is reinterpreted and made meaningful in the contemporary context.

We should also draw on other religious traditions. For example, the great Jain and Buddhist tradition of non-violence, the Christian commitment to charity and service, the Islamic stress upon social equality, and the Sikh tradition of brotherhood and sacrifice are all valuable elements in our cultural heritage which must be imaginatively mobilized to bring about a new orientation in our educational philosophy. At the same time, the scientific spirit of free and fearless enquiry into the universe in which we live, which is in no way incompatible with the Vedāntic heritage, needs to be nourished and nurtured.

The creative reorientation of our education system, both its outer structure and its inner spirit, represents one of the most exciting challenges for the remainder of this century. Indeed, we should be able to provide an educational model not only for ourselves but for the entire developing world, which is desperately seeking a new synthesis between the traditional wisdom of the East and the technological progress of the West.

13

Declaration on Nature: The Hindu Viewpoint

In the ancient spiritual traditions, man was looked upon as part of nature, linked by the indissoluble spiritual and psychological bonds to the elements around him. This is very much marked in the Hindu tradition, probably the oldest living religious tradition in the world. The Vedas, those collections of hymns composed by great spiritual seers and thinkers which are the repository of Hindu wisdom, reflect the vibrance of an encompassing world-view which looks upon all objects in the universe, living or non-living, as being pervaded by the same spiritual power.

Hinduism believes in the all-encompassing sovereignty of the divine, manifesting itself in a graded scale of evolution. The human race, though at the top of the evolutionary pyramid at present, is not seen as something apart from the earth and its multitudinous life forms. The *Atharva-Veda* has the magnificent Hymn to the Earth (*Bhūmi-Sūkta*) which is redolent with ecological and environmental values. The following verses are taken from this extraordinary hymn:

> Earth, in which lie the sea, the river and other waters,
> in which food and cornfields have come to be,
> in which lives all that breathes and that moves,
> may she confer on us the finest of her yield.
> Earth, in which the waters, common to all,
> moving on all sides, flow unfailingly, day and night,
> may she pour on us milk in many streams,
> and endow us with lustre.
> May those born of thee, O Earth,

be for our welfare, free from sickness and waste,
wakeful through a long life, we shall become bearers of
tribute to thee.
Earth my mother, set me securely with bliss
in full accord with heaven,
O wise one,
uphold me in grace and splendour.

Not only in the Vedas, but in later scriptures, such as the Upaniṣads, the Purāṇas and subsequent texts, the Hindu viewpoint on nature has been clearly enunciated. It is permeated by a reverence for life, and an awareness that the great forces of nature—the earth, the sky, the air, the water and fire—as well as various orders of life including plants and trees, forests and animals, are all bound to each other within the great rhythms of nature. The divine is not exterior to creation, but expresses itself through natural phenomena. Thus, in the *Muṇḍaka Upaniṣad* the divine is described as follows:

Fire is his head, his eyes are the moon and the sun;
The regions of space are his ears, his voice the revealed Veda;
The wind is his breath, his heart is the entire universe;
The earth is his footstool,
Truly he is the inner soul of all.

Turning to the animal world, we find that animals have always received special care and consideration. Numerous Hindu texts preach that all species should be treated as children. In Hindu mythology and iconography, there is a close relationship between the various deities, and their animal or bird mounts. Each divinity is associated with a particular animal or bird, and this lends a special dimension to the animal kingdom.

In addition, according to the Vaiṣṇava tradition, the evolution of life on this planet is symbolized by a series of divine incarnations beginning with the fish, moving through amphibious forms and mammals, and then on into human incarnations. This view clearly holds that man did not spring fully formed to dominate the lesser lifeforms, but rather evolved out of these forms himself, and is, therefore, integrally linked to the whole of creation.

This leads necessarily to a reverence for animal life. The *Yajur-Veda* (13.47) lays down that 'no person should kill animals helpful to all. Rather, by serving them, one should attain happiness.'

This view was later developed by the great Jain Tirthankara, Lord Mahāvīra, who regenerated the ancient Jain faith that lives down to the present day. For the Jains *ahiṁsā* or non-violence is the greatest good, and on no account should life be taken. This philosophy was emphasized more recently by Mahatma Gandhi who always spoke of the importance of *ahiṁsā* and looked upon the cow as a symbol of the benign element in animal life. All this strengthens the attitude of reverence for all life including animals and insects.

Apart from this, the natural environment also received the close attention of the ancient Hindu scriptures. Forests and groves were considered sacred, and flowering trees received special reverence. Just as various animals were associated with gods and goddesses, different trees and plants were also associated in the Hindu pantheon. The *Mahābhārata* says that 'even if there is only one tree full of flowers and fruits in a village, that place becomes worthy of worship and respect'. Various trees, fruits and plants have special significance in Hindu rituals.

The Hindu tradition of reverence for nature and all forms of life, vegetable or animal, represents a powerful tradition which needs to be renurtured and reapplied in our contemporary context. India, the population of which is over eighty per cent Hindu, has in recent years taken a special interest in conservation.

What is needed today is to remind ourselves that nature cannot be destroyed without mankind ultimately being destroyed itself. With nuclear weapons representing the ultimate pollutant, threatening to convert this beautiful planet of ours into a scorched cinder unable to support even the most primitive lifeforms, mankind is finally forced to face a dilemma. Centuries of rapacious exploitation of the environment has finally caught up with us, and a radically changed attitude towards nature is now not a question of spiritual merit or condescension, but of sheer survival.

This earth, so touchingly looked upon in the Hindu view as the Universal Mother, has nurtured mankind up from the slime of the primeval ocean for billions of years. Let us declare our determination to halt the present slide towards destruction, to rediscover the ancient tradition of reverence for all life and, even at this late hour, to reverse the suicidal course upon which we embarked. Let us recall the ancient Hindu dictum: 'The earth is our mother, we are all her children.'

14

The Ethics of Conservation

Ethical values are in reality those which conduce towards the welfare of all beings. The interpretation of these values, however, can differ in important ways. Welfare can be defined in terms of a single community, religious group, race, economic class, commercial interests or nation state. Through history human beings have interpreted ethical values in all these different dimensions, and, indeed, the clash between opposing concepts of welfare has been largely responsible for the blood-stained annals of the human race. It would require the latest generation of computers to work out the amount of suffering and misery, torture and slaughter, that human beings have meted out to each other in the name of ethical and religious values. Our own century has seen the nadir of inhumanity. Millions have perished in wars and concentration camps, in gas chambers and nuclear explosions. Even as we meet here, fellow human beings are killing each other in the name of what each side considers to be an ethical value.

It is against this chilling background that we have to consider the whole question of the ethics of conservation. Before we turn our attention to conserving nature, it would perhaps be worthwhile to spend a little time trying to conserve the human race. For those of us who come from the developing world, the sight of mighty nuclear powers gleefully brandishing their terrible weapons at each other is extremely disturbing. One nuclear warhead today packs explosive power equal to a thousand of the bombs that obliterated Hiroshima and Nagasaki forty years ago; and, on a conservative estimate, there are now 50,000 such nuclear warheads in existence. May I, with great respect, ask this distinguished audience whether talk of nature conservation really has much significance unless this dreadful threat can be removed?

It is now obvious that a nuclear conflagartion would not only destroy human civilization as we know it but endanger all forms of life on earth. Despite all the arguments marshalled by the proponents of a so-called 'limited' nuclear war, a series of recent scientific reports has made it quite clear that the dangers are too terrible to contemplate. And the most disturbing feature is that a conflict can now be started even without the two superpowers formally declaring war upon each other. An accident, a malfunctioning computer, a fight of wild geese, a ruthless group of terrorists, any one of these could trigger off calamity.

This whole question of nuclear weapons is far too important to be left only to generals and politicians. If the big catastrophe strikes, I can assure you that dedicated conservationists will not be spared from the effects of deadly nuclear radiation. Therefore, those of us who are committed to the preservation of life upon this planet and to furthering the welfare of humanity can no longer evade the unpleasant task of unequivocally confronting the dilemma of man in the nuclear age. It is a matter of great satisfaction that the World Wildlife Fund has expanded its vision beyond the animal kingdom into wider dimensions of the natural environment. May I suggest that it should also move in the other direction, and strengthen its interest in the survival of *Homo sapiens*, the race to which we happen to belong.

This is the first ethical imperative that faces us. Closely linked to this is the whole area of conserving the natural environment. The development of nuclear weapons with unprecedented destructive power has not taken place as an isolated phenomenon. In fact, it has been the culmination of a whole world-view which has dominated Western civilization ever since the renaissance. This has been described as the Cartesian-Newtonian-Marxist paradigm, because the underlying thesis of these great philosophies is the dualistic-materialistic world-view which has so completely dominated Western civilization, and, through it, our entire planet.

I do not for a moment wish to denigrate the tremendous achievements of science and technology over the last few centuries. The transformation of agricultural and industrial production; the breakthroughs in all branches of science, specially medicine and surgery; the communications revolution that has converted this world into a global village in our very lifetime; the astounding adventure into space through which man has landed on the moon and is reaching out to the planets and even the stars beyond; all these represent a truly remarkable achievement of the human mind. However, as always, against the brightest light there falls the darkest shadow. With all its wealth and technology, two-thirds of the human race today lives below what can be considered a satisfactory standard of living, and one-third are in fact below the poverty line. Even as we meet here, in this beautiful town of Assisi sacred to the memory of St. Francis who loved all beings, millions of children go to sleep hungry, their bodies stunted, their minds distorted by malnutrition and lack of medical facilities. Ten days' expenditure on armaments can abolish hunger on this planet.

The great achievements of science and technology have not only been unable to meet the requirements of the human race, but have also been gained at a terrible price. The last few centuries, and this one in particular, have witnessed an unprecedented destruction of the natural environment. Man's ability to intervene in the environment has increased tremendously, but unfortunately there has been no commensurate growth in wisdom and understanding. As a result of this divergence, there has been what can only be described as a ruthless and rapacious plundering of our planet, based upon materialist philosophies which deny the spiritual dimension of Mother Earth and look upon her as merely a material substance to be manipulated at will.

Hundreds of thousands of square miles of forest have disappeared, taking with them many species of fauna and flora. The atmosphere has been poisoned particularly in the great urban and industrial concentrations, so that in many cities it is becoming increasingly difficult to breathe clean air. There is reason to believe that the ozone layer surrounding this planet is becoming dangerously attenuated, the possible effects of which we still know very little. Continued testing of nuclear weapons releases a steady stream of radiation into the atmosphere, the cumulative results of which will only unfold in the decades ahead and in the lives of generations yet unborn. The disposal of nuclear wastes now represents a major hazard in several countries. The tragic accident at Chernobyl is only a faint warning of what lies ahead for mankind if we persist in our present path.

The great oceans, which were the repository of the earliest life forms and from which all creatures originally emerged, have been heavily polluted. The increasing use of chemical fertilizers and pesticides have poisoned the earth, and endangered the entire food chain. Numerous species have become extinct, and many others are on the verge of disappearing. The strange doctrine that our race is in some way specially entitled to destroy other species so as to establish its 'sovereignty' over the earth has distorted human consciousness down through the corridors of time. Tens of millions of animals are slaughtered every year for food, or perish in agony in laboratories, and this in civilizations which claim to abhor animal sacrifice. The anthropocentricity of modern civilization has now reached neurotic proportions, so that ultimately the race itself is in danger of committing collective suicide.

In this whole context, the ethics of conservation become very clear. It is now no longer a question of attaining spiritual merit or performing a good deed for our personal satisfaction or salvation. We have reached the stage where it is essential for our own survival, and that of generations yet unborn, to adopt conservation as a central commitment of the entire human race. The splendid work being done by the World Wildlife Fund which, to quote a shining example, co-operated so effectively with the Government of India in Project Tiger—surely one of the world's most successful conservation projects—is a heartening example of what can be achieved if men and women of devotion, dedication and firm resolve decide to undertake an ethically desirable venture. However, against the grim backdrop that I have sketched, this can only be described as a small pilot project.

What is needed at this juncture is a concerted commitment by governments, voluntary organizations and individuals the world over to call a halt to our suicidal march towards terricide, and, even at this midnight hour, to reverse the whole process of thinking, and begin the long, slow march back to sanity. Developing nations, in particular, must resist the temptation to follow blindly the industrial and commercial policies of the developed world without paying careful attention to the ecological factors involved in economic growth. Ecological planning must be built into the whole process of industrialization, and ecological values should become part of educational curricula throughout the world. The insights of the great religious traditions of mankind, which will find expression in the five declarations being prepared here in Assisi, should be spread widely through mass media—the press and radio, television and cinema.

Ancient myths often powerfully illuminate the human

predicament, and there is the Hindu myth of the Churning of the Milky Ocean which speaks to us today across the millennia, symbolizing as it does the dangers that lie in a mindless quest for ever-increasing possessions.

It is a sobering thought that we are a privileged generation, not only because we may be the first to see the dawn of the third millennium after Christ but because we may be the last to inhabit this earth. Our survival now depends upon our capacity to make a major transition of consciousness, equal in significance to the earlier ones from nomadic to agricultural, and agricultural to industrial society. We must transit to complementarity in place of competition, convergence in place of conflict, holism in place of hedonism. We must, in short, move rapidly into a new, global consciousness to replace the present fractured and fragmented consciousness of the human race. This, as I see it, is the true significance of the ethics of conservation.

15

Transition to Global Consciousness

While thinkers and seers from the very dawn of civilization have spoken of the necessity for peace—mark, for example, the exquisite *śānti pāṭh* from the *Ṛg-Veda*—the fact remains that, for as long as we have any record, the annals of the human race have been violent and blood-stained in the extreme. The history of all races and nations is full of battles and wars, whether these are internal conflicts or external invasions. It would require the latest generation of computers to work out the amount of bloodshed and deaths inflicted by human beings upon each other through all ages. The causes of these conflicts have been many and varied. Some wars have resulted from the ambition of individuals or groups to dominate society; others from an attempt to fight against injustice and tyranny. There have been wars flowing from the megalomania of tyrants, and also wars of national liberation and freedom. Sometimes it is possible to demarcate those guilty of starting conflicts; often the issues are so complex that a clear-cut verdict is virtually impossible. But the fact remains that war has always been a major factor in human affairs.

Our own century has seen the nadir of inhumanity. Millions have perished in two world wars and hundreds of regional conflicts, in concentration camps and gas chambers, in atomic explosions and correction camps. Despite the so-called march of civilization, human casualties in war have shown no sign of decrease. Indeed, with each technological advance, the number of people involved in conflicts also increases, and whereas in ancient times it was usually only the combatants who were killed, now whole populations are annihilated in the struggle. The obliteration of Hiroshima and Nagasaki by atomic weapons just forty years ago marked the culmination of this process, and opened out a new era of danger for all mankind. With the dawning of the nuclear age, there has been a qualitative change in the whole situation. Today a single nuclear warhead packs explosive power equal to a thousand of the bombs dropped on Japan in 1946, and on a conservative estimate there are now fifty thousand such nuclear warheads on this small planet. A nuclear war between the superpowers, therefore, no longer threatens only the two sides but will almost certainly lead to the destruction of human civilization as we know it, the virtual annihilation of the human race and probably all higher forms of life upon this planet. It will, in fact, amount to terricide, the destruction of the planet.

In this context, it should now be clear that a major war can no longer be looked upon as an acceptable way of settling international disputes. Peace and international understanding are now not merely a moral necessity but a categorical imperative for the sheer survival of the human race. The ancient vision of the seers regarding the establishment of peace on earth must now be converted into reality, if mankind is to survive into the next millennium and benefit from the benign application of the amazing advances in science and technology that have taken place over the last few decades. Any philosophy which evades this central question of possible nuclear annihilation cannot claim to cope with the dilemma of mankind in the nuclear age. Once this is clear, it follows that we must elucidate a world-view which can deal effectively with the present situation.

I submit that such a comprehensive world-view is, in fact, available to us in the Vedānta. There are five principles which, taken together, can constitute the broad framework within which a comprehensive philosophy of world peace can be developed. Briefly stated, these are as follows. The first concept is that the entire cosmos is permeated by the same spiritual power: *Īśā vāsyam idaṁ sarvaṁ yat kiñca jagatyāṁ jagat*. There is no ultimate dichotomy between matter and energy, and, though energy may manifest itself in a million different ways, its inner essence is essentially the same. Secondly, it follows that the divine light is present in all beings, and the higher up we move on the ladder of evolution the more powerful does this power manifest itself in consciousness. *Homo sapiens* being at present at the apex of the evolutionary pyramid on this planet, the light of the divine manifests itself in all human beings regardless of their race or religion, creed or nationality: *Īśvaraḥ sarvabhūtānāṁ hṛddeśe 'rujna tiṣṭhati.* Thirdly, if all human beings represent a spark of the divine, then all humanity is, in fact, an extended family: *Vasudhaiva kuṭumbakam*. Fourthly, if that is so, then the highest good is to be found not in the domination of one race, religion or nationality over another, but in a co-operative commonwealth in which the welfare of all beings is ensured: *Bahujana sukhāya bahujana hitāya ca*. Finally, it also follows that all religions and creeds are but partial approaches to the totality of truth, and none can claim a monopoly of wisdom. As the *Ṛg-Veda* has it: *Ekaṁ sad viprāḥ bahudhā vadanti*.

A world-view based upon these Vedāntic principles could reverse the present trend towards destruction, and, even at this late hour, help mankind to begin the movement back to sanity. Although the principles find eloquent expression in the Upaniṣads, they are, in fact, universal and by no means the property of any particular religion. The five principles of the Buddha Panchsheel, the Jain creed of *ahiṁsā*, the Christian doctrine of Universal Love are all reflections of the same spiritual awareness. Indeed, we must remember that vast numbers of people today do not even profess or follow any formal religion, but that does not make them in any way less committed to human survival. What is required is a carefully structured educational campaign at the global level, utilizing all the power of the mass media—radio and television, newspapers and journals, books and pamphlets, cinema and stage—to put across to the vast mass of humanity the utmost urgency of preventing a nuclear holocaust. Universal values must be built into the educational curricula of nations, and we in India, with our unique combination of spiritual vision and scientific excellence, can blaze the trail in this regard.

In our country there have been many attempts to build international organizations designed to ensure peace, but so far these have proved to be disappointing. The plight of UNESCO is particularly tragic. Envisaged as the conscience of humanity, it has become a battlefield of international tension and conflict. One of the problems is the painful fact that nationalism itself, which has been such a powerful and potent force in human affairs for many centuries, cannot now continue in its pristine form without grave danger to humanity. In the global village, bristling as it is with nuclear weapons, we simply cannot afford the luxury of a hundred competing nationalisms. In the same way, as tribal loyalties were transcended in the nation states, national barriers will also have to be transcended in some form of global organization, if we are to survive into the future. Indeed, as a symbolic gesture, it would be desirable if all passports are stamped 'Planet Earth' and then the name of the country, a reminder that despite our differing nationalities we all inhabit the same small planet. At the turn of the century, Sri Aurobindo took up the great *mantra* of *Bande Mātaram* (Hail to the Mother) from Bankim Chandra and converted it into a potent instrument for national liberation. Now eighty years later, we have to move towards the broader concept of *Bhavāṇī Vasundharā* and not only *Bhavāṇī Bhāratī*, Mother Earth and not only Mother India.

Such a transcendence of nationalism is not as unrealistic as it may appear at first sight. Already the communications revolution, linked with satellite technology, has made possible instant contact between any two parts of the earth. A sports event in one city is visible throughout the world at the very moment that it occurs; a famine in Africa can trigger off a worldwide campaign for a massive raising of funds; an inter-religious ceremony in a basilica can be witnessed by all humanity regardless of creed or religious denomination. Television and video breakthroughs are bringing human beings together in a way quite inconceivable even three decades ago. What President Reagan or President Gorbachev says can no longer be confined to their respective countries, but becomes world property. Howsoever hard nations may try to build barriers, the very dynamics of the present age tends to break them down. In language and music, in dress and diet, and in a hundred different ways we can see the outlines of a world civilization arising before our very eyes.

Amidst the conflicts and discords of our times a new world civilization is struggling to be born, though we are too close to the event to appreciate the immensity of the change that is coming about. The emergence of what I call the Global Consciousness will involve an even more dramatic paradigm shift than the earlier ones from nomadic to agricultural, and from agricultural to industrial civilization. What is more, due to technological progress time itself has telescoped, so that the changes which previously involved many centuries must now take place within a few years.

It is my conviction that we stand today on the threshold of immense changes in human consciousness, a virtual metamorphosis into a new and dazzling dimension, though whether we will have the wisdom to survive the change or will blow up our planet before it is completed, remains to be seen. Such changes are seldom peaceful, and often extremely unpleasant for those involved in the process. We admire the transformation of an ugly, land-bound caterpillar into a beautiful airbound butterfly, but the process of change must be a terrifying one for the creature concerned. In a way, the entire human race is now going through such a transformation. and those of us who claim to be intellectuals must play a leading role to ensure the rapid spread of universal values and the establishment of peace and international understanding, so that the transition is completed with our world still intact. In the immortal words of Maulānā Jalāl-al-Dīn Rūmī:

> Wherever I go there are torches and candles.
> Wherever I turn there is tumult and shouting.
> For the world tonight is heavy and in travail,
> Striving to give birth to the eternal world.

16

The Need for Human Unity

There comes a time, which comes but rarely in human history, when mankind stands poised between the weight of the past and the challenges of the future; when the old collapses and the new struggles desperately to be born; when the promise of a higher consciousness begins to unfurl its potentialities, but the forces of hatred and destruction cast their ominous shadow over generations yet to come; when knowledge grows apace but wisdom languishes; when science and technology give us incredible gifts, but also open the floodgates to unimaginable destruction; when we have within our grasp the possibility by the end of this century of abolishing poverty and hunger, illiteracy and unemployment from the face of the earth, but when all the fruits of human history and civilization could by then have been abolished in a nuclear conflagration destroying not only the human race but all life on our planet. It is a tragic irony that Mother Earth, which has nourished and sustained consciousness for a billion years up from the slime of the primeval ocean, is today herself imperilled by the human race which is in the vanguard of evolution.

Coming as we do from different climes and races, we are gathered in this beautiful and gracious hall of worship, the Cathedral of St. John the Divine in the heart of the world's greatest city, dedicated to the author of the great revelation that flowed from his vision on the Island of Patmos, to invoke the grace of the divine upon humanity. Representing many religious faiths of mankind, we are united in our conviction that a divinity pervades the cosmos—*īśā vāsyam idaṁ sarvaṁ yat kiñca jagatyāṁ jagat*—as the Upaniṣad has it, and that each human being on this planet, regardless of creed or denomination, partakes in some mysterious way of divine grace and divine potential. What is required at this critical juncture is that the many streams of our separate aspiration should merge into a unified prayer for peace and well-being, so that this may evoke a powerful and effective response from the divine power to save mankind from total destruction. Śrī Kṛṣṇa in the *Gītā* clearly says that whenever the human race is in real danger a decisive divine intention takes place for the re-establishment of *dharma* or righteousness on earth.

A creative symbiosis, a merging of the positive elements in each great religion, could even at this midnight hour dispel the darkness and release the psychic energies so urgently needed to meet the global crisis. This is borne out by a contemporary revelation in the astonishing book *The Present Crisis* by Pandit Gopi Krishna who passed away only a few weeks ago. This not only graphically portrays the danger of annihilation, but predicts that nuclear war can be averted if enough people become aware of and grow into the higher consciousness. Other great thinkers of our time, notably Sri Aurobindo in the East and Teilhard de Chardin in the West, have spoken eloquently of the crisis that looms ahead and the evolutionary leap that is required to overcome it.

Hinduism, the religion based on the Vedas, the most ancient living scripture available to man, has placed before us the noble idea of the oneness of mankind—*vasudhaiva kuṭumbakam*—and proclaims the divinity inherent in each human being, the essential unity of all religions and the brotherhood of the family of man. We must rediscover the core of divine power that resides in each individual, that underlies all creeds and dogmas, that cuts across all the artificial barriers man has so painstakingly erected and that holds within it the key to our survival and spiritual evolution. It is these truths that we must rediscover, for, as Jesus rightly said, 'Ye shall know the Truth and the Truth shall make you free.' And, as the Upaniṣad proclaims: *Satyam eva jayate nānṛtaṁ* (Truth, alone prevails, not falsehood).

At this moment of supreme peril let us cleanse our minds and hearts of bitterness and suspicion, for to survive we must forge together a higher consciousness that embraces all the religions of man including the non-believers, so that our children and theirs can flourish into the millennium ahead. Many are the wars that have been waged in the name of God, millions are the human beings who have perished and continue to perish in these conflicts, while the forces of atheism also extend their sway over large segments of the human race. Let us now, we who call ourselves men and women of religion, wage peace with the same zeal with which we once waged war, so that the era of human conflict may pass into the pages of history and we may embark on a new adventure of love and co-operation, of mutually assured welfare rather than mutually assured destruction. Let us not wait for the day after, but spread the message of peace and harmony to the ends of the earth of the day before, now, when we can still respond to the beauty of music and the ennobling experience of creative art; when our hearts can still resonate with the wisdom of great literature and the sovereign vibration of love.

And let us so reorganize planetary resources that the two-thirds of humanity still struggling at subsistence level is assured of the material and intellectual inputs necessary for a decent civilized existence; so that millions of children do not go to sleep at night hungry and underfed, or grow to adulthood with stunted minds and bodies; so that millions do not perish from communicable diseases, including new and virulent strains that baffle medical science, or waste away from malnutrition until their very humanity is reduced and distorted. All this can be achieved if even ten per cent of the world's resources now consumed by increasingly lethal weapons of overkill are diverted for peaceful purposes, for we must remember that talk of peace loses much of its meaning unless it is accompanied by justice and freedom for every human being, because each person is unique and has the potentiality of making a unique contribution to human civilization.

The air is thick with foreboding and dark clouds of conflict seem to be gathering on the horizon. And yet those of us who tread the inner path must keep faith amidst the encircling gloom. Thousands of years ago a great seer of the Upaniṣads proclaimed in ecstasy: 'I have seen the great being shining in splendour on the other shore beyond the darkness.' Let all of us gathered here open our deepest selves to the light and the power of that great being, so that we are irradiated by divine luminosity and develop the wisdom to act in such a way that our beautiful planet, so lovely and yet so fragile, shall become not a burnt-out cinder circling the sun into eternity but the cradle of the greater man reflecting the power and the glory of the higher consciousness.

17

The Way to Peace

Throughout human history mountains have been looked upon as sacred because of their grandeur, and also because their upward thrust symbolize the aspiration of the human soul for unity with the divine. In India, it was from the great Himalayan range that, millenia ago, self-realized sages composed the thousands of beautiful hymns known collecitvely as the Vedas. These provide the foundations of Hinduism, the religion that I have the honour to represent at this Religious Summit. It is, therefore, particularly appropriate that this meeting under the patronage of the widely revered Venerable Etai Yamada should be associated with Mount Hiei, believed to be the cradle of Buddhism in Japan, and with this beautiful city of Kyoto, your great cultural capital. Coming as I do from India, the land where from the dawn of civilization the spiritual sun has been shining in all its splendour, I bring fraternal greetings to this land of the Rising Sun. May this meeting of representatives drawn from all the great world religions prove to be an important landmark in the structuring of the global consciousness, so urgently needed if humankind is to survive in this nuclear age.

Humanity today is in the throes of a transformation as significant as the earlier ones from nomadic to agricultural, from agricultural to industrial and from industrial to post-industrial civilization. With the extraordinary quantum leap in science and technology over the last few decades, an entirely new process has been initiated which can be described as 'globalization'. While national, ethnic, religious, ideological and other divisions remain, there is a clearly discernible movement towards globalization—in politics, in economics, in communications and in cultural patterns. The terrible bombs thrown over forty years ago on Hiroshima and Nagasaki heralded the dawn of the nuclear age. If mankind is to survive into the centuries ahead and if this beautiful planet is not to be destroyed, it is necessary that a new global civilization should emerge which cuts across all barriers and unites the human race into a single family. For this the prime requirement is world peace.

While the movement towards globalization is gathering momentum, the global consciousness that is required to sustain the new civilization has still not emerged adequately. Thus, a most dangerous situation has arisen, caused by the lag between the growth of globalization and its acceptance by the vast masses of humanity, particularly political leaders. It is here that the great religious traditions of the world have a crucial and urgent role to play. While religion has been a fountain-head of great inspiration in many creative spheres of life—music and dance, philosophy and the fine arts, literature and architecture—it has also been a source of tremendous internecine strife. But despite this history of conflict the great world religions do provide invaluable insights into a higher form of human consciousness, which need to be creatively rearticulated in the light of present requirements.

Running like a golden thread through the religious traditions of the world are the concepts of peace, human brotherhood and divine compassion, which today need to be recaptured so that they can become a crucial input into the new consciousness that is struggling to be born. Coming as I do from the Hindu tradition, I would like to place before this distinguished gathering five universal principles found in our scriptures—the Vedānta—which, taken together, represent a comprehensive and enlightened approach to the problems of humanity. Firstly, there is the concept of the all-pervasiveness of the divine, whether it is our tiny planet or the billions of galaxies in this infinite universe. The second concept is that each and every individual, irrespective of religion or nationality, race or ideology, embodies a spark of this divinity, and that the highest goal of life is to fan this spark within each one of us into a blazing fire of spiritual realization.

Thirdly, if all human beings are potentially divine, then the entire human race represents a single extended family; and, in the final analysis, the inner spiritual link that binds human beings together is stronger than the outer differences which divide them. The fourth insight is that all true religious aspiration must lead to essentially the same goal. If a divinity exists—whether worshipped as immanent or transcendent, as male or female, as visible or invisible—it cannot ultimately be different just because of the accident of our birth. Certainly, it can reveal itself in a million different forms, just as the sun can reflect itself in a thousand separate pools of water without itself being divided. But though it may appear in different ways, the divine truth is essentially one.

Fifthly, the goal of human life is a dual one: the spiritual release of our individual souls from bondage, and also the welfare of society and the world. This welfare is not interpreted in any narrow racial or religious terms; it is defined as the welfare of the many, the happiness of the many. Thus, our spiritual quest must manifest not only in our internal spiritual practice but also in our external activity devoted to peace and human welfare.

These five universal concepts of Hinduism collectively represent an alternative ideology to the present disruptive philosophy, well summed up by the acronym MAD, Mutually Assured Destruction. Similar universal principles can no doubt be abstracted from the other great religious traditions represented here. Indeed, one of the concrete results of this meeting could well be a unique publication that presents universal principles drawn from all the great religious traditions of the world so as to spread the message of global consciousness and peace to all humanity.

Friends, we stand today at a crucial crossroads of destiny. The old is dying, and the new is struggling to be born, and it falls to our generation to seek the golden bridge whereby humanity can cross the dark and perilous waters that surround us. When we gather on the holy Mount Hiei, let us pray to the divine spirit to give our minds clarity, our hearts compassion, and our bodies vigour, so that together we can move into the next phase of evolution on Planet Earth. As the seer of the Upaniṣads said thousands of years ago: 'I have seen that great being shining like the sun beyond the darkness. It is only by knowing this that we can overcome death, this is our bridge to immortality.'

APPENDIX

Muṇḍaka Upaniṣad

Introduction

If the Vedas, to paraphrase Kālidāsa, can be compared to the mighty Himalayas stretching majestically from the Hindu Kush in the West all the way across to the Eastern sea, like some gigantic measuring rod against which the world's great traditions will have to be gauged, then the Upaṇisads may be likened to those great Himalayan peaks which stand in splendour reflecting on their eternal snows the sparkling glory of the sun of wisdom. They have rightly been described as the supreme expression of the Hindu mind, indeed one of the high watermarks of the human spirit since the dawn of civilization. A record of the deepest spiritual experiences of a whole series of *ṛṣis* or sages across many centuries, they are, as Sri Aurobindo puts it 'documents of revelatory and intuitive philosophy of an inexhaustible light, power and largeness and, whether written in verse or cadenced prose, spiritual poems of an absolute and unfailing inspiration, inimitable in phrase, wonderful in rhythm and expression'.

The traditional classification of the Vedas by Western scholars into the *karma-kāṇḍa* dealing with ritualistic action and sacrifice, and the *jñāna-kāṇḍa* concerned with philosophy cannot be considered sacrosanct. Vedic hymns are by no means merely ritualistic in the sense that they are used only for purposes of the sacrificial *yajñas*. In fact, if rightly interpreted, they contain the deepest spiritual truths veiled in an intricate and imposing symbolism. Nonetheless, the Upaniṣads do constitute the Vedānta, or the culmination of the Vedas, both because chronologically they come at the end of the Vedic collections and also because of the sublime philosophical nature and superb poetical structure that they present.

As is frequently the case with Sanskrit, a rich, many-splendoured language, the word Upaniṣad can be interpreted in more than one way. The literal meaning is 'sitting down near', and describes the disciples sitting around the *guru* as he expounds the *brahmavidyā*, the Science of Brahman. This is in interesting contradistinction to Socrates and his disciples who, apparently, preferred to conduct their philosophical discussions while walking up and down the pathways of the Academy, thus earning the name of 'peripatetic' philosophers. By extension, the term Upaniṣad could mean 'the secret doctrine' or 'the saving wisdom' to be imparted only to those disciples who followed the monastic discipline and were thus entitled to sit near the master. In a more abstract sense, the Upaniṣads are referred to in the *Muṇḍaka* itself as 'the great weapon, the mighty bow' through which the individual soul (the Ātman) can be sped towards the goal of Brahman and become one with it. Ādi Śaṅkarācārya takes the word Upaniṣad to mean that knowledge by which ignorance is loosened or destroyed.

Taken together, it is clear that the Upaniṣads represent a unique corpus of philosophical thought and spiritual experience. In the Hindu tradition, there is not the curious dichotomy that we find in the West between philosophy and religion, the former being merely a mental formulation not necessarily connected with spiritual vision and experience. The Upaniṣads, in fact, flow from the spiritual vision and realization of the masters, who express their experience in superb prose and poetry. There are various views regarding the number of Upaniṣads, the traditional belief being the auspicious number one hundred and eight. The great Śaṅkarācārya commented upon eleven—*Īśā, Kena, Kaṭha, Praśna, Muṇḍaka, Māndūkya, Taittirīya, Aitareya, Chāndogya, Bṛhadāraṇyaka* and *Svetāśvatara*—which are generally accepted as being the principal Upaniṣads. These range from short, cryptic texts such as the *Īśā* which has only eighteen verses, to the great *Bṛhādāraṇyaka* which runs into many hundreds.

The texts have been composed over several centuries. Without entering into the scholarly dispute about their chronology, one might generally accept the view that they date from about 1000 B.C. down to the first or second century after Christ. The orthodox Hindu tradition, of course, is that the Vedas are timeless, and this is certainly true as far as the Vedāntic teachings are concerned as they have a universality that places them beyond the limitations of time and geographical location. While many of the texts are anonymous, a common feature of Hindu philosophy and iconography, a number of historical personages figure in the Upaniṣads, notably the great King Janaka of Mithilā and the sage Yājñavalkya, whose dialogues form such a striking feature of the *Bṛhādāraṇyaka*, the Upaniṣad of the Great Forest.

It is impossible to describe the inner luminosity of the Upaniṣads. The *ṛṣis* or seers speak with the authority of authentic spiritual experience, 'not as the scribes'. There are two qualifications laid down for the teacher—he should be *śrotriya* or well-versed in the scriptures, and also *brahmaniṣṭha* firmly based on the realization of Brahman. In other words, he must combine intellectual ability with spiritual experience, knowledge with wisdom. Then and then only was he considered qualified to impart the secret doctrine. On their part, the disciples, whether young acolytes resident in the hermitage or distinguished citizens—rulers, householders, merchants—had also to be dedicated to the quest for truth with humility and devotion. Acolytes had to live under strict discipline and perform penance and austerities before they were considered capable of receiving the teaching.

The teaching itself, sublime and multifaceted, runs like a crystal stream emanating from the lofty heights of the Himalayas, dancing in ecstasy down the glittering slopes, widening into broad, life-giving rivers, and finally merging into the radiant ocean of wisdom. It is a stream that is never-ending, arising as it does from the springs of spiritual power deep within the heart of the earth, and flowing down across the millennia as the sacred Gaṅgā itself meanders through the matted locks of Śiva Mahādeva before appearing on earth as the benefactor of humanity—a rainbow bridge to immortality.

Mankind today is poised precariously at a crucial crossroads in its long and tortuous history on this planet. Over the last few decades there has been an explosion of knowledge, resulting in all the glittering achievements of science and technology. And yet there has been no parallel growth in wisdom, and the erosion of traditional cultures has proceeded apace. As a result, mankind today stands on the verge of destruction, unable to cope with its own technological ingenuity. A nuclear holocaust is now very much within the realms of possibility—some would say probability—and with each day that passes nuclear arms continue to multiply and this planet moves closer to the edge of the precipice. At a time like this, we turn to the great scriptures to see whether we can derive from them a viable philosophy, capable of comprehending and confronting the dilemma of man in the present age of nuclear weapons in the global village. The Upaniṣads, though composed thousands of years ago, present a philosophy of life and human existence that is startlingly relevant in the present context.

There are five fundamental concepts that could perhaps be considered to constitute the foundations of the Vedāntic world-view, all of which find their expression and elucidation in the Upaniṣads. The first is the all-pervasiveness of the divine—*īśāvāsyam idaṁ sarvaṁ yat kiñca jagatyāṁ jagat*—the view that all creation, whether this tiny speck of cosmic dust that we call our world or the billions of galaxies that stretch endlessly into the chasm of time, is in the ultimate analysis a manifestation of the same divine power. Thus, despite the multitudinous manifestations in this space-time continuum, there is ultimately no dichotomy between mind and spirit, between matter and energy, between the human and the divine.

The second concept flowing from this is that the divine, which is all-pervasive, resides hidden but is discoverable in what we may call consciousness, specially in human consciousness which at present appears to be the highest broad level of evolution. As the *Gītā* has it: *Iśvaraḥ sarvabhūtānāṁ hṛddeśe 'rjuna tiṣṭhati* (the lord resides in the heart of all beings). This implies that despite differences of caste and creed, race and religion, nationality and ideology, the entire human race is held together by a deep and fundamental inner spiritual bond.

With this we may link the next concept that all members of the human race in reality belong to a single, extended family—*vasudhaiva kuṭumbakam*. In view of the blood-drenched history over the last several thousand years—it would require the very last generation of supercomputers to calculate the slaughter and torture that human beings have inflicted upon each other in the name of religion and ideology—this concept would appear to be absurdly romantic. And yet, on deeper thought, it becomes clear that unless this view is adopted there is really little hope of man being able to survive for long into the next century. The mechanical, exteriorized attempts at human unity—whether through the United Nations, UNESCO or any other multilateral organization—have failed precisely because of the lack of an inner, unifying philosophy.

The fourth Vedāntic concept is that of the ultimate unity of all religions and ideologies—*ekam sad viprāḥ bahudhā vadanti* (the truth is one, the wise call it by many names). True, the history of mankind down to the present moment is replete with the most frightful massacres and strife, not only between religious groups but between tribes, nation states and conflicting ideologies. Millions have died on opposing sides, carrying with them to the end the conviction that they were fighting for right and justice, for truth and God as they understood those terms. But the Vedāntic doctrine gives an alternative scenario. Could it be that all these lesser formulations are, in fact, simply fragmentary approaches to a single, unified truth flowing from differing ethnic, economic, geographical and political backgrounds? Are we not like the blind men in the fable who touched different parts of the elephant and then flew at each other in a rage, because their descriptions—true in themselves—did not match?

Finally, there is the concept of welfare, not of any particular person or group or class, but of all creation. As the ancient prayer goes: *Sarvepi sukhīnaḥ santu, sarve santu nirāmayāḥ* (May all beings be happy, may all beings be free from fear). Here welfare is described not in limited terms but as all-embracing, covering not only the human race but also what, in our arrogance, we call 'lower' beings—animals and birds, insects and plants, as well as 'natural' formations, such as mountains and oceans. In addition to the horrors that mankind has perpetrated upon its own members,we have also indulged in a rapacious and ruthless exploitation of the natural environment. Thousands of species have become extinct, millions of acres of forest and other natural habitat laid waste, the land and the air poisoned, the great oceans themselves, the earliest reservoirs of life, polluted beyond belief. And all this has happened because of a limited concept of welfare, an inability to grasp the essential unity of all things, a stubborn refusal to accept the earth not as a material object to be manipulated at will but as a shining, spiritual entity that has over billions of years nurtured consciousness up from slime of the primeval ocean to where we are today.

These five concepts, then, represent an alternative philosophy for the nuclear age. While Vedāntic in origin and expression, they are by no means confined to Hinduism. They are universal in their sweep and applicability, and can provide an invaluable input into the new, holistic, global consciousness that, despite the discords and conflicts of our age, is desperately struggling to be born. Indeed, it is as a small offering to this great *yajña* of global transition that this study of one of the most beautiful and sublime of the Upaniṣads has been undertaken.

The word *Muṇḍaka*, etymologically, derives from a razor and, by extension, can be taken to refer to a person who has shaved his head. This was common among young students who were sent to the forest hermitages, or *āśramas*, to study at the feet of a master. It could, indeed, refer to all monks who, in the Eastern tradition, shave their heads after donning the ochre robe. This would imply that the teachings of this Upaniṣad are intended for novices or monks, who have dedicated their lives to finding the eternal reality behind waking consciousness and material objects. However, another interpretation could be that the Upaniṣad presents the higher wisdom in such a sharp and lucid manner that it shaves off or removes the crust of ignorance with which we are surrounded, and enables us to realize the clear light of the divine. Accepting both the interpretations, it would be correct to say that the *Muṇḍaka Upaniṣad*, while certainly representing a teaching that valued renunciation above worldly involvement, nonetheless expresses the eternal Vedāntic truths with great effectiveness and in unforgettable imagery.

The Upaniṣad belongs to the *Atharva-Veda* and is a rather short one, comprising only sixty-four verses divided into three chapters with two sections each. Each section is a compact presentation of a fundamental Vedāntic concept, compressing into few verses a great wealth of wisdom and illumination. Its setting is in the forest hermitage of a great seer Aṅgiras, who is approached by an eminent householder, Śaunaka, with what has become one of the most famous questions in the history of human thought. 'Revered Sir,' he asks, 'what is that knowledge whereby everything in the world becomes known?' In reply to this leading question, the seer propounds in brief compass the whole Vedāntic world-view.

In translating and commenting upon the Upaniṣad I have been greatly helped by Dr. Radhakrishnan's scholarly work on the Upaniṣads, the excellent commentary by Swāmī Śarvānanda in the Upaniṣad series brought out by the Sri Ramakrishna Math, the lectures of two contemporary Swamis for whom I have the highest personal regard—Swami Ranganathananda and Swami

Chinmayananda, the deeply intuitive comments of Sri Aurobindo—surely, one of the greatest seers of modern times—and the extraordinary work, *The Yoga of the Kathopanishad*, by the late Sri Krishna Prem. None of these eminent persons, however, can in any way be held responsible for such errors of interpretation as this essay may contain.

The reason for my undertaking to write on an Upaniṣad is twofold. Firstly, I have derived immense pleasure and guidance from this text, and felt that I should share this with a wider audience. Secondly, there is an unfortunate impression prevalent in India and abroad that the Upaniṣads are too abstruse and difficult for the general reader, and should, therefore, be left severely alone as the preserve only of scholars and academicians. This is simply not true. Indeed, the *Bhagavad-Gītā* which, along with the Upaniṣads and the *Brahma-Sūtras*, makes up the *prasthāna-trayī* or the three foundations of Vedānta, is a much more complex text than most of the Upaniṣads, but this has not prevented it from becoming a seminal work for all those interested in the Hindu view of life. it is my hope that this modest study of one of the most illuminating of the Upaniṣads will help introduce a glowing text to a wider audience and, thus, contribute towards the development of the deeper wisdom so urgently needed if mankind is to survive in this nuclear age.

PEACE INVOCATION

Aum, O worshipful Ones, may our ears hear that which is auspicious, may we, well-versed in the sacrifice, see with our eyes that which is auspicious. May we, singing your praise, enjoy our allotted span of life with strong limbs and healthy bodies.

May Indra, extolled in the scriptures, Pūṣan, the all-knowing, Tārkṣya, who protects us from harm and Bṛhaspati, who protects our spiritual lustre, grant us prosperity and further our welfare.

Aum, Peace, Peace, Peace.

Traditionally, each Upaniṣad begins with one or more Vedic verses which set the tone, as it were, for the teaching that is to follow. These verses, when chanted in the correct manner, produce a powerful impact which it is virtually impossible to capture in a translation. The prayers are directed towards various Vedic gods, but it is important to realize that these are simply various manifestations of the same supreme spiritual being, the Brahaman, and not, like in the Greek pantheon, independent gods. Indeed, the Upaniṣads contain several verses where this important fact is stressed again and again, lest the underlying monism be misunderstood for an apparent polytheism.

Vedic verses generally begin with *Aum*, a word which is considered to be the closest audio-visual symbol of the divine. One whole Upaniṣad, the *Māṇḍūkya*, is devoted to *Aum*, and indeed it is looked upon as the symbol par excellence of the Brahman: *Aum ity eka akṣaraṁ brahma.* Briefly, it may be mentioned that *Aum* is made up of three syllables—*A*, *U* and *M*—plus an invisible but clearly discernible fourth resonance. This has been interpreted in a variety of creative ways. For instance, it represents the entire gamut of sounds that can be produced by the human voice, beginning with *A* when the mouth opens and ending with *M* when it closes. Again, the three syllables could stand for the three states of consciousness—waking, sleeping and deep sleep—along with the transcendent fourth dimension of spiritual awareness. Similarly, they could be taken as representing the three *guṇas*—*tamas* (dark inertia), *rajas* (passionate activity) and *sattva* (harmonious purity)—through which in varying combinations we are constantly passing, again with the fourth dimension that enables us to rise above these limitations.

Aum is a word sacred not only to the Hindus but also to the Buddhists, the Jains, and the Sikhs. It is generally believed that it also has close etymological and spiritual links with the *Āmen* and *Amēēn* of Christianity and Islam. It is, thus, a powerful symbol of spiritual and gnostic life the world over. It is often looked upon as a symbol of the original divine vibration from which the universe sprang into being—'in the beginning there was the Word', as the Old Testament puts it or, perhaps, as a faint echo of the original 'Big Bang'. A whole science of Tantra has developed in India around various *mantras* or combination of sounds, all of which revolve in some way around *Aum*. If chanted in a certain manner for a prolonged period, it creates a sort of vibratory field which is conducive towards the study of the deeper truths that lie behind scriptural texts. Also, if one is following that particular path, it helps in unlocking the powerhouse of spiritual energy that is believed to reside at the base of the human spine known as the *kuṇḍalinī śakti* or serpent power.

Chapter I
SECTION 1

1. Aum, Brahmā, the creator of the universe, the protector of the world, arose before all the gods. He taught the knowledge of Brahman, which is the foundation of all knowledge, to his eldest son Atharvan.
2. That knowledge Atharvan imparted in ancient times to Aṅgiras. He in turn taught it to Satyavāha, son of Bhāradvāja, and the son of Bhāradvāja passed it on to Aṅgiras, the science thus descending from the greater to the lesser sages.

The origins of knowledge, in most ancient traditions, are believed to lie in the very act of creation. Cosmogenesis, the bursting forth of matter into manifestation, is not looked upon as merely a physical phenomenon but rather as the result of a divine will, of pure spirit taking upon itself the burden of matter, of the one deciding to become the many. The creation of our universe over which Brahmā presides is symbolized in Vedic cosmology as the bursting of the cosmic egg, the Hiraṇyagarbha, the spiritual parallel to what scientists now call the 'Big Bang'. It should be noted, though, that Brahmā is not to be confused with the Brahman. The former is simply the aspect of power that presides over the creation of this universe, while the latter is the all-pervasive consciousness that permeates countless billions of possible universes—*anantakoṭi brahmāṇda*.

The gods—in the Vedic sense, the Devas or shining ones—represent a later stage of manifestation. Again, a semantic confusion is to be avoided. The word 'God', as used in the West, is closer to the Hindu concept of *īśvara*, the personified Brahman. The Devas could perhaps be considered more like the Archangels in the semitic religions. These verses, thus, trace the genealogy of the spiritual wisdom back to the very dawn of creation. It is characteristic of Hindu philosophy, as well of its art and architecture, that the great masters often choose to remain anonymous or, if their names do figure, they make it clear that they are not creating a new philosophy but simply expounding in fresh idiom the perennial wisdom that has come down through the ages. They look upon themselves as inheritors and trustees of priceless treasure which they wish to enrich and pass on to their disciples.

The end of the second verse can be interpreted in two ways.

The translation I have given implies that the teaching descended from the great spiritual beings down to human teachers. The alternative reading would be 'both the higher and the lower knowledge'. This interpretation also fits the context, as will be clear in subsequent verses.

> 3. Saunaka, the renowned householder, once approached Aṅgiras with reverence in the manner laid down by the scriptures, and asked:'Venerable Sir, what is that, knowing which, everything becomes known?'
> 4. To him Aṅgiras replied: 'The knowers of Brahman declare that there are two kinds of knowledge to be acquired—the higher as well as the lower.
> 5. Of these the lower consists of the *Ṛg-Veda*, the *Yajur-Veda*, the *Sāma-Veda*, the *Atharva-Veda*, phonetics, ritual, grammar, etymology, metrics and astronomy. And the higher is that by which the imperishable is attained.

It is significant that the master here is not instructing one of his celibate disciples, but, rather, a man who has achieved distinction in the outer world, evidently a man whose wealth and position have not overwhelmed his desire for spiritual enlightenment. The traditional division of Hindu life was into four periods of twenty-five years each—first the Brahmacarya, when the student was expected to remain celibate and pursue his studies under a qualified master; then Gārhasthya, the life of a householder when he would marry, raise a family and undertake such professional activities as suited his background; then Vānaprastha, when there would be a period of gradual detachment, a deepening of the spiritual quest, a graceful transition to old age, and, finally, Sannyāsa when he would sever all bonds with society, don the ochre robe and wander at will totally dedicated to the search for the divine.

This pattern, which, incidentally, is based on the Vedic concept of a hundred years as the full human life-span, was obviously an ideal only partially followed by society. Nonetheless it did give a certain spiritual chronology to human life specially when juxtaposed with the four *puruṣārthas*, or goals of life—*dharma* (the religious-philosophical foundation), *artha* (material wealth), *kāma* (sensual enjoyment) and *mokṣa* (spiritual liberation). Śaunaka clearly was transiting from the householder's stage, where he had made his mark in society, to the next one in which his quest or wisdom had led him to the hermitage of Aṅgiras. It is mentioned that he approached the master *vidhivat*, which we have translated as being in accord with the scriptures. What is evidently implied is that he approached him with humility and reverence, a prerequisite for spiritual quest. Not only does such an attitude evoke a positive response from the teacher, it also puts the seeker in a receptive frame of mind conducive to absorbing the teaching that he is about to receive.

Śaunaka now asks his famous question, the reply to which constitutes the rest of the Upaniṣad. The purport of his question is to discover that knowledge which forms the basis of all other knowing. The world we live in, consisting of what the Chinese call 'the hundred thousand things', is so vast and varied that it is impossible for any individual to know more than a tiny fraction of current knowledge. This was true thousands of years ago, and is even truer now with the recent information explosion linked with the new technology. However, there has always been the tradition of a secret knowledge, a philosopher's stone which can open the key to illumination, an alchemical formula to convert the dross of our normal consciousness into the gold of mystical awareness, and it is about this wisdom that Śaunaka asks Aṅgiras.

The master begins his reply with the celebrated statement about the two kinds of knowledge, the higher and the lower, or what we could call knowledge and wisdom. Significantly, he defines the lower knowledge in terms of the four Vedas and the six recognized branches of intellectual study in those times. Considering that the Vedas are the most sacred of Hindu scriptures, believed by the orthodox to be the voice of the divine itself, it is remarkable that Aṅgiras relegates them to the lower knowledge. Quite clearly, what he is saying is that any purely intellectual perception, even one so sublime and multifaceted as that of the Vedas, cannot in itself constitute real spiritual illumnation. For that what is required is the spiritual perception of the immutable, imperishable, eternal Brahman.

The spiritual realization, ultimately, is beyond verbalization or intellectualization. It is the state, as the *Ṛg-Veda* has it, 'where words along with the mind fall back, unable to attain'. A common misconception among intelligent people, whether in the age of the Upaniṣads or today, is that by mere intellectual gymnastics they can arrive at spiritual illumination. The mystic tradition throughout the world tells us that this is not so. The human intellect is certainly a marvellous instrument for grasping and manipulating the lower knowledge, but when it comes to spiritual illumination the mind has at some stage to be transcended or transmuted into the higher consciousness. This brings a direct perception of the divine power that permeates the entire cosmos, both in its universal aspect as Brahman and in its individualized aspect as the Ātman within each one of us. Such knowledge is not mediated by the senses or mental activity, and is characterized by an intuitive immediacy overwhelming in its impact.

> 6. That which is invisible, ungraspable, without origin or attributes, which has neither eyes nor ears, hands nor feet; which is eternal and many-splendoured, all-pervading and exceedingly subtle; that imperishable being is what the wise perceive everywhere as the source of creation.

There is a dilemma built into the very texture of a truly spiritual utterance. On the one hand, as has been mentioned, the experience is supraintellectual and, therefore, almost impossible to verbalize. On the other, it has to be expressed in words, because that is the generally prevalent mode of transmitting thoughts from master to pupil. This double-bind is particularly acute in the Upaniṣads, which deal largely with suprarational concepts. It is for this reason that the language of paradox and even contradiction has often to be used, so that the disciple sees that words can never be a substitute for experience, that they bear the same relation to the actual realization that a map does to the actual land that it seeks to delineate.

In this verse we have two sets of descriptions regarding the Brahman. The first are a set of six negative attributes, saying what the Brahman is not. Considering the basic Vedāntic tenet that the Brahman pervades everything, this may appear to be contradictory, but the intention clearly is to make the point that the imperishable Brahman is not something that can be restricted or limited within any particular manifestation, anthropomorphic or any other. Then follow four attributes which stress the eternal, all-pervasive aspect of the divine. Between these two seemingly opposed descriptions, some sense of what the seer is trying to convey comes across.

The implication regarding the changing and evanescent character of manifestation—the world of *nāmarūpa* (name and form) is clear.

The Hindu word for the manifested world is *saṁsāra* which means 'that which constantly changes'. What the Vedāntic seers realized was that behind this constant process of change there was an unchanging reality which, nonetheless, could become manifest to us in states of purified consciousness. Further, we ourselves contain in some way a direct access to that higher consciousness, because, while our bodies last for only a few decades, the Ātman within us is immortal and indestructible as is the Brahman of which it is a part.

> 7. As the spider sends forth and gathers in (its web), as herbs sprout upon the face of the earth, as hair grows upon the head and body of man, so from the immutable springs forth the universe.

Here, in three simple, almost homely, similies, the teacher attempts to illustrate the fact that this entire universe, with all its myriad and multifaceted manifestations, is a natural and spontaneous emanation from the Brahman, the unchanging, imperishable divine basis for all existence. This is a clear refutation of the often misunderstood concept of *Māyā*, where the universe is considered to be an illusion. While it has no existence independent of the Brahman, as our three similies suggest, it does have a dependent existence that is certainly not illusory.

The deeper question of cosmogenesis, of why the universe is created at all, is not directly touched upon in this verse, except that it hints at a recurrent, spontaneous process, not a unique, one-shot event. Also, the underlying Hindu view of time as being cyclical rather than linear is clearly indicated, because the three processes of a spider weaving its web, of plants growing upon the earth and of hair on the human body are all recurrent and repeated phenomena. In the next two verses the cosmological question is tackled at a deeper, more fundamental level.

> 8. By concentrated meditation, Brahman expands; from him matter is born, from matter life, mind, truth and immortality through works.
>
> 9. From Brahman, the all-seeing, the all-knowing, whose energy consists of infinite wisdom, from him is born Brahmā, matter, name and form.

The transmutation of the infinite, formless, eternal Brahman into the manifested cosmos in which everything is constantly changing represents the mystery of creation. Caught as we are within the space-time continuum, it is virtually impossible for us in our normal state of consciousness to answer the question as to why creation took place at all. In their forays into the higher consciousness, the Vedic seers seem to have had the insight that the entire cosmos is but a manifestation of the divine ground, the Brahman. The interesting notion of Brahman expanding into the cosmos could perhaps be linked with a 'Big Bang' at some point in time, except that there could be an infinite number of such bangs each resulting in a cosmos and, also, regardless of how often the Brahman manifests, it does not detract from or dilute its transcendent dimension.

In these two verses, we are given a broad picture of cosmogenesis, which begins when the supreme self-conscious being plunges into the opposite pole and bursts into material manifestation. From there in slow stages lasting billions of years life emerges, then mental consciousness evolves until we come to the human race which is entangled endlessly in works. However, there is the significant indication here that these works themselves can be the pathway to immortality. Thus, the Vedāntic world-view is essentially positive and life-affirming. Man is not a sinner, hopelessly condemned to eternal suffering until redeemed by a saviour, but, rather, a product of evolution itself who can work out his own salvation through involvement in outer and inner activity in this universe of name and form.

Chapter I
SECTION 2

1. This is the truth; the rituals which the seers beheld in the sacred hymns are elaborated in the three Vedas. Ye lovers of the truth, perform them constantly, for they are your paths to the world of good deeds.
2. When the sacred fire is well kindled and the flames begin to move, offer your oblations with faith between the two portions of fire.

Dealing with what in the first section has been termed the lower knowledge, the Upaniṣad now proceeds to a statement that the ritualistic works elaborated in the Vedas are in their own sphere true and valid. The predominant mode of prayer for the early Aryans was the pouring of offerings into the sacred fire, looked upon as the intermediary between the human and the divine powers. The fire sacrifice was mainly in the form of melted butter, although other ingredients were also used. In the deeper sense, the sacrifice was an exquisite symbol of the inner offering that lies at the heart of the spiritual quest, but in the outer sense also it was believed to bring great rewards in present as well as future lives. It was considered a good and meritorious action, and elaborate texts developed which laid out in meticulous detail the *modus operandi* of these sacrifices or *yajñas*.

The first verse mentions 'three Vedas', the *Ṛg, Sāma* and *Yajur*, the *Atharva-Veda* evidently being a later compilation. It can also be interpreted as meaning 'in the *tretā* age', which refers to the second of the four ages or *yugas* through which the earth passes—the *Satya, Tretā, Dvāpara*, and *Kali yugas*—in which there is a steady descent and decline of *dharma* until at the end of the *Kali-yuga* there is a *pralaya*, or destruction, and the cycle begins all over again. We are at present living in a *Kali-yuga*, although opinions differ as to how near we are to the final destruction. Given the incredible amassing of nuclear material over the last few decades, enough now to destroy not only mankind but all life on this planet many times over, it seems that we are nearer the end than is generally believed. But, then, we must also be nearer the new beginning, the dawning of the next *Satya-yuga*!

In the second verse, there is the intriguing statement that the oblation should be made 'between the two portions of fire'. This could simply mean that they should be poured when the fire is brightly burning and not merely smouldering, or between the northern and the southern portions of the sacrificial platform. On a more esoteric level however, it could refer to the inner symbolism of the sacrifice in which the fire is that mystic power, the *kuṇḍalinī*, present in every human body. In this interpretation the two portions of the fire would be the two channels—the *īḍā* and the *piṅgalā*—flowing on either side of the central *suṣumṇā* channel which carries the fiery power from the base of the spine up to the thousand-petalled *cakra* in the cortex. This is in line with the *Śatapatha Brāhmaṇa* which narrates how the gods prevailed over the demons, though both were offspring of Brahmā, because, while the latter performed the sacrificial rites externally, the Devas interiorized them, thus becoming immortal and invincible.

3. For those whose fire sacrifice is not accompanied by the rites to be performed at the new moon and the full moon, at the four months of rain and at the first harvest, which is without guests and without offerings to all the gods, or which is performed contrary to scriptural injunctions; for such their hopes are destroyed in all the seven worlds.

Given the premise that the sacrifice is a potent means for the achievement of desirable ends, even though these may be material possessions, social status or political power and not the greater bliss of spiritual enlightenment, it follows that it has to be performed with scrupulous regard to the correct rituals and methodology laid down in the scriptures. These include seasonal offerings, feeding of guests and other practices associated with the sacrifice. If these are not followed, the sacrifice is flawed and will either bring no result or even a contrary and negative outcome.

It must be remembered that these minute details built into the fire rituals were not created in a casual or arbitrary manner. They emerged as a result of careful and meticulous experimentation by many generations of sages over several centuries. This could be compared with a complex experiment in nuclear physics. Unless the details worked out by scientists through repeated experimentation are carefully followed, the result is likely to be either nil or, sometimes, an unexpected explosion with disastrous consequences.

The word *atithi* in Sanskrit for guest is interesting. It literally means one who comes without fixing a date, an unexpected visitor. In many mystical traditions the world over, the stranger who appears on an auspicious occasion carries a magic mantle, and it was looked upon as a good omen if some person of wisdom and austerity arrived during a sacrifice and consented to partake of the sacrificial meal.

The 'seven worlds' referred to in this verse probably denote the traditional seven states of consciousness—*bhūr, bhuvar, svar, maha, jana*, *tapas* and *satya*—starting from the material and rising all the way up to the spiritual. The drift seems to be that an incorrect rendering of the fire sacrifice can have adverse effects on many levels, and that either this should be left severely alone or performed with due diligence and devotion. The worlds could also be taken to mean places or states of consciousness that the Ātman experiences after the death of the physical body.

4. The black, the fierce, the swift-as-mind, the crimson, the

smoke-hued, the scintillating, the many-splendoured—these are the seven swaying tongues of the fire.
5. Whoever performs the rites and makes the offerings into these shining flames at the proper time, these in the form of the rays of the sun lead to where the lord of the gods resides.

In powerful language the Upaniṣad portrays the leaping tongues of fire, symbolized as seven aspects of the Sakti, the feminine power that quickens the universe. While the all-pervasive Brahman is generally alluded to as 'It', beyond gender, the motive force behind creation is, in the ancient Hindu tradition, referred to as a feminine power. It is significant that unlike the Semitic religions which postulate a male god, Hinduism is deeply aware that, if the divinity is to be worshipped in an anthropomorphic form, it will have to combine both the male and the female aspects, with the female taking precedence similar to that of the mother over the father. Thus, Lakṣmi is linked with Nārāyaṇa, Gaurī with Saṅkara, Sītā with Rāma, Rādhā with Kṛṣṇa and so on.

In the present context, the fire is looked upon as the seven-hued goddess, the *sapta-mātrikā* or seven-mothers who are worshipped in many rituals. The goddess, while maternal towards her devotees, also has a terrible aspect. She is both Kāli and Durgā—the benign protectress of the righteous but also the dark destroyer of the wicked. Both these aspects are evident in the seven names by which the fire-goddess is invoked in this verse.

The Upaniṣad then proceeds to state that, if the sacrifice is performed at the proper time with the proper rituals, the offerings are in a subtle, invisible form carried through the rays of the sun and reach the 'lord of the gods'. In the Hindu heavenly pantheon which, it must be remembered, is far below the great trinity of Brahmā-Viṣṇu-Maheśa, the chief of the gods or Devas is Indra. It is he, in Vedic symbolism, who rides upon the divine, six-tusked white elephant Airāvata and gives battle to the Asuras, or the powers of the darkness. He holds the thunderbolt, and a large number of Vedic hymns are addressed to him, particularly those praying for victory in battle.

Within their intrinsic limitations, therefore, the rituals bear fruit. But, as will be sharply pointed out soon, these heavenly rewards are mere trifles when compared with the supreme bliss of spiritual liberation.

6. The radiant ones cry, 'Come with us, Come with us', as

> they carry him up on the rays of the sun. They speak pleasant words of sweetness and honour, saying 'This is the holy world of Brahmā gained by your good work'.

The rewards to be gained by the performance of good deeds, whether through the fire sacrifice or any other, are, indeed, pleasant. These can be thought of in terms of terrestrial enjoyment or heavenly enjoyment after death. Yet, the fatal flaw in both these is that they are evanescent. Viewed, not in the context of a single human life-span but in the infinitely larger time dimension of a cosmic cycle, these rewards turn out to be fleeting, and when the effect of good work is repaid, as it were, through such enjoyments, the individual has once again to tread the inner path towards salvation.

The treasures that we can store up, whether on earth or in heaven, are not eternal and incorruptible. In fact, they soon wear out, and, even if the process of earning them through good deeds is repeated again and again through the long aeons of time, it will still bring the individual not closer to spiritual enlightenment than he was before. It is for this reason that the Upaniṣad, having first praised good work and vouchsafed for the efficacy of fire sacrifice, now proceeds with startling abruptness to decry these and, instead, to point to a different path that leads to salvation.

> 7. Verily, frail are these rafts of the eighteen sacrificial forms, which represent only the inferior work. The ignorant who acclaim them as the highest good fall repeatedly into the domain of old age and death.
> 8. Though they consider themselves to be wise and learned, they are fools wandering aimlessly like the blind led by the blind.

Seldom in spiritual literature does one come across such a sudden and radical change of emphasis. Apart from being sublime philosophers, the seers of the Upaniṣads were great teachers and used the Sanskrit language to perfection. By first describing the benefits of sacrificial work, Aṅgiras makes his point even more effective by demolishing them and describing those who follow that path as fools. According to the Vedānta, such works can never break the cycle of birth and death in which the Ātman is caught. They can lead to increased prosperity and fame, but ultimately old age and death catch up with us inexorably.

It needs to be pointed out that the Upaniṣadic teaching here extols the path of renunciation and decries mere sacrificial works. This does not mean that all work is negated. Indeed, the *Bhagavad-Gītā*, which, in a way, is a logical offshoot of the Upaniṣads, points out that work, if performed with devotion and dedication to the divine and without selfish motives, can also be a potent means of spiritual realization. It would appear that in the Upaniṣadic times there was a school of thought, as there is today, that held material possessions to be the *summum bonum* of human existence. It is against this attitude that the seer comes down with such severity.

The 'eighteen forms of the sacrificial work' can also be read as 'eighteen members'—the sacrificer, his wife and the sixteen priests who are required for an elaborate and expensive ritual. Eighteen has a deep symbolic significance also—note the eighteen chapters of the *Bhagavad-Gītā* and the eighteen days of the *Mahābhārata* war.

9. Revelling in multifarious ignorance, such people think they have achieved the goal of life. But, being bound to passions and attachment, they do not attain knowledge and sink down in misery when the effects of their good deeds are exhausted.
10. Such bewildered minds regard sacrifices and good works as most important and do not know any greater good. Having reaped in heaven their rewards of good deeds, they enter again this world or even a lower one.

Unsparing in his criticism of those who seek heavenly rewards by the performance of rituals and good deeds, Aṅgiras again points out that the rewards gained thereby are fleeting, and after they are exhausted they leave the individual soul no better off than it was before. Indeed, because of the hubris that often accompanies such work, the soul may even have to be reborn in a 'lower world'. This could mean that they are reborn on earth in a less fortunate position than when they began, or, perhaps, in some other world even less conscious than ours.

There are, as modern cosmology has now confirmed, hundreds of millions of stars like the sun in our own milky way galaxy, and hundreds of millions of galaxies in the observed universe. For us, to hold the view that this tiny planet of ours is the only cradle of human life is ridiculous. How can we presume to strait-jacket the infinitely creative power of the Brahman with our arrogant and obsolete geocentricity?

A word needs to be said about the 'good deeds' mentioned in

these verses. Apart from the fire sacrifice, these deeds fall into two categories. *Iṣṭa* includes the fire ceremony, austerity, truthfulness, learning and teaching the Vedas, hospitality and the feeding of animals and birds, while *pūrta* consists of sinking of wells, construction of temples and water tanks, laying out of gardens and planting of trees, feeding the poor and other such benevolent activities. It can well be argued that such desirable and beneficial acts should be encouraged rather than condemned, because they are far preferable to selfish and cruel deeds to which the bulk of mankind is so addicted. Indeed, Aṅgiras' condemnation of these activities is difficult at first sight to appreciate.

However, the key to understanding this lies in the concept of spiritual liberation which is the cornerstone of the Vedāntic world-view. When compared to the bliss of liberation, any material or mental enjoyments earned by good deeds pale into insignificance as do even the brightest stars when the sun rises in all its majesty. The seer does not condemn the 'good deeds' as bad in themselves which obviously they are not, but simply points out vehemently that their worth is temporary and limited when compared with the other path which he now proceeds to expound.

> 11. But those who live in the forest leading a life of austerity and faith, tranquil, wise and keeping the mendicant's rule, they, purged of all impurities, go by the solar gate to where the immutable, imperishable being dwells.

In sharp contradistinction to the path of heavenly rewards mentioned in earlier verses, the seer now goes on to state that it is only by renouncing worldly possessions and desires that real immortality is to be gained. Clearly, this path is only for those who are prepared to spend their lives in a hermitage or as wandering monks, and it is curious that the teaching is being imparted to Śaunaka who has earlier been described as 'a great householder'. It is not recorded whether Śaunaka actually renounced the world after receiving this teaching.

The tradition of the two paths, one radiant and resplendent like the sun, the other pale and feeble like the moon, is to be found in many of the world mythologies, both Eastern and Western. As the most dramatic object in the sky and, very literally, the source of all life and light on this planet, the sun is par excellence the ideal symbol of the divine. One of the best known *mantras*, the *gāyatrī*, is directed at the sun and prays for spiritual illumination, and the Upaniṣads contain many beautiful verses in praise of it.

The 'immutable, imperishable being' of course is the Brahman. The basic argument of these verses is that, as long as we remain caught in the net of the senses, so long will we shuttle between heaven and earth; or, to put it another way, between birth and rebirth, because our very desires will inexorably pull us back again and again. It is only if we alter course drastically and, renouncing worldly attractions, turn all our energies and aspirations to the inner path, then we can obtain release from this cycle and attain the supreme state of being.

> 12. Having examined the worlds gained by deeds, the wise seeker should become indifferent to them, for the eternal cannot be attained by work. To know that, let him approach with humility a *guru* who is learned in the scriptures and established in the Brahman.
>
> 13. To such a seeker, whose mind is tranquil and senses controlled, and who has approached him in the proper manner, let the learned *guru* impart the science of Brahman through which the true, imperishable being is realized.

The First Chapter of the *Muṇḍaka Upaniṣad* closes with the important statement that the real science of Brahman, what has been called the higher knowledge, can be imparted only if two essential prerequisites are present. There must be a seeker who is humble, genuinely devoted to the spiritual quest; and who, having tasted or witnessed the material joys of life, has seen that their worth is fleeting and, therefore, no longer craves for them. And there must be a *guru* who is not only well versed in the scriptures but, even more important, firmly established in the divine consciousness.

This is to be carefully noted, because, though the turn towards spirituality is generally to be welcomed, we often find these days that unripe disciples and unbalanced *gurus* combine to produce a great deal of confusion and sometimes cause real damage. There is actually a book written some years ago by a lady from the West entitled *Hunting the Guru in India*, as if he were some rare trophy to be shot, beheaded, and carried back in triumph across the seven seas. The word *guru* means one who dispels darkness, and the tremendous reverence shown to the *guru* in the Hindu tradition is because, while our parents give us physical birth, it is the *guru* who dispels the darkness of ignorance and helps our spiritual rebirth into the light.

It can well be objected that, since it is not possible for a seeker to judge the spiritual worth of the *guru*, how can he be sure that he has made the right choice? This is a good question; the only answer is that ultimately we have to be guided by our inner intuition, instinct, sixth sense or whatever it is that we call that special phenomenon which all of us encounter from time to time. There is no assurance that our choice will be correct, but if the aspiration is pure, that is, if we are genuinely devoted to the divine and not simply looking for a subtle stratagem to bolster our egos, then there is really no danger.

Many people learn from more than one master, some from reading the scriptures or from a dream. If correctly understood, these are all fingers pointing inward towards the divine *guru* seated in our hearts. The *guru* points the way; he can, to apply a statement from political science, 'encourage, guide and warn', but he cannot do the work for us. The inner path is one that has, in the final analysis, to be trodden alone. The *guru* dispels the darkness so that we can see the way ahead, but he or she cannot do the actual walking in our place. Sometimes, after our long sojourn in the dark, the light is too bright for us, and, instead of illuminating the path, it only dazzles and disorients us. Sometimes, when we see the path winding precariously up precipitous slopes to the mountain-top, we are aghast and draw back into the shadows. It is too difficult, we say, too hazardous. We are reminded of Arjuna who asked Śrī Kṛṣṇa on the battlefield: 'What will happen if we leave the security of our present lives and fail to reach the goal?'

Śrī Kṛṣṇa's answer is the only one that can be given. No truly spiritual activity will ever go in vain. The night of death may descend on us long before we reach the summit, yet every step taken is a step gained; and, though it may take a thousand lifetimes, the moment will surely come when the wonderful hour strikes and we stand face to face with what another Upaniṣad calls 'the great being, shining like the sun on the other shore beyond the darkness'. And the only way to cross the turbulent ocean of *saṁsāra* is the *brahmavidyā*, the higher knowledge, the rainbow bridge to immortality.

Chapter II
SECTION 1

1. This is the truth. As from a blazing fire thousands of fiery sparks leap out, just so, my beloved, a multitude of beings issue forth from the imperishable and, verily, fall back into it again.

Using the graphic description of a great fire from which millions of sparks are constantly arising and falling back, the seer now proceeds to give a description of the Brahman, the imperishable, eternal being that is the very source and foundation of all manifestation. The ten verses of this section are all directed towards attempting to describe what is essentially beyond verbalization, and they forcefully make the point that everything that exists owes its being to the divine ground. From that great matrix they emerge; and, whether their span is a billionth of a second or a billion centuries, it is to that same ground that they ultimately return. In the final analysis, there is no dualism. Birth and death, light and darkness, day and night, good and evil, joy and sorrow—all the dualities that are so striking in the manifested cosmos are ultimately reconciled and united in the one imperishable being.

The cosmic dance of Śiva is eternal; it has no beginning and no end because it transcends space and time. In one hand of Naṭarāja is the drum, the creative sound from which spring countless universes; in the other is the sacred fire into which, in the fullness of time, these universes disappear. At every moment a billion galaxies spring into existence, and a billion disappear into the endless mystery of that great being. Our own world, which we consider so large and abiding, is but a grain of sand on the endless beach of eternity, and we ourselves infinitesimal sparks from the mighty fire. And yet each spark is illuminated with the fiery element; each one of us embodies in some mysterious fashion the divine spark of consciousness. And because we do, we have the unique possibility of a conscious participation in the divine bliss.

2. The divine being is formless, eternal and pure, pervading within and without, anterior both to life and mind. He transcends even the highest immutable.

3. From him are born life, mind and the senses; ether, air, fire, water and the all-supporting earth.

4. Fire is his head, the sun and moon his eyes, space his ears,

> the Vedas his speech, the wind his breath, the universe his heart. From his feet the earth has originated; verily he is the inner self of all beings.

The divine being is the origin, the support, the foundation, the inner spirit of all that exists. This fundamental Vedāntic insight is the very essence of higher wisdom. The word God, as it is generally used in the West, is really much closer to the later Hindu concept of *īśvara*, the personified, anthropomorphic manifestation of the divine. The Brahman of the Upaniṣads is a very much wider and deeper concept. Long before the elements were created, long before life and then mind began manifesting themselves, the immutable being was there, radiant with the splendour of a million suns. Without that great being there could be no creation, no time, no space, nothing.

> 5. From him comes the fire fuelled by the sun; from the moon the rains which nourish herbs upon the earth. (Nourished by them) the male casts his seed into the female; thus are these many beings born of the divine being.
> 6. From him are born all Vedic hymns, of the *Ṛg, Sāma* and *Yajur*, the sacrificial chants and the sacrifice; the ceremonies and the sacrificial gifts; the time of the sacrifice, the sacrificer and the worlds purified by the moon and illuminated by the sun.

The process of the origin of all beings from the divine Puruṣa is described in these verses. The entire cycle of creation, the delicate and intricate web of causal relationship through which the human species and all its transactions with nature are governed, all ultimately derive from the great being. From him spring the heavens, the sun and moon cause clouds to form which, raining upon the fertile earth, produce herbs. Men live on these plants, either directly or through animals which feed on them, and secrete semen. When this is cast into the womb of the woman, living beings come into being and the mysterious cycle begins afresh.

There is, thus, a direct causal relationship between the divine and earthly life. The Vedāntic view is not that God sits in some seventh heaven, aloof and detached from his creation, only judging human follies on doomsday. On the contrary, we are all very literally part of his own divine power. The very processes that have brought us into being and that which pervades us as well as our universe are but manifestations of his immense all-pervasive divinity.

The Vedic chants which, when the Upaniṣads were taught, represented the entirety of the religious tradition, and the whole intricate network of sacrificial rituals and practices were all clearly seen as flowing from the divine being. It is this unifying vision that, unlike in ancient Greece, prevented the Vedic system from dissolving into an ultimately sterile polytheism.

7. From him are born the many gods and celestial beings; men, beasts and birds, the in-drawn breath and the out-breath; rice and barley; austerity and faith, truth, chastity and the law.
8. From him also are born the seven senses; the seven flames and their fuel; the seven oblations and the seven worlds in which move the life-breaths; seven and seven which dwell in the secret place of the heart.

There are many orders of beings, not only human, animal and vegetable but super and suprahuman. These include a whole spectrum of celestial beings, gods and demigods or, in Christian terminology, archangels and angels. Just because they are not generally visible to the naked eye, it is wrong to assume that they do not exist. Taking an example from the science of medicine, we know that for millennia germs and viruses were invisible, yet they continued to fulfil their functions even before they were 'discovered'. It is interesting that in this verse a number of different categories are mentioned together—gods and barley, rice and chastity. The point clearly is that everything, whether what we would call an abstract idea or a concrete object, is within the realm of manifestation and derives its existence from the divine being. The neat intellectual categorization to which we are so prone has no ultimate validity.

The seer has mentioned the in-breath and the out-breath. At one level, breathing is the most fundamental of all activities, without which most creatures including man simply cannot stay alive in material manifestation. But there is a deeper significance; one of the major insights of the *ṛṣis* was that, if properly regulated and accompanied by an appropriate *mantra* and psychological conditioning, the breath can open doorways into vastly enhanced states of consciousness. It is not possible here to do more than simply mention this, and to point out that subsequent seers, specially the great Patañjali who composed the *Yoga-Sūtras*, have elaborated this technique whereby control of the breath—*prāṇā-yāma*—holds the key to 'stilling the modifications of the mind'.

Verse eight again is redolent with symbolic meanings not apparent at first reading. Indeed, as a general comment it should be said that it is a mistake to bring a purely intellectual approach to bear upon a study of the Upaniṣads. Certainly, we must strive for intellectual understanding, but there are deeper meanings and resonances to which we must also open ourselves, and which do not necessarily come out at first reading. The figure seven has in many mystic traditions a special significance. Why, for instance, are there seven days in the week in all civilizations of which we have any record? The decimal system has been explained by the fact that we are born with ten fingers, but then why not five or ten days to a week? The 'seven senses' are often explained as two eyes, two ears, two nostrils and the mouth, but this is unsatisfactory because these comprise four—sight, hearing, smell, and taste—and not seven senses. Perhaps a better reading would be to add touch and two other extrasensory modes of perception. The 'seven flames' have already been personified in an earlier verse as seven powers of the Śakti, the multi-splendoured goddess.

Again, the 'seven worlds' are well known in Vedāntic literature as seven states of consciousness, but what mysteries lie within the seven breaths which dwell in the secret places of the heart will have to be unravelled by each one of us for ourselves. Suffice it to say that within this human frame, and deep in the recesses of our heart, can be found the secret of the ages, the philosopher's stone that can change the dross metal of our normal consciousness into the gold of spiritual realization; the elixir of immortality which carries us to the other shore beyond the darkness. This 'heart', of course, is not the one with which cardiac surgeons are familiar, which can now be transplanted from a dead to a living person. The 'secret place' referred to in this verse is the mystical heart, said to be located ten finger-breadths above the navel, when the spiritual life-blood pours out from eternity.

9. From him are all these mountains and the oceans; from him the multifarious rivers flow; from him also are all the herbs and juices which, together with the elements, support the inner soul.

10. Verily, that great being is all this universe—sacrificial works, austerity and knowledge. O handsome youth, he who knows this immortal being as seated in the secret caverns of the heart cuts asunder the knot of ignorance even during this life on earth.

The Vedānta does not accept an incurable dichotomy between matter and energy, body and spirit. The elements that make up our universe, the very fluids that circulate within our bodies are themselves manifestations of the divine. The invisible inner soul—the *antarātman*, itself a spark of the divine fire—is held in a physical form by the elements which, in their turn, flow from the divine. The difference, thus, is not between a divine and a non-divine manifestation, but between various gradations of evolution beginning with the primordial elements and growing into forms that progressively manifest the divine spirit.

'Verily that great being is all this universe' is a statement that sums up the quintessence of the Vedantic viewpoint, and it is important to remember that the same verse goes on to say that this great being can be discovered within the secret caverns of the heart even here when we are in a physical birth. The importance of this statement cannot be overemphasized. If the Upaniṣad had merely given the majestic, all-embracing definition of the divine and left it at that, we might have been led to believe that it is simply not possible for us to comprehend, far less actually experience it while we are in the body. In many religious traditions, the confrontation with the divine is conveniently postponed until after death. Not so in the Vedānta, which holds that, given the right conditioning and aspiration, which need lifetimes to nurture, it is possible to realize the great, all-pervasive divine being as seated within our own hearts. The roads leading to this magnificent denoument are many: one can go through the *Jñāna-mārga*, the way of wisdom; the *Bhakti-mārga*, the way of devotion; the *Karma-mārga*, the way of action; the *Rāja-mārga*, the way of mysticism; or through a combination of all these. And any genuine religious teaching, if sincerely and diligently followed, can lead us there—*ekaṁ sad viprāḥ bahudhā vadanti* (truth is one, the wise call it by many names)—as the *Ṛg-Veda* has it. But it can be done, and, once the divine presence is actually felt within the mystic heart, the great knot of ignorance, the primeval unknowing through which all of us have passed for millennia since our spiritual adventure began, is finally rent asunder.

That is the divine moment, the glorious upshot of a million lives. It may come, as the Veda has it, like a flash of lightning against a dark-blue thunder cloud —*nīla toyada madhyastha vidyullekhaiva bhāsvara*—or, as the *Gītā* puts it—with the splendour of a thousand suns rising simultaneously in the sky. The great mystics of all the religious traditions known to mankind have testified to this amazing phenomenon, the birth of the divine within the human, of the eternal spirit within matter. They have sung of this in different tongues and climes, in various ages and aeons; but all have been trying to express the Great Experience when we become not merely intellectually or emotionally aware of the divine but actually find it pulsating within the deepest recesses of our being.

Chapter II
SECTION 2

1. The Brahman is the mighty foundation, manifesting deep in the secret cavern of the heart. In it are established all that breathe, and move and see. Know this both as being and non-being, as the supremely desirable, greatest and highest of beings beyond all understanding.

2. Luminous, subtler than the subtle, the imperishable Brahman is the abode of the worlds and all their peoples. It is life, it is speech, it is mind. It is reality and immortality. O beloved one, it is this which must be pierced; know it.

It is reiterated that the mighty Brahman manifests within the mystic heart and pervades all things. It is also added that Brahman is 'both being and non-being', which means that it pervades the visible as well as the invisible, the manifested as well as the unmanifested reality. The point here is that even this entire wondrous creation, involving an infinite number of galaxies, does not exhaust the power of the Brahman. He is all this, but also all that is unmanifested or that can at some point become manifest. The whole question of creation or cosmogenesis is a fascinating one. The Upaniṣads would seem to suggest that the Brahman really has no beginning and no end: It is *anādi-ananta*. There was never a time when it was not, nor will it ever cease to be. In some way, impossible perhaps to express within semantic limitations, the great being has always been there. The real wonder is that such an unthinkably resplendent power can manifest itself within human consciousness, although beyond mere intellectual 'understanding'. It is, indeed, an achievement of great importance, because in the splendour of its radiance all else pales into insignificance.

Mind, through which we seek to understand the world in which we live; speech, through which we seek to express our deepest thoughts and perceptions; life itself, the *elan vital* which energizes our being—all flow from the Brahman. It is subtler than atoms and subnuclear particles, because they, as much as the Himalayas which they combine to form, are manifestations of the great power that surges through the cosmos unto eternity. This, then, is the reality which the disciple has to grasp, and it is this alone which leads to immortality. It should be noted that in the Hindu system immortality does not mean merely survival after death. That, in fact, is taken for granted. It means the realization of the divine, which enables us to transcend both birth and death, to free ourselves from the wheel of *karma* around which all manifested beings revolve.

This is the reality which, says the *guru*, has to be perceived, penetrated. The word used in the Upaniṣads by the teachers when they address their disciples is *saumya*, which has been variously translated as 'handsome youth', 'beloved friend', 'dear one' 'fair son', and so on. It is a term of great tenderness and endearment. The Upaniṣadic teaching is not some grim command issued by an aloof divinity to a cringing disciple far below. It is a loving gift, an affectionate transmission of wisdom from one human being to another for whom he feels infinite love, compassion and tenderness. The *guru* seeks to guide, not command; encourage, not browbeat; inspire, not intimidate.

> 3. Having taken as a bow the great weapon of the secret teaching, one should fix in it the arrow sharpened by constant meditation. Drawing it with a mind filled with That (Brahman), penetrate, O good-looking youth, that imperishable as the mark.
> 4. The *pranava* (*aum*) is the bow; the arrow is the self; Brahman is said to be the mark. With heedfulness is It to be penetrated; one should become one with It as the arrow in the mark.

These celebrated verses are among the best known in the Upaniṣadic corpus, and rightly so because they express in clear and powerful imagery the significance of the Vedāntic teaching. The translation of these verses is taken bodily from a remarkable book by Sri Krishna Prem *The Yoga of the Kathopanishad*, in which that great seer, born an Englishman, expounds the inner meaning of the Upaniṣad with a combination of deep intuition and wide-ranging scholarship. He has translated Upaniṣads as 'the secret teaching' which, indeed, is one of its several meanings.

In these striking verses the Upaniṣads, referred to collectively as embodying the spiritual wisdom, are likened to a great bow and this, in turn, is equated with the sacred syllable *aum*. Elsewhere in Vedāntic literature is the statement *aum ity eka akṣaraṁ brahma* (the one syllable *aum* is the Brahman) and a popular stanza refers to *aum* as the giver both of sensual enjoyment and spiritual liberation. The Upaniṣads, therefore, in their most fundamental aspect as *aum* are to be used as the bow, the individual soul as the arrow and the Brahman, the great being, as the target. The bow is to be drawn with 'heedfulness', with an unfaltering and undistracted awareness. The divine is not something which can be achieved along with others, a sort of a by-product of a generalized activity. It has to become the clear focus of our aspiration, and the arrow, our inner self, must also be constantly sharpened by meditation and spiritual practice.

If the goal is not clearly seen, if the arrow is blunt or crooked, if the drawer of the bow is distracted and disturbed, then there is no way in which the target can be hit. It is only if the target is clear, the arrow sharp and eager, the drawer of the bow calm and undistracted, that the great being can be penetrated or, as a great European mystic has put it, the flight of the alone to the alone can take place. When this happens, the soul becomes one with the divine, the Ātman merges with the Brahman, the dualities of birth and death, of joy and sorrow, of good and evil, of man and God, disappear.

That this process does from time to time take place is testified to by the prophets and saints, seers and mystics of all the great religious traditions of humankind. That it is a supremely difficult task is also clear; as Śrī Kṛṣṇa says in the *Gītā* only one in many thousands even hears of the teaching, and of them only one in many thousands actually achieves the goal. And yet this should not be a source of discouragement. Rather, knowing that what a human being has done once another can do again, we must with redoubled vigour bend all our energies to the spiritual quest so beautifully described in these verses.

5. He in whom are in-woven the sky, the earth and interspace, along with the mind and all the life-breaths, know him as the one self and desist from other utterances. This is the bridge to immortality.
6. Where all the nerves and arteries come together like the spokes of a chariot wheel at its hub, there, moving within the heart, he becomes manifold. Meditate on that self as *aum*; may your passage to the other shore beyond the darkness be pleasant and auspicious.

One of the major hindrances to the spiritual path is verbosity, the endless talk and disputation which lead to nothing more than sterile intellectual gymnastics. The intellect is a marvellous instrument invaluable within its own sphere of rationalization. But the spiritual reality, as has been said before, is essentially supraintellectual. The mind can take us up to a point, but beyond that it becomes a positive hindrance. Therefore, the sage advises the disciple that, once he has grasped the tremendous, all-encompassing nature of the Brahman in which all the outer and inner dimensions of space are comprehended, he must desist from idle chatter and futile speculation. The higher knowledge is the bridge to immortality, and once this is glimpsed the disciple must start preparing himself for the great journey, and not merely sit at this end of the bridge and argue endlessly about the crossing. As the Chinese saying goes: 'A journey of a thousand miles starts with a single step.' Intellectual disputation is often an elaborate psychological ploy to conceal our reluctance to take that crucial first step.

Changing the metaphor, the seer again reiterates the fact that the Brahman manifests itself in the secret heart, where all the channels of the body meet—not only the nerves and arteries which are known to medical anatomy, but the subtler, invisible channels that carry the vital energy through our bodies. The human body is surely one of the most complex and marvellous structures that ever existed, and within it are dimension upon dimension of visible and invisible mechanisms which, between them, enable us to be vital, living, thinking, feeling, human beings. The simile of the spokes of a wheel meeting at the hub is a powerful one. However fast the wheel may rotate and wherever it may travel, its centre remains the hub without which the whole structure would collapse into a jumble of twisted metal.

'Meditate on the self as *aum*', says the seer again, and wishes his disciple a safe and auspicious passage to the other shore beyond the darkness. This is a statement of great significance; it shows what the *guru* can do and what he cannot do. He can point out the way, inspire and guide the disciple lovingly on the path, help to save him from the myriad temptations and dangers that lie on the journey. But the actual travelling has to be done by the disciple himself. A *guru* cannot be a substitute for the *sādhanā*, the sustained work and effort on many levels, which alone can actually move us along the inner path. This path, as all the mystics of the world testify, involves at some point a journey across the dark and turbulent ocean. This can be interpreted in intellectual terms as referring to the darkness of ignorance or the turbulence of emotions which is certainly one of the meanings. It could also mean the inner state of the soul as it moves out of ordinary waking consciousness into the psychic and spiritual realms. At another level, it could refer to the after-death states of being which formed such an important element in many civilizations, notably in that of ancient Egypt and of Tibet.

The essential point is that the inner path and its divergences are constantly upon us, and we have at every moment to make a choice. Robert Frost in his poem 'The Road not Taken' says:

> Two roads diverged in a yellow wood
> and sorry I could not travel both
> and be one traveller, long I stood
> and looked down one as far as I could
> to where it bent in the undergrowth,
> Then took the other. . . .

And Sri Krishna Prem in his glowing work, *The Yoga of Bhagavad Gita*, speaks of these inner paths in these memorable words:

> Two are the Paths, there is no third for man.
> Cleave to the self in Yoga or lose yourself in matter.

Brief is the choice, yet endless, too, for at each point the way is forked; one can go up or down. Now should the choice be made, while yet the heart is flexible with life, for in that after-state the mind is fixed, fixed like a death-mask, by its previous thoughts.

There but a ghostly shade of choice remains. Sped by its former thoughts and deeds, the soul will either sink through dread illusions to rebirth in matter, or it will rise past heavenly realms of light, stopping at none till it attains the goal, the deathless and supreme eternal state.

> 7. The omniscient, the all-wise, whose glory is reflected here on earth, is the self enthroned in the luminous city of Brahman, his etherial heaven. Firmly established in mind, seated in the heart, he controls life and body. The wise by the higher knowledge see him clearly as the radiant, blissful, immortal.

The Brahman is self-resplendent and luminous, and all the glories that we see on earth—the splendour of the sunrise, the wonder of the starry skies on a moonless night, the moon itself waxing and waning to the rhythm of the ages, the blue of the sky and the green of the forest—all these are but faint reflections of its lustre. He is seated in the brain, where he builds up the thought; he is found in the deep cavern of the heart from where he controls life and body. The force that resides in the tiniest atom with the capacity to destroy a city is the same whose smile kindles the universe.

With the normal eye, the ordinary consciousness, he cannot be seen. At best he can be thought about, written about. But just as a map of an unknown continent may be useful in giving us some idea of its shape and topography but in no way enables us actually to see it, so do the mere intellectual ideas about the divine help to some extent in giving us a faint idea about it but does not entitle us to its realization. For that, the Vedānta teaches, what is required is the higher knowledge, the *Brahmavidyā*. When that knowledge dawns, the great being shines forth through every pore of our being as the blissful, the immortal. As Sri Aurobindo puts it in one of his poems entitled 'Who':

> He is lost in the heart, in the cavern of nature,
> He is found in the brain where he builds up the thought.
> In the pattern and bloom of the flowers he is woven,
> In the luminous net of the stars He is caught.
> In the strength of a man, in the beauty of woman,
> In the laugh of a boy, in the blush of a girl.
> The hand that sent Jupiter spinning through heaven,
> Spends all its cunning to fashion a curl.

8. When the Great Being is seen as both the higher and the lower, then the knot of the heart is rent asunder, all doubts are dispelled and *karma* is destroyed.
9. In the highest golden sheath dwells the Brahman—stainless and indivisible. He is the light of all lights; it is he that the knowers of the self realize.

What actually happens when the beatific vision dawns upon the individual? This is difficult to describe, as difficult as explaining to one, who is blind, the colours of a rainbow. And yet some indications can be given, and three are mentioned here in our text, each referring to a different dimension of the personality—physical, emotional and intellectual. These correspond to the three knots well known on the spiritual path—the knot of Brahmā which ties the Ātman to the sensory world and particularly the body; the knot of Viṣṇu which binds it to the desire world, the world of the emotions; and the knot of Śiva, the knot of the mind which binds us to the world of thought, the final bastion of our separate ego-centric selfhood. These three knots, says the Upaniṣad, are rent asunder when the divine is seen; seen integrally, not only in the higher but in the lower, not only there above but here below, not only in spirit but in matter.

The Brahman, although permeating all manifestation, dwells specially in the highest or deepest sheath of consciousness. In the Hindu tradition, the Ātman is encased in five sheaths, the physical, the vital or ethereal, the emotional, the intellectual and, finally, the blissful, the *ānandamaya kośa*. It is within and beyond this fifth and inmost sheath that the Brahman shines out in all its glory; stainless, because by its nature it is beyond contamination; indivisible, because being all-pervasive it cannot be divided or fragmented.

This Brahman, says the seer, is the light of all lights, the truth of all existence, the inner power behind all that has been, is and is to be. It is this Brahman that the knowers of the self, the realized ones, know.

10. There the sun does not shine, nor the moon and the stars; there these lightnings do not shine, how then this earthly fire? Verily, everything shines only after his shining; his shining illuminates this entire cosmos.
11. Verily, the immortal Brahman is everywhere; in front and

behind, to the north and the south, above and below; verily, Brahman alone is this great universe.

At the conclusion of this chapter the seer bursts into an ecstasy of realization. Many of the Upaniṣadic verses are cryptic and mysterious, specially when they seek to describe the spiritual vision. Here Aṅgiras seems to imply that neither the celestial lights—the sun, the moon and the stars—nor the terrestrial lights—flashes of lightning and the sacred fire—can be said to illuminate the Brahman, because it is the Brahman itself that is the source of all these lesser lights. He, shining, causes everything else to shine. This fundamental truth is reiterated throughout the Vedāntic texts, lest the seeker gets carried away by the limited splendour of the lesser powers. These powers are certainly worthy of worship, whether they are the earthly illuminations, the celestial ones, or the Devas—the shining ones—themselves. But, in the final analysis, they are to be worshipped, because they are brilliant manifestations of the all-encompassing, all-illuminating Brahman.

The various lights referred to could also be taken to mean the flashes of inner illumination which the disciple often encounters as his consciousness alters with the progress of spiritual disciplines and arousal of the *kuṇḍalinī* power in the spine. The mystical tradition reaffirms that such flashes, intermittent at first and then gradually growing into a steady blaze, are frequently associated with the spiritual path. In this reading, what the seer is saying would be that the disciple must not get stuck with any of these preliminary stages, howsoever glorious they may appear after the darkness of 'normal' consciousness, but must always remember that these lights are simply faint reflections of the light of Brahman which kindles the universe.

In the last verse, we have a rhapsodic statement about the all-pervasiveness of the radiant Brahman. Above and below, in all directions, within and without, there is nothing else. All that we look upon as 'real', our 'too-too solid flesh', the earth itself that has nurtured our race from the dawn of history, everything is seen to be but as the surface of a bubble, devoid of weight or density. Wherever we look we see only the divine Brahman, because, in truth, we ourselves have become one with it or, to put it in another way, it is the Brahman which looks at itself through our eyes. No more are we tied with strong knots to the body, the emotions or the mind. As Śiva's great arrow pierced the three cities of iron, silver and gold within which the demon of false individuality sought to take shelter, so does the light of Brahman invade and pervade all our citadels one by one, until we are naked in the overwhelming glory of its illumination. And it is then that we realize that all this magnificent and resplendent universe is, indeed, Brahman itself.

Chapter III
SECTION 1

1. Two beautiful birds, closely bound in friendship, cling to a common tree. Of these one eats the delicious fruit with relish, while the other looks on without eating.
2. Seated on the same tree, one of them—the personal self—grieves on account of its helplessness. But when he sees the other—the worshipful lord in all his glory—then his sorrow passes away from him.

After the great ecstasy of the last few verses, in which the unsurpassing radiance of the all-pervasive Brahman is sought to be described, one could well assume that the highest attainment having been reached there is really no need for the teacher to proceed further. Had this flight into the Brahman been the final goal, the Upaniṣad could well have ended with the Chapter Two. Why, then, does it continue the teaching? Evidently because, despite the tremendous vistas described earlier, the disciple is still far from ready for the actual flight; and, therefore, the teacher has once again to come down to earth, as it were, and to address the disciple at his level. The same situation occurs in the *Bhagavad-Gītā*, which does not end with the great vision of the Eleventh Chapter but continues to convert that tremendous attainment into permanent spiritual progress.

The seer now descends from the vastness of the previous vision to a simple but telling allegory of two birds seated on the same tree. The tree is the body, and the two birds are the Ātman and the Brahman, or the Jivātman and the Paramātman, both of whom reside there. Or, to put it differently, below and beyond our surface personalities is the real self which is the spark of Brahman from the great fire referred to earlier in this Upaniṣad. These two are described as being indissolubly linked in friendship; because, in fact, the Jivātman, due to its bondage in the three great knots of the body, the emotions and the mind, looks upon itself as different, but, in reality, is inseparably linked to the Paramātman much as the reflection of the sun in a bowl of water is to the sun itself.

The lesser self is said to eat the fruits of the tree with relish, meaning thereby that it partakes of the unending treadmill of *karma* and hence gets caught up in the cycle of duality—of joy and sorrow, birth and death. This ultimately brings it to a point of satiation and helplessness. *Na vittena tarpaṇīyo manuṣyo* (Man is never satisfied with wealth), says another great Upanisad. The quest for material possessions, for sensual enjoyment, for emotional gratification is ultimately a self-defeating one. Howsoever overjoyed we may be at some gain in these spheres, there are always spectres that, consciously or unconsciously, haunt our victory like Banquo's ghost at Macbeth's banquet. Disease, old age and death—these three await all embodied beings at some point in their lives; and even if, by some stroke of signal good *karma*, we are able to avoid the first, then the second is there; and if we avoid the second, the third, death, comes inevitably at the last.

The greatest of emperors, the richest of tycoons, the most glamorous of playboys, the most seductive of *femmes fatale*, all, in the end, fall into the widespread net of death. And when, having tasted the material joys of life, one is suddenly brought face to face with harsh reality, a sense of helplessness sets in. It is at this stage that if one is fortunate enough to have imbibed the teaching, one turns for help to the other bird, our higher self unencumbered with karmic burdens and convolutions, that has all this time been serenely sitting on the same tree looking at us with love and compassion.

He was there all along ever since we reached the stage of human consciousness and began the long and complicated process of *karma* lasting for aeons, but we did not know of him till now. He has always been closer to us than breathing, nearer than hands or feet but we have not recognized him. As Sri Aurobindo puts it:

The Master of man and his infinite lover,
He is close to our hearts had we vision to see.
We are blind with our pride and the pomp of our passions.
We are bound in our thoughts where we hold ourselves free.

And then, one day, dejected and despondent, discouraged and disillusioned, we throw down our weapons as Arjuna did on the battlefield of Kurukṣetra, and turn in despair to our friend and comrade, the charioteer of our lives, the great being who, though he exceeds the splendour of a million suns, is yet seated within us in a form like unto ours. And when we look up at our greater selves, at the one who is the true recipient of devotion, a miracle occurs. Our sorrow passes away from us; we realize in a flash that the sweet and bitter fruits we have been eating birth after birth, age after age, are the real cause of our bondage, and that for release all we have to do is to surrender our false ego, to open ourselves to the power and the light and the glory of the great being who resides within our deepest consciousness.

> 3. When the seer sees the golden-hued lord, the great being, who is the maker of the world and the source of Brahmā the creator, then the wise one, shaking off good and evil, free from stain, attains unity with the Supreme.
> 4. Verily, it is the divine spirit that shines forth in all beings. Knowing this, the wise one desists from unnecessary talk. Sporting in the self, delighting in the self, yet involved in outer activity, such a one is the greatest among the knowers of Brahman.

The simile of the two birds is now projected onto the human condition. When, after long striving, we finally reach the point of being able to 'see' the higher self of which our lower selves are reflections, then do we become 'seers' in the true sense of the term. At that point the conventional distinctions between 'good' and 'evil' disappear. These were important in their own sphere, the sphere of conventional life and its attendant social and moral mores which, incidentally, differ drastically from age to age, from civilization to civilization. But when the higher being is seen, these realms are transcended, and the seer, shaking off the dark stain of the polluted lower consciousness, attains unity with the great being. He is described as golden-hued, refulgent with divine light, and as 'the one who created the creator, Brahmā'. In other words, he is prior to the creation as we know it and, therefore, *ipso facto*, the source of Brahma himself.

Once again the great truth is proclaimed—verily, it is the divine spirit that shines forth in all beings. And one who knows this, who has realized the Brahman within and without, ceases from unnecessary talk and disputation. People who talk incessantly about the path, who argue endlessly about the superiority of their respective faiths or *gurus*, are often so busy with their intellectual gymnastics that they hardly have actually any time to move forwards on the inner quest. As Fitzgerald puts it in his superb recreation of Omar Khayyam:

> Myself when young did eagerly frequent
> Scholar and saint, and heard great argument
> About it and about, but evermore,
> Came out by the same door wherein I went.

Sincere exposition of the sacred texts, or genuine discussion about the path is one thing. Indeed, such *satsaṅga* is useful in clarifying many issues that perplex us. But it must be realized that ultimately we have to go beyond words, beyond verbalization, into an experiential dimension. And, according to the Vedānta, the highest attainment is when the seer, delighting in the bliss of self-knowledge, is yet involved in outer activity—*kṛyāvān*. This is a profoundly significant statement, which places the whole teaching in a new light and makes it relevant for all times. Had it not been made, it would have meant that the only way to liberation was to give up all worldly activity, retire to a hermitage and spend the rest of our lives striving to realize the Brahman.

Certainly, that path is open for *sannyāsins*, for those who are prepared to renounce worldly affairs. But here we have a clear-cut reiteration that outer activities are not in any way inconsistent with intense inner activity, a point which many centuries later was made a central theme by Śrī Kṛṣṇa in the *Bhagavad-Gītā*. Indeed, the Upaniṣad describes such persons who have attained the divine realization and continue to be active as the 'highest' among the knowers of the Brahman. This explains the great reverence given to the *rājarṣis* (the royal sages) in the Hindu tradition. Pre-eminent among these was King Janaka of Mithilā, who appears in the Upaniṣads in his own right as a realized soul, and is specifically mentioned by Śrī Kṛṣṇa in the *Gītā* as having attained enlightenment through actions.

5. The self within the body, pure and resplendent, is attained through the cultivation of truth, austerity, right knowlege and

> chastity. When their impurities dwindle, the ascetics behold him.
>
> 6. Truth alone triumphs, not untruth. By truth is laid out the divine path along which sages, their desires fulfilled, ascend to where truth has its supreme abode.

The gaining of the self is, after all, no easy matter. It involves a constant process of purification, not only of the body through dietary and sensual restrictions, but more importantly of the mind, both conscious and subconscious. The alchemical symbolism of transmuting the lead of normal consciousness into the gold of spiritual realization through a constant process of heating and purifying is relevant here. Unless we go through the fire, as it were, we cannot burn away the dross in which we are enmeshed through the millennia ever since our human adventure began in the mists of time. Four requirements are mentioned: truth, which means an unswerving commitment to that within us which infallibly shows the way; austerity, which means a concentration of energy towards the spiritual goal undistracted by outer temptations; wisdom, which means the insight and disrimination necessary to keep unwaveringly to the spiritual quest; and chastity which implies sensual continence.

These four between them constitute a whole discipline and framework for spiritual quest. The fourth was generally expected only of the *sannyāsins* or monks, not of householders who could hardly be expected both to raise a family and abstain from sex. However, even for them, a certain discipline and conservation of psychic energy was required. The powerful, primeval sex drive is a force which cannot be thwarted with impunity. It can be sublimated, not repressed without doing grave psychological damage. The Tantra, in fact, turns the sexual urge itself into a powerful vehicle for spiritual quest.

In the sixth verse we come across the celebrated words 'Truth alone triumphs', which is the motto inscribed on the seal of the Indian nation. By 'truth' here is obviously meant not the conventional sense of that word but the overriding sense which, as Mahatma Gandhi pointed out, was equivalent to God. Truth is both the divine path or, in an alternative reading, the path laid out by the gods, which really comes to the same thing, and also the supreme goal.

It should be noted, firstly, that the path is an ascending one, in the sense that it does involve a conscious effort to fight against the downward current of inertia and entropy in which we all find ourselves caught. If we simply float along, we will inevitably drift downstream, imperceptibly at first, but then with increasing speed as we crash to our doom in the rapids and waterfalls ahead. Therefore, the Vedas exhort *caraiveti, caraiveti* (move on, move, on), and another great Upaniṣad, the *Kaṭha*, exhorts us 'to awake, arise and cross the difficult and dangerous razor-edged path'. Secondly, it is only when our lower desires have been fulfilled, or sublimated, that we can really undertake the journey. If we attempt it while still overloaded with the heavy baggage of physical and emotional cravings, of psychological and intellectual confusions, we will hardly be able to walk a few steps before we stumble and fall.

And yet, whatever our weaknesses, we have to start moving. Far above us, and deep inside, is the blazing truth, although in the beginning it may appear just a tiny flicker within the encircling gloom. This truth, as has been said, is both the path and the goal. Gradually, as we move onwards and upwards, new vistas unfold; the radiant sun grows brighter until, finally, at the crossing, the rainbow bridge appears which takes us to the other shore beyond the darkness where the great being shines with the splendour of a million suns.

> 7. Vast, divine, beyond all thought processes shines the Brahman; subtler than the subtle, further than the furthest. Yet is it nearer than the nearest, and the seer sees it within the secret heart.
>
> 8. He cannot be grasped by the eye, by speech, nor by the other sense organs. Nor can he be revealed by penance and austerities. Only when the mind becomes calm and purified by the grace of the higher knowledge does one, meditating, behold the great, indivisible being.

The human mind is a marvellous instrument; in its subtlety and complexity it is, indeed, a miracle of evolution. And yet, as has been reiterated throughout the Vedāntic texts, the mind by itself is unable to behold the Brahman, because it is Brahman itself that activates the mind. The same is true of speech and other sensory organs, as is strikingly portrayed in the parable of the *Kena Upaniṣad* where the gods are unable to comprehend the Brahman who appears before them as a spirit. They all look outwards, while the Brahman lies within and behind their capacity to function. It is further away than each incredibly distant quasar that unfolds before the startled eyes of radio-astronomers, because wherever anything exists at all it is due to the radiance of the Brahman. Yet it is near, nearer to us than our bodies themselves, and, therefore, can be perceived glowing within the secret cavern of the heart.

Austerity and penance, intellectual study and learned disputation, are all valuable elements on the spiritual path. They can prepare and pacify our consciousness, but they cannot *in themselves* take us to the supreme being. For that we will need to turn our purified consciousness inwards, to reverse a billion years of natural evolution in which the senses reach outwards, and to see what it is that energizes the senses, what is it that activates the mind, what it is that lies behind our ego-consciousness.

This looking inwards is often most effective in a quiet, harmonious atmosphere conducive to meditation. It was for this reason that the ancient seers chose mountain caves and the banks of lakes, deep forests and sylvan glades to set up their hermitages. In this day and age, with the hustle and clamour of modern civilization and the growing pollution of the natural environment, it is becoming increasingly difficult to find such quiet retreats. Yet deep within us, if only we can find it, is an abode of silence which is always available. Even in the full flood of outer activity, the very thick of the daily battle, it is possible to detach a part of our consciousness so that it continues to search within for the divine guest who lives in our inner citadel. In some way, also, this turning inwards has to carry over into the sleeping state, because in that shadowy realm also we can continue our search.

> 9. The subtle Ātman within the body, pervaded by the five-fold life force, is to be known by thought. The mind is constantly pervaded by the senses; when it is purified, the self shines forth.
> 10. Whatever world the man of purified mind desires, whatever desires he wishes to fulfil, all these he attains. Therefore, let whoever is desirous of prosperity worship the man of self-realization.

Our consciousness in this physical body is pervaded by the five senses and the sensory inputs being constantly received through them. This is so universal that some materialistic philosophies look upon the five senses as the sole mode of knowledge and do not accept any higher reality. However, the Hindu tradition has always been aware of the fact that beyond and behind the senses is the mind, which itself is the reflection of the deeper reality, the Ātman-Brahman complex. The purification of the mind, therefore, is the first step towards self-realization. When this is achieved, it gives not only a mastery over the senses, which are then seen to be powerful but subordinate elements of the personality, but also over material objects and attainments.

Such mastery brings with it a plenitude of what are generally known as psychic powers or *siddhis*. The mind of a seer is much more powerful than that of an ordinary man, as, for example, is the beam of a finely crafted torch with a strong lens in comparison with the same bulb without this equipment. It is, therefore, believed that such a person can successfully apply his will power to the attainment of any worldly or material end if he so desires. Subsequent texts, specially Patañjali's celebrated *Yoga-Sūtras*, deal with these psychic powers at some length. It is also generally believed that an undue involvement in or demonstration of such powers becomes ego-inflationary and thus a hindrance to further progress on the spiritual path.

However, some great masters do use these powers for benign, non-selfish purposes; to help a disciple, for example, or alleviate the sufferings of someone in pain or deep distress. It is for this reason that the seer advises people in search of prosperity and good fortune to worship and serve such masters in order to earn their blessings and grace. Since the quest for material wealth has been roundly condemned earlier in the Upaniṣad, this advice may appear to be slightly out of place; but it should be recalled that Aṅgiras is speaking not with an ascetic but with Śaunaka, a great householder, whose *dharma* involves the creation of wealth by legitimate means.

Chapter III
SECTION 2

1. The man of self-realization knows the supreme Brahman upon which the universe is based and shines radiantly. The wise who, free from desire, worship the Brahman pass beyond the seed of rebirth.
2. Whoever in his mind longs for the objects of desire is born

> again and again for their fulfilment; but one whose desire for the Brahman is fully satisfied, for such a perfected soul all his desires vanish even here in this life.

Desire is the basis of the constantly turning wheel of existence; it is the seed that leads to birth after death, and death after birth, and until the whole drama is fully played out and the individual soul has overcome this burning thirst. In Hinduism and Buddhism this insatiable desire is known as *triṣṇā*, and it is this that compels us to seek desperately for material and sensual fulfilment. The Vedic seers realized very clearly that this desire is in the nature of a fierce fire, and each offering into it, far from appeasing its appetite, will further fan the flames. Thus our unfulfilled desires carry their impressions, or *saṁskāras*, from life to life, and force us to be reborn again and again for their fulfilment.

This process will continue into infinity unless we, in our wisdom, reverse the process. It is this reversal that is at the heart of the spiritual quest, a looking inwards to the source of our consciousness rather than outwards towards the objects of desire. It may appear as if our desires are ours alone; but, if we step back and analyse ourselves, we will see that, these are, in fact, great tidal waves in which we allow ourselves to be washed away. Seeing the Brahman in ourselves and in all things, we must gradually start moving from the outside in. Then only can there be a release from the cycle of *saṁsāra*, the wheel of death and change to which all creation is strapped.

It is significant that the seer clearly states the possibility of liberation even in this life. *Esoteric* religions talk of heavens after death where, if we dutifully follow their particular teachings, we will all dwell happily ever after. The Vedānta, however, postulates the concept of the *jīvanmukta*, one who is liberated in this very life. If we have not achieved spiritual realization while yet alive, the act of dying by itself is not likely to bring this about. Hence the constant reiteration in the Upaniṣads of the importance of following the spiritual path to its source *now*, while we are still embodied and endowed with consciousness and wisdom. Indeed, the whole Vedāntic teaching, as the *Gītā* points out, is *pratyakṣāvagmaṁ*, something which can be actually experienced right now in our lifetimes, not something to be postponed until after death.

> 3. Not by discourses, nor by intellectual analysis, nor through

much learning can the Atman be attained. He is attained only by one whom he chooses; to such a one the Ātman reveals its own form.

4. This self cannot be attained by one without strength, nor by the careless, nor through improper austerities. But the wise who strive by all these means enter into the abode of Brahman.

As has been said earlier in the Upaniṣad, while intellectual disputation, rationalization and scriptural study are useful for the lower knowledge, they are not able to take us through the barrier that separates our consciousness from the divine. They have not to be negated but transcended by a different *kind* of wisdom which involves direct perception and realization of the all-pervasive Brahman. That can be attained only by one whom he chooses or, in an alternative reading of the text, by one who longs for it with his whole heart. In effect the difference between the two interpretations is not as sharp as may appear on the surface. The first reading, 'by one whom he chooses', is the basis for the doctrine of grace. But this grace itself is not capricious and arbitrary, it is invoked when there is a genuine and overwhelming aspiration from below.

Again, the Ātman is not to be won by a person devoid of 'strength'. This could mean physical stamina, because the intense psychological activity involved often throws a heavy strain upon the body, as has been demonstrated in the lives of great saints such as Śrī Caitanya and St. Francis of Assisi, Sri Ramakrishna and Sri Ramana Maharshi. But even more important than physical strength is psychological strength and emotional stability. It must be remembered that after all spiritual achievement is no mean task; it involves a total reorientation of our inner and outer perspectives. Sri Aurobindo would go further and say that it involves a transformation in the very cellular and molecular structure of our bodies.

Carelessness is the worst enemy on the path, as dangerous as it is to a climber attempting to scale the great Himalayan peaks. In fact, the imagery of climbing a great mountain is peculiarly appropriate to illustrate the spiritual quest. The higher we get the more difficult and dangerous the ascent becomes; and a single false step which in the plains would involve only a minor inconvenience can, at those heights, send us crashing down precipitous slopes. There we simply cannot afford the luxury of carelessness as we proceed towards the divine. At each moment our consciousness must be alert and attuned; nor should we allow ourselves to be so carried away by the euphoria induced by the glorious new vistas opening up at every turn that we allow ourselves to slip or stumble.

Similarly, improper and excessive austerities are not to be encouraged. Both in the Eastern and the Western mystical tradition there are instances of undue torturing of the body as a means to spiritual realization. This is to be avoided, and the Upaniṣads, the *Bhagavad-Gītā* and the Buddha point out that at some stage these become counter-productive. Indeed, if Sujātā had not brought him a bowl of sweetened rice at a critical moment, Siddhārtha would have perished, and one of the world's greatest teachers would never have shed his light upon suffering humanity. What is needed is a combination of strength, attention and balanced austerity—the reverse of the three weaknesses mentioned earlier. These combine to help the culmination of the quest, the entry of the Ātman into the supreme abode of the Brahman.

> 5. Having attained the self the seers are fully satisfied with wisdom, perfect in their souls, non-attached and tranquil. Having realized the all-pervasive everywhere, these disciplined souls verily enter into the Brahman.
> 6. Firmly established in the Vedāntic wisdom through the *yoga* of renunciation, their consciousness purified, these seers at the end of time achieve immortality and liberation in the world of Brahman.

These verses reiterate the central theme of the Vedānta that by means of the higher knowledge it is possible for human beings first to refine and purify their inner consciousness and then, ultimately, to enter into the radiance of the Brahman. The purification involves renunciation of desire and the cultivation of inner tranquillity, while the illumination implies spiritual realization in this very life. In verse six the term *parāntkāle* can be translated, as we have done, as 'the end of time' or, alternatively, 'at the time of death'. The question of what happens to a liberated soul after the death of the body is a complex one which is the object of considerable Upaniṣadic literature, notably the famous *Kaṭha Upaniṣad* with its celebrated dialogue between the boy-seeker Naciketas and Yama, the god of death.

There would seem to be three possibilities: the spirit can merge in the bliss of the divine for ever; it can continue to function in a benign manner for the sake of humanity, from the astral rather than the physical level; or it can voluntarily seek rebirth in a human form so as to help suffering mankind and sweeten the bitter sea of sorrow. In any case, once the Ātman and the Brahman have become one, the individual soul is released from the necessity of blind and instinctive rebirth.

7. Gone are the fifteen parts into their foundations; the sense into the corresponding deities; the deeds and the intellect into the supreme, immutable being.

8. As flowing rivers disappear into the ocean, losing their separate name and form, even so the seer, freed from name and form, becomes one with the effulgent being, the highest of the high.

When the great liberation is attained, the material and astral constituents of the human body go back into the matrix where they came—ashes to ashes, dust to dust, molecule to molecule, atom to atom. In the Hindu systems of philosophy, there are several categorizations of the constituent units that make up the physical, astral and psychological body of man. It is significant that in verse seven the word used for senses is Deva or the shining ones, thereby implying that it is the divine powers themselves that, reflecting the light of the Ātman, glow forth through our senses. Far from denying or denigrating the senses, the Hindu tradition sees them as manifestations of the divine powers; and, indeed, it is nothing short of divine that we have the power to think, to see, to hear, to smell, to taste and to touch.

How much poorer our lives become if even one of these senses is lost. And yet, in our arrogance and ignorance, we denigrate these great gifts, either through ascetic refusal or hedonistic over-indulgence. But, divine though they may be, the senses are not the source of consciousness. That lies in the Ātman; and when it achieves oneness with the Brahman, then the body with all its marvellous mechanisms is no longer needed, and its constituent units go back into the great ocean from where they arose.

As rivers arise from different parts of the earth, bear different forms and different names through their long and tortuous journeys and ultimately merge into the great ocean in which it is no longer possible to identify them as separate waters, so does the realized soul, when oneness with the Brahman has been achieved, get freed from the individual labels that it has borne through countless lives and find freedom and fulfilment in that radiant being, the highest of the high. The simile of the river and the ocean is most appropriate. The rivers themselves are ultimately derived from the ocean through the rain that feeds them, and for long periods they bear a separate location and name of their own. Thus, the divine Gaṅgā issues from the heart of the Himālayas, and for thousands of kilometres retains its name and form, varying at every moment and from season to season. Yet ultimately it merges into the ocean and once that happens it ceases to exist there as a separate entity.

The water is, of course, still there, but it is no longer labelled nor constricted by narrow banks. Rather, its work fulfilled, it merges calmly into the ocean from where its molecules originally sprung. In such a way, says the Upaniṣad, the individual Jīva is born again and again until by its *karma* and the grace of the higher knowledge it finally achieves the supreme being. The dewdrop slips into the shining sea; the human journey is complete; spiritual evolution has reached its supreme goal.

> 9. Verily, he who knows the supreme Brahman himself becomes Brahman. In his lineage none is born who knows not the Brahman. He crosses beyond sorrow, he crosses beyond sin. Liberated from the knots of the heart, he becomes immortal.

The bridge to immortality has now been crossed. By knowing, in the deepest and most integral sense of that word, the supreme Brahman, the seer himself becomes a part of that divine radiance. His body will still continue to exist for as long as his previous *karma* requires; but even when embodied his consciousness is one with the divine, and after he sheds the body he is under no compulsion to assume another unless, as a deliberate act of compassion, he decides to do so.

The statement that no one in his *kula*, translated as lineage or family, is born who does not know the Brahman is rather difficult to interpret. It can hardly be taken literally in the sense that all present and future descendants will become knowers of the Brahman. The individual Jīva has its own *karma*, and the network of outer family relationship is a transient and ever-changing one. What is probably meant is spiritual lineage. It will be recalled that when the Buddha, having attained enlightenment, returned as a monk to his father's kingdom of Kapilavastu and was sternly asked by the king as to why he was setting aside his family traditions, he answered that his real lineage was the line of Buddhas who had always laboured for the welfare of mankind.

The enlightened ones do, indeed, constitute a race apart, a race based not on colour or creed, sex or religion, but upon spiritual realization. This great community transcends time and location. Every great civilization in one period or the other, and some down to the present day, continue to produce men and women of spiritual realization. Some have been worshipped as *avatāras* and prophets, some revered as philosophers and saints, still others have lived out their lives in silent radiance, unknown to all except a handful of close associates. Some have been learned and eloquent, others illiterate and largely silent. But whatever the outer variations, inwardly they have crossed beyond sin and sorrow, the knots of their hearts have been sundered, they have become immortal.

> 10. This very doctrine is declared in the Vedic verse; to them alone who perform the rites, who are well versed in the scriptures, who are firmly grounded in the Brahman, who tend the sacred fire with devotion, who have duly performed the rite of the head, should this knowledge of the Brahman be imparted.
> 11. This is the truth imparted to his disciples in ancient times by the seer Aṅgiras. Let no one who has not performed the rite study this. Salutations to the great seers! Salutations to the great seers!

The Upaniṣad now ends with the mystic exhortation that the higher knowledge is not to be imparted to one who is not intellectually, psychologically and spiritually qualified to receive it. This admonition is necessary, not because of a desire to be secretive or, elitist, but for the very good reason that imparting this knowledge to the unqualified would be useless or, worse, downright dangerous. Useless because without the required discipline, devotion and perseverance, the teaching would be totally wasted—in Biblical phrase, a casting of pearls before swine. It would either not be understood at all or, even if grasped by the surface mind, would fail to make any deeper impact. It could also be dangerous, because in these rarefied realms a little knowledge is, indeed, a dangerous thing. It would be safer to send a substandard electrician to repair a nuclear reactor than to let those of unripe or hostile minds dabble with the great truths expounded in the Upaniṣad.

Hence the qualifications of the disciple are enumerated, and, interestingly enough, the first two—being well versed in the scriptures and firmly founded in the Brahman—are the same as those for the teacher mentioned in the Chapter One. Although the disciple would not be expected to have these qualities in the same degree as the teacher, they are nonetheless essential for a successful crossing of the rainbow bridge. Two more qualifications are added: that they duly tend the sacred fire, both the outer sacrificial one and the more profound inner *kuṇḍalinī*, and also that they should have performed the *sirovrata*, the rite or discipline of the head.

This can be interpreted in several ways. At one level it can simply mean one who has shaved his head or, in other words, renounced the world and donned the ochre robe of a mendicant. This interpretation is sought to be justified on the ground that the whole Upaniṣad is called the *Muṇḍaka* which, as has been mentioned at the outset, could refer to the shaven heads of the *sannyāsins*. However, it is also specifically mentioned in the text that the disciple to whom the seer Aṅgiras is expounding the secret teaching is not a *sannyāsin* at all but a great householder. Another explanation is that it refers to a special rite mentioned in the *Atharva-Veda* which involves carrying fire on the head.

Once again, however, we have to look deeper below the surface meaning to try and find the real significance. The *kuṇḍalinī śakti*, the fiery serpent power that lies dormant at the base of the human spine can under certain conditions be aroused and led upwards along the spine, irradiating various *cakras* or centres on the way, until it bursts in splendour into the cortex and illuminates the highest of these *cakras*, the thousand-petalled lotus in the head. Surely, this is the rite or ceremony of the head to which the seer refers, and which, indeed, is a rare achievement.

This, then, is the secret teaching, the luminous truth imparted by Aṅgiras in ancient times. Truly, such realized seers are the salt of the earth, the highest evolution of humanity, the saviours and torch bearers of mankind. To such sages humanity owes a profound debt of gratitude, and to them it bows again and again in love and reverence.

Index

Abhinavagupta, Ācārya, 15
Ambedkar (Dr.) B. R., 37
Ananda Math, 34
Aṅgiras, 51, 62, 142, 145–47, 154–56, 179, 185–86
Arjuna, 10–11, 17, 61–63, 67–68, 81–89, 158, 174
Arya Samaj, 28, 94
Āśrama(s), 8, 10, 66, 104–06, 142
  Brahmacarya, 8, 146
  Gārhasthya, 8, 146
  Vāṇaprastha, 8, 146
  Sannyāsa, 8, 146
Asuras, 59–60, 60, 153
āsurī śakti, 48, 56
Āśutoṣa *see* Śiva
Atharvan, 144
Ātman, 5–7, 9, 19, 25, 43, 46–47, 51–53, 55, 63, 67, 81, 86–87, 149, 152, 154, 166, 170, 172, 178, 181–82, 183
Aurobindo, Sri, 28, 34, 36, 61, 66–67, 82, 85, 89, 94, 128, 131, 137, 169, 173
Autobiography of a Yogi, 106
Ayappan *see* Mohinī

Bāla Kṛṣṇa *see* Kṛṣṇa, Śrī
Bande Mataram, 34
Besant, Mrs Annie, 28
Bhagavad-Gītā (*see* also *Gītā*), 4, 6–7, 10–11, 13–14, 37–38, 45, 59, 61–63, 72, 84, 88–89, 96, 143, 155, 172, 175, 182
Bhandarkar, R. K., 27, 94
Brahmā, 7, 16, 18, 43, 145, 149, 151, 154, 174
Brahma-Sūtras, 7, 14, 60, 88, 143
Brahman, 4–6, 9, 11, 18–20, 25, 45–47, 51–53, 55, 87, 90, 138–39, 144, 150, 153, 155, 157, 159–60, 164–67, 169–72, 175, 177, 179, 180–86
Brahmo Samaj, 27, 93
Buddha, 12, 15, 182, 184–85

Caitanya, 24, 88, 181
Chatterjee, Bankim Chandra, 29, 34, 128
Chatterjee, Gadadhara *see* Ramakrishna, Sri
Chinmayananda, Swami, 38, 78, 84, 143
Chisti, Khwaja Moinuddin, 21
Coomaraswami, Ananda, 104

Dādu, 22
daivi śakti, 48, 56
Dalai Lama, His Holiness, 73, 110
Dance of Shiva (*The*) *see* Coomaraswami, Ananda
Dattātreya, 18,
Devas, 59–60, 70, 145, 153, 171, 183
Doors of Perception (*The*) *see* Huxley, Aldous
Durgā, 17, 18, 153
Dutta, Narendranath *see* Vivekananda, Swami

Einstein, 81
Essays on the Gita, 35, 89

Fate of the Earth (*The*), 71, 80

Gandhi, Mahatma, 28, 36–38, 61, 82, 94, 99, 108, 119, 176

Gaṇeśa, 18
Gangeshwananda, Swami, 38
Gaurī, 153
Gautama, 15
Gītā (*see* also *Bhagavad-Gītā*), 10–12, 61–68, 81, 115, 140, 164, 166, 175, 180.
Gīta-Govinda, 23
Gopikrishna, Pandit, 131
Granth Sāhib, 22

Hanumān, 18
Heisenberg, 81
Hiroshima, 45, 56, 70, 120, 125, 134
Huxley, Aldous, 91

Indra, 18

Jaimini, 15
Jayadeva (also *Gīta-Govinda*), 23
jñāna-kāṇḍa, 137
Jñāneśvara, 24, 61
Jñāneśvarī, 24
Jung, C.G., 91

Kabīr, 21–22, 38
Kālī, 17, 153
Kālidāsa, 50, 138
Kāma-Sūtra (also Vātsyāyana), 9
Kamban, 27
Kanāda, 15
Kapil, 15
Karma-kāṇḍa, 137
Karmayogin, 34
Kārtikeya, 18
Kashmir Saivism, 15
Koestler, Arthur, 72
Kṛṣṇa, Śrī (also Kṛṣṇa) 4, 10–13, 17, 23–25, 61–64, 66–68, 81, 89, 131, 153, 158, 175
kuṇḍalinī, 19, 38, 91, 171, 186

Lakṣmī, 17
Lalleśvarī, 24
Life Divine (*The*), 35

Ma, Anandamayee, 106
Madhva (also Madhvācārya) 6, 14, 61
Mahābhārta, 7, 12, 61, 67, 119, 155
Maharshi, Sri Ramana, 28, 32–33, 99, 180
Mahāvīra, 15
Mahiṣāsura, 17–18
Mai, Yashoda, 38
Manu-Smṛti, 7, 96
Mātā, Śrī Dayā, 106
Mīrābāi, 24, 38
Mohinī, 18
Muktananda, Swami, 78
Müller, Max, 28
My Experiments with Truth, 37

Nagasaki, 45, 56, 70, 120, 126, 134
Nānak, 22
Nārāyaṇa, 153
Naṭarāja *see* Śiva
Nikhilananda, Swami, 38
Nyāya, 15

Paramhansa, Yogananda, 38, 78, 106
Pārthasārathi *see* Kṛṣṇa
Pārvatī, 17, 18
Patañjali, 10, 15, 19, 161, 179
Plato, 30, 51, 57, 60, 80, 115
Prabhavananda, Swami, 38
Prabhupāda, Swami Bhaktivedanta, 38, 78
Prarthana Samaj, 27, 94
Prem, Sri Krishna, 38, 142, 166, 168
Present Crisis (*The*) *see* Gopikrishna, Pandit
Purāṇa 7, 28, 60, 118
Puruṣārtha, 8,
  artha, 8, 146,
  dharma, 8–9, 66–67, 94, 146, 179
  kāma, 8–9, 146
  mokṣa, 8–9, 146
Pūrva-Mīmaṁsā, 15

Rādhā, 17, 153
Radhakrishnan, Dr., 142
Rāma, Śrī (also Rāma) 12, 16–18, 23, 37, 53, 94
Rāmacaritamānasa, 23
Ramakrishna, Sri, 28–30, 32–33, 88, 94, 181

Rāmānanda, 21
Rāmānuja (also Rāmānujācārya) 6, 14, 21, 61
Rāmāyaṇa, 7, 23, 60
Ranade, M. G., 27, 93
Ranganathananda, Swami, 38, 142
Ravidāsa, 21
Roy, Raja Rammohun, 27, 93
Rūmī, Maulānā Jalāl-al-Dīn, 129

Śakti, 162
Samudra-Manthana, 44, 59, 69, 80
  Airavata, 59, 70, 153
  garala, 59, 70
  Kalpavṛkṣa, 59, 70
  Kāmandhenu, 59, 70
  Mahālakṣmi, 70,
  Uccaiḥśravā, 59, 70
Śaṅkarācārya, Ādi (also Śaṅkara), 6, 14, 32, 35, 52, 61, 88, 104, 138
Saṅkaradeva, 24
Sāṅkhya, 15
Sarasvatī, 17
Saraswati, Swami Dayananda, 28, 94
Śarvānanda, Swāmī, 142
Śatapatha Brāhmaṇa, 151
Śaunaka, 51, 142, 146–47, 179
Savitri, 35
Sen, Keshub Chunder, 27, 29
Sītā, 17
Śīva, 12, 15–16, 18, 43, 65, 70, 77, 88, 159, 171
Śiva Mahādeva *see* Śiva
Śiva Purāṇa, 66, 89
Sivananda, Swami, 38
Sivaya Subramaniya, Swami, 104, 106
Socrates, 30, 51, 115, 138
Śrīmad-Bhāgavatam, 7, 66, 88
Sufi, 21, 41
Suradāsa, 23
Sūrya, 18

Tagore, Devendranath (also Adi Brahmo Samaj), 27, 29, 93
Tagore, Rabindranath, 21
Tantra, 15, 19, 90, 144
Theosophical Society, 28
Tilak (Lokmanya), B. G., 34, 61, 94
Tirukural, 14
Tiruvalluvar, 14
Tukārāma, 24
Tulsīdāsa, 23

Upaniṣad, 3–4, 7, 10–11, 14, 18, 35, 40, 45–46, 50–54, 56–58, 60–63, 65, 84, 87–88, 96, 99–101, 115, 118, 127, 130, 132, 137–40, 142–44, 147–48, 150, 153–55, 157–58, 160–66, 170–73, 175–76, 179–82, 184–85
  Aitareya Upaniṣad, 52, 62, 138–39
  Chandogya Upaniṣad, 5, 52, 138
  Īśā Upaniṣad, 42, 52, 138
  Kaṭha Upaniṣad, 3, 5, 52, 92, 138, 177, 182
  Kena Upaniṣad, 52, 138
  Māṇḍūkya Upaniṣad, 18, 52, 138, 144
  Muṇḍaka Upaniṣad, 3–4, 20, 37, 46, 51–52, 54, 62, 94, 118, 137–38, 142, 157.
  Praśna Upaniṣad, 52, 138
  Śvetāśvatara Upaniṣad, 5, 52, 57, 138
  Taittriya Upaniṣad, 52

Uttara-Mīmāṁsā, 15

Vaiśeṣika, 15
Vallabhācārya, 61
Vālmīki, 23
Varṇa, 9
  Brāhmaṇa(s), 9, 13, 66
  Kṣatriya(s), 9; 13, 66
  Śūdra(s), 9, 66
  Vaiśya(s), 9
Varuṇa, 18
Vedānta 3, 29, 32, 44–45, 47, 50, 54–56, 60, 81, 96, 126, 134, 137, 154, 163, 169, 175, 180, 182
  Advaita, 6, 14
  Dvaita, 6
  Viśiṣṭādvaita, 6
Vedas, 1–3, 7, 13, 15, 35, 50, 60, 99, 117–18, 131, 133, 137–38, 147, 150, 156, 164, 178

Atharva-Veda, 1, 3, 75, 117, 142, 146, 151, 186
Āyur-Veda, 39, 95
Ṛg-Veda, 1–3, 40–41, 46, 54, 125, 127, 146–47, 151, 160, 163
Sāma-Veda, 1, 146, 151, 160
Yajur-Veda 119, 146, 151, 160
Virat Hindu Samaj, 83, 85, 95–97
Viṣṇu, 12, 15–16, 18, 88
Vivekananda, Swami, 28, 30–33, 40, 79, 82, 94, 96, 101, 103
Vṛndāvana, 13, 23, 68
Vyāsa, 15

Woodroffe, Sir John (Avalon, Arthur), 90

Yajña, 2, 50, 137, 151
Yājñavalkya, 62, 139
Yoga, 9, 39, 53, 65–67, 84, 87
Bhakti-yoga, 10, 46, 53, 65, 81
Jñāna-yoga, 10, 46, 53, 65, 87–88
Karma-yoga, 10, 46, 53, 65, 87, 89
Rājā-yoga, 10, 46, 53, 65–66, 87, 89
Yoga-Sūtras, 1, 19, 66, 90, 162, 179
Yoga of Bhagavad Gita (The) see Prem, Sri Krishna
Yoga of Kaṭhopanishad (The) see Prem Sri Krishna
Yugas, 7, 151
Dvāpara, 7, 151
Kali, 7, 8, 65, 151
Satya 7, 151
Treta, 7, 151